Governing Financial Services in the European Union

The global financial crisis that reached its peak in late 2008 has brought the importance of financial services regulation and supervision into the spotlight.

This book examines the governance of financial services in the EU and explains where the power lies in the policy-making process. It covers the main financial services – banking, securities, payments systems, clearing and settlement. Addressing the politics and public policy aspects of financial market integration, regulation and supervision, it conducts a theoretically informed and empirically grounded analysis of financial services governance from the establishment of Economic and Monetary Union and the launch of the Financial Services Action Plan in 1999 to the present day. It also assesses the EU responses to the global financial crisis.

Providing a reliable and unique insight into the politics of financial services regulation in the EU based on an extensive programme of interviews with policy-makers and stakeholders across Europe, the book will be of great topical interest to students and scholars of European Union studies, political science and political economy.

Lucia Quaglia is Senior Lecturer in Contemporary European Studies at the University of Sussex, UK. She is the author of *Central Banking Governance in the European Union: A comparative analysis* (also published by Routledge).

Routledge/UACES Contemporary European Studies

Edited by Tanja Börzel, *Free University of Berlin*,
Michelle Cini, *University of Bristol*, and
Roger Scully, *University of Wales, Aberystwyth*,
on behalf of the University Association for Contemporary European Studies

The primary objective of the new Contemporary European Studies series is to provide a research outlet for scholars of European Studies from all disciplines. The series publishes important scholarly works and aims to forge for itself an international reputation.

Governing Financial Services in the European Union

Banking, securities and post-trading

Lucia Quaglia

Routledge
Taylor & Francis Group

LONDON AND NEW YORK

First published 2010
by Routledge
2 Park Square, Milton Park, Abingdon, Oxon, OX14 4RN

Simultaneously published in the USA and Canada
by Routledge
270 Madison Avenue, New York, NY 10016

Routledge is an imprint of the Taylor & Francis Group, an informa business

Typeset in Times New Roman by
Book Now Ltd, London
Printed and bound in Great Britain by
CPI Antony Rowe, Chippenham, Wiltshire

British Library Cataloguing in Publication Data
A catalogue record for this book is available from the British Library

Library of Congress Cataloging in Publication Data
Quaglia, Lucia, 1973–
Governing financial services in the European Union: banking, securities,
and post-trading/Lucia Quaglia.
    p. cm.—(Routledge/UACES contemporary european studies)
Includes bibliographical references and index.
1. Financial services industry—European Union countries. 2. Banks and
banking—European Union countries. 3. Corporate governance—European
Union countries. I. European Union. II. Title.

HG186.A2Q34 2010
332.1094—dc22   2009037932

ISBN10: 0–415–56418–2 (hbk)
ISBN10: 0–203–85552–3 (ebk)

ISBN13: 978–0–415–56418–2 (hbk)
ISBN13: 978–0–203–85552–2 (ebk)

Contents

Tables

Acknowledgements

Fieldwork for the research for this book was funded first by the British Academy (SG 45759) and later by the European Research Council (Grant 204398 FINGOVEU) – and their financial support is gratefully acknowledged. The primary research could not have been completed without the help of many practitioners and experts in several financial institutions, interest organisations and private companies based in Brussels and several European countries. I was able to benefit from forthcoming and helpful interlocutors, who generously gave me their time, despite their very busy diaries, and who were willing to share some of their insights with me. Some of the persons interviewed were also available to read parts of my text, providing valuable comments. I am very grateful to all of them. It was agreed with all the interviewees that, although I could use the information they gave me, comments would not be individually attributed. I am sure they would not agree with all the evaluations expressed in this book: all errors, omissions and interpretations are mine.

In order to gain access to the relevant primary documents I have used the website of the European Commission (DG Internal Market), in particular to reconstruct the policy-making process of the main pieces of legislation and other policy measures concerning financial services in the EU. I have also consulted the websites of the European Central Bank, the Committee of European Securities Regulators, the Committee of European Banking Supervisors, the Basel Committee on Banking Supervision, the European Parliament, and the main EU and national associations, private firms, national finance ministries and supervisory authorities, especially the UK Treasury and the Financial Services Authority. In addition I have benefited from the newsletters (and similar documents) produced by policy-makers and stakeholders.

Since I started my research, several academics have generously given me their advice, and some have commented on parts of the book, conference papers and other publications in which some of the findings were presented. In particular, I would like to thank Chad Damro, Kenneth Dyson, Enrik Enderlein, Rob Eastwood, Peter Holmes, David Howarth, Patrick Leblong, Huw Macartney, Ivo Maes, Michael Moran, George Pagoulatos, Eliot

Posner, Claudio Radaelli, Jim Rollo, Tal Sadeh and Amy Verdun. I also wish to thank the participants of the UACES conference in Edinburgh, the EUSA conferences in Los Angeles and Austin, the APSA conferences in Chicago and Washington, the conference organized by the Hertie School of government in Berlin, and two research seminars at the University of Sussex.

I am grateful to the UACES series editors, Tanja Boerzel, Michelle Cini and Roger Scully, the commissioning editors at Routledge, Heidi Bagtazo and Lucy Dunne, for their interest in my project, and Caroline Richmond for her copy-editing on behalf of Book Now. I wish to thank the *European Journal of Political Research* and the *Journal of European Public Policy* for permission to use some of the material from articles I had previously published in these journals, specifically: Quaglia, L. (2007) 'The politics of financial service regulation and supervision reform in the European Union', *European Journal of Political Research*, 46, 2: 269–90; and Quaglia, L. (2009) 'Political science and the Cinderellas of Economic and Monetary Union: payments services and clearing and settlement of securities', *Journal of European Public Policy*, 16, 4: 623–39.

My fellow colleagues at the Sussex European Institute contributed to providing a stimulating and supportive environment in which to carry out my research. This book was completed while I was visiting fellow at the Robert Schuman Centre for Advanced Studies at the European University Institute. Last, but by no means least, I would like to thank my family and friends.

Dr Lucia Quaglia
Brighton, July 2009

Abbreviations

BaFin	Bundesanstalt für Finanzdienstleistungsaufsicht
BCBS	Basel Committee on Banking Supervision
BIS	Bank for International Settlements
CEBS	Committee of European Banking Supervisors
CEIOPS	Committee of European Insurance and Occupational Pensions Supervisors
CESR	Committee of European Securities Regulators
CPSS	Committee on Payment and Settlement Systems
DG	Directorate-General
EBC	European Banking Committee
EC	European Community
ECB	European Central Bank
ECOFIN	Economic and Financial Affairs Council
EEA	European Economic Area
EFC	Economic and Financial Committee
EMU	Economic and Monetary Union
EP	European Parliament
ESCB	European System of Central Banks
EU	European Union
FSA	Financial Services Authority (UK)
FSAP	Financial Services Action Plan
FSB	Financial Stability Board
FSC	Financial Services Committee
FSF	Financial Stability Forum
G7, G10	Group of Seven, Group of Ten
IAIS	International Association of Insurance Supervisors
IASB	International Accounting Standards Board
IIMG	Inter Institutional Monitoring Group
IMF	International Monetary Fund
IOSCO	International Organisation of Securities Commissions
JF	Joint Forum
MEP	member of the European Parliament
MiFID	Market in Financial Instruments Directive
MNC	multinational corporation
OECD	Organisation for Economic Cooperation and Development
QMV	qualified majority voting
SEA	Single European Act
SME	small and medium enterprise
TARGET	Trans-European Automated Real-Time Gross Settlement Express Transfer System
TARGET2 Securities (T2S)	Trans-European Automated Real-time Gross Settlement Express Transfer System 2 Securities
TEU	Treaty on European Union

1   Introduction

The global financial turmoil that began in 2007 and gained full force in the autumn of 2008 brought into the spotlight the importance of financial services regulation and supervision. Although this is not a book on those global financial troubles – the project was well under way before the first signs of the crisis erupted – the research is very topical because, in order to shed some light on that situation, it is necessary to gather a better understanding of how financial regulation is made, who are the main players, how they define their regulatory preferences and how they exert their influence in the rule-making process, as well as the effects of all this on the regulatory outcomes – i.e. the rules set in place.

This project examines the governance of financial services in the European Union (EU) in banking, securities markets and post-trading activities – it explains where the 'power' lies in the rule-making process. Paraphrasing Dahl (1961), it addresses the question of 'who governs financial services' in the EU, how and why. Since governance is, inherently, multi-level, the book not only explores the politics and public policy aspects of financial regulation and supervision in the EU, it also concisely evaluates how such processes interact with international and national policy-making in this area.

In the multi-level governance of financial services, the EU level is paramount because EU rules, unlike international regulatory agreements, are legally binding and national financial legislation in the member states is shaped by, or at the very least incorporates, EU legislation. This has been the case particularly over the last decade, when the project of the completion of the Single Market in financial services gained momentum and a host of new rules were issued by the EU.

The volume has two main goals, which are both exploratory and explanatory. The first goal is to map and explain the complex institutional framework underpinning the governance of banking, securities markets and post-trading activities in the EU, analysing how it interplays with regulatory and supervisory arrangements in international arenas and selected countries. This mapping exercise is a challenging and worthwhile activity in its own right, given the intricacy of the multi-level institutional framework in place and the vast number of committees, of various types, at work.

The second goal is to analyse the EU policy-making processes in the financial sector and their outcomes: the main policy-makers and stakeholders involved; their resources and influence on the policy process and outcome; the relations between the public authorities and industry; and the role of 'experts' and policy paradigms in framing 'technical' policies. The assessment is conducted in a multidimensional policy space, taking into account the interplay between international, EU and national financial services regulation.

The research is both academically interesting and policy relevant. In academia, there is a considerable gap in the literature in political science. Two path-breaking studies on the politics of financial market integration in the EU were conducted in the mid-1990s, by Josselin (1997) and Story and Walter (1997), focusing mainly on specific member states rather than the EU as a whole, and stressing the intergovernmental character of the negotiations concerning the Single Market in financial services (see also Underhill 1997; Coleman and Underhill 1998). Armstrong and Bulmer (1998) and Jabko (2006) examined the coming about of the 1992 project and the governance of the Single Market as a whole, dealing only marginally with financial services, one important reason being that market integration and regulation in the EU lagged behind in this sector in the period covered in their study. Apeldoorn (2002) focused on the activities of the European Round Table in the same period, hence it does not cover the last decade. Academic research has not kept pace with the new developments since the relaunch of the Single Market in financial services in 1999, especially in political science. Whereas lawyers and economists have analysed specific aspects of financial services regulation in the EU (Ferran and Goodhart 2001; Ferran 2004; Moloney 2002; Padoa-Schioppa 2004b), a comprehensive public policy analysis of financial services governance over the last crucial decade is still lacking.

In the last few years, several journal articles and book chapters have dealt with specific aspects of financial services governance, without, however, providing a complete picture. Posner (2005, 2009a) has investigated the creation of the European Association of Securities Dealers Automatic Quotation System (EASDAQ), which was a common stock market for start-up enterprises operating on a pan-European basis and the opening of new markets in several European countries in the mid-1990s, emphasising the role played by the European Commission. More recently, he has focused on the 'transatlantic regulatory dialogue' and disputes concerning securities markets (Posner 2009b).

Grossman (2004, 2005) has focused on banking policy, and particularly the activity of banking associations and their interactions with their respective national governments. Mügge (2006), Bieling (2003, 2006) and Macartney (forthcoming) have identified transnational capital and multinational financial companies as the main drivers in the making of the Single Market in the financial sector over the last decade. Macartney and Moran (2008), Moran and Macartney (2009) and Posner (2007) have taken stock from recent developments concerning financial market regulation and supervision in the EU.

In a study of networks of regulators, Coen and Thatcher (2008) have analysed the activity the Committee of European Securities Regulators (CESR), which is a 'Lamfalussy committee', as explained in Chapter 3. De Visscher *et al.* (2008) have also scrutinised the functioning of the so-called Lamfalussy committees in the securities sector, and Quaglia (2008c) has extended this analysis to the committees in the banking sector. All these works provide some useful insights, though in a piecemeal fashion. A systematic cross-sectoral study of financial services governance in the EU is needed.

This research is also policy relevant. As the global financial crisis has demonstrated, the governance of financial services has far-reaching economic and political repercussions, and the politics of financial services regulation is a very topical subject of broad public interest. The financial sector is a core part of national economies in the EU and has been one of the most dynamic areas of EU regulatory activity in the last decade or so. At the same time, this policy area is often perceived or deliberately presented as being 'technical', receiving limited public scrutiny, whereas politics is omnipresent in the process. Since accountability and transparency of financial services governance have of late become a matter of great public interest, this volume contributes towards opening up and informing public discussion.

Thematic context of the research

Five main sets of developments, taking place in the European, international and national arenas, have had far-reaching repercussions on financial services governance in the EU, providing the background to this research.

First, there was the relaunch of the Single Market in financial services with the Financial Services Action Plan (FSAP) issued by the European Commission in 1999, discussed in more detail in Chapter 3. The FSAP was a five-year plan that contained a set of forty-two legislative measures (see Mügge 2006). Moreover, the final stage of Economic and Monetary Union (EMU) in 1999 and the physical introduction of the single currency in 2002 gave new momentum to financial market integration, with clear repercussions on the configuration of the financial services industry, which has undergone national and cross-border consolidation (ECB 2004a; Deutsche Bank 2004a). This was followed by increasing interpenetration between the main segments of the financial sector, on account of the growth of securitisation of banking activities, the creation of other financial instruments, such as credit derivatives or collateralised debt obligations, and the formation of financial conglomerates (CEC 2002c; Group of Ten 2001; De Nicoló *et al.* 2003).

The Lamfalussy framework, which was agreed in 2001 with a view to improving financial regulation and supervision in the EU (on the Lamfalussy reform, see Mügge 2006 and Quaglia 2007), and the establishment or restructuring of the committees that underpin such a framework, were partly a response to the changes taking place in Europe, and partly a response to international trends and global competition, as discussed in Chapter 3. Moreover, the institutional framework and hence the policy processes in the financial sector in the EU are still in flux, particularly following the global financial crisis in 2007–8 (see Chapter 8). For example, the report of the de Larosière Group (2009) proposed a series of far-reaching institutional changes, such as the creation of the European Systemic Risk Council and the European System of Financial Supervisors, even though it fell short of proposing a single EU regulator.

Second, important (though non-legally binding) international agreements concerning financial regulation have been negotiated from the late 1990s onwards. For instance, the 'Core Principles for Effective Banking Supervision' were agreed in 1997 in Basel and the 'Basel II Accord: Revised International Capital Framework' was signed in 2004, as discussed in Chapter 4 (see Wood 2005; Quaglia 2008b; Underhill and Zhang 2008). Moreover, new regulatory and supervisory fora – such as the Financial Stability Forum established in Basel in 1999 (Porter 2005; Drezner 2007) – were created, with a view to coordinating the activities of national regulators and supervisors and in order to step up the cooperation between international regulatory and supervisory bodies dealing with different segments of the financial sector. This body came to the fore in leading the response to the global financial turmoil in 2007–8 (Angeloni 2008), as explained in Chapter 8. More generally, the crisis renewed policy-makers' interest and public concern for the stability of the financial system, highlighting some open issues concerning the arrangements for financial stability in the EU.

Third, many EU countries have reformed their domestic frameworks for financial regulation and supervision in the last decade. Some of the most noticeable examples were the UK, Germany, Belgium, the Netherlands and Ireland, as well as some of the new member states (for an overview, see Masciandaro 2005; Masciandaro and Quintyn 2007; Westrup 2007; Quaglia 2008d). Several of these reforms moved towards a similar model of supervision, namely, a single supervisor for the entire financial sector, within or outside the central bank. It should also be noted that there are differences even among the countries that established a single financial supervisor. For example, in Germany the central bank retains some responsibility for banking supervision, unlike in the UK. However, different macro-regional models of supervisory authorities persist within the EU (Lütz 2004; Busch 2004). The most noticeable alternative to the 'Anglo-German model' outlined above is the 'Mediterranean model', which assigns an important supervisory role to the central bank. At any rate, the field of financial services remains a very sensitive issue for the member states, as suggested by relatively slow and often painstakingly negotiated progress made both in the EU and internationally.

Fourth, the augmented complexity of governance in this area has led to an increased reliance on the private sector for the provision of information and expertise; the issuing of private (soft) regulation; and the self-monitoring and self-enforcement of agreed norms. Intensive consultation with financial sector associations, interest groups, individual companies and experts has taken place internationally (Porter 2005; Underhill and Zhang 2008). In the EU, this is generally led by the European Commission. For example, the Commission's *Green Paper on Financial Services Policy* was followed by intensive and extensive public consultation (principally with market participants) and, in the light of the responses received, the *White Paper on Financial Services Policy* was issued in 2005 (CEC 2005a, 2005b). Moreover, the so-called Lamfalussy committees, discussed in Chapter 3, consult industry in a systematic manner (Quaglia 2008c).

Internationally, the Basel Committee on Banking Supervision (BCBS) published several consultation papers on the Basel II Accord from 1999 through to 2002 and received hundreds of responses, which were then incorporated in successive amendments of the accord (Wood 2005; Underhill and Zhang 2008). Furthermore, in-depth consultation takes place at the national level both before and after important EU and international negotiations (Quaglia 2008b), and monitoring and enforcement of regulation is sometimes delegated (at least partly) to the private sector, mainly to private sector associations, as in the case of the Code of Conduct on Clearing and Settlement and the Single Euro Payments Area, discussed in Chapter 6.

Finally, financial governance has become a matter of interest outside the restricted circle of the policy-makers, the stakeholders and the experts involved. This increased public salience is linked to the fact that policy failures in this sector directly affect citizens in their capacity as bank account holders, small investors, insurance holders, pensioners, and so on, as underscored by recent financial scandals in several European countries (Westrup 2007). There is also growing concern among the public about the transparency and accountability of the institutions and policy-making processes in this area (for an overview, see Masciandaro and Quintyn 2007), which feeds into the broader debate on the democratic deficit of the EU and, more generally, democracy and legitimacy in global finance (Porter 2005, Underhill and Zhang 2008).

Caveats and limitations

There are three main caveats concerning this research. First, it does not deal with all financial services. A traditional classification of financial services comprises 1) banking, including financial conglomerates; 2) securities markets; and 3) insurance. Post-trading activities, which include payment services and the clearing and settlement of securities, can broadly be seen as part of banking and securities markets, respectively. Nonetheless, these activities became an important policy area in their own right after the establishment of EMU and the Single Market in financial services. They have been almost completely overlooked by the academic literature reviewed above, partly because they are rather 'technical' (hence, perhaps, the presumption that their regulation is not 'political'), partly because, before the establishment of EMU and the FSAP, EU regulatory activity had been minimal in this field. The politics of these seemingly technical activities is explored here.

The regulation of insurance services in the EU is not examined for several reasons (on recent developments on insurance regulation, see Quaglia 2009d). For a long time, insurance was not considered as a financial service *stricto senso* and, indeed, it was regulated in many countries not by the finance ministry but by the social affairs ministry, the ministry for industry, or the ministry for economic activities. Second, banking and securities markets have been dealt with together in previous studies of financial sector governance (see Coleman 1996; Josselin 1997), whereas insurance is generally treated separately. Finally, and perhaps more substantially, it would have been overambitious to treat the governance of all financial services in one volume. Indeed, there is a trade-off between the scope of the research and its depth. I have preferred to develop an accurate analysis of EU rule-making processes of three highly interconnected financial services – banking, securities markets and post-trading activities – corroborated by substantial empirical evidence, rather than stretching the research to cover insurance regulation.

The second caveat is that this research focuses at the EU level. The national level is dealt with rather succinctly and only whenever this is necessary to understand the policy preferences and strategic actions of national actors and forces interacting at the EU level. The research does not cover the implementation of EU legislation and soft measures in the member states, which would be an interesting project in its own right. Following the same logic, the international level is mentioned only whenever this is directly relevant to explain developments in the EU.

The third caveat is that this is not a book about the specific legal content of EU legislation or an economic cost–benefit analysis of EU rules. It is, instead, a book on policy-making in the financial sector, even though the following chapters do discuss the content of the EU rules adopted and some political economy considerations that influenced the regulatory process.

The overall argument in brief

This book provides a 'pluralistic' picture of financial services governance in the EU. In contrast to the commonly held view about the power of big (transnational) financial capital, an interpretation often supported by the media and some international political economy literature, it is argued that power is diffuse in the policy-making process concerning EU financial services regulation. This is reflected in the regulatory outcomes, which are often the product of (at times rather odd) compromises, and sometimes results in an incoherent set of rules, which, together with the fragmentation of the arrangements for financial stability, weakened the EU response to the global financial market turmoil of 2007–8.

Certain public policy-makers – the largest member states, the European Commission, the European Parliament (EP) – and some private stakeholders, such as the largest financial associations and big companies, are more influential than others (albeit, not always), especially at certain stages of the policy process. However, their preferences are often dissimilar, and hence the policy process involves complex negotiations, characterised by the formation and interaction of variables and fragmented coalitions of public and private actors. Certain policy-makers and stakeholders might have the upper hand in the making of one specific directive, but not of others.

The oldest supranational authority, the European Commission, is most influential at the *agenda-setting* stage of the process, especially in rule-shaping – that is, deciding whether (or not) to propose legislation (with the limitation that, if the Commission does not have the support of a critical mass of member states, it is unlikely to table proposals) and the broader content and scope of that legislation. The Commission is also influential in the adoption of EU implementing legislation through the Lamfalussy process, albeit assisted by committees of member states representatives and national supervisors.

The national political authorities (the governments of the member states) are influential at the *decision-making* stage, when, however, a second supranational authority, the EP, has co-decision power and has been very willing to make use of it. In the negotiation of EU directives and soft rules, national governments tend to defend the interests of their own financial sector and their institutional prerogatives, even though the public authorities in the member states and national industries are sometimes internally divided. The national technical authorities (namely, financial supervisors) are collectively part of the so-called Lamfalussy committees, hence they are particularly influential at the *implementation* stage.

Both intergovernmentalism and supranationalism need to pay more attention to the role of industry (the 'market') in financial services governance in the EU (Mügge 2006; Apeldoorn 2002) in a way that goes beyond the study of lobbying activities. The public authorities at both the EU and the national level actively seek interaction with industry in this complex and highly technical policy area, as they need access to information and expertise that market players have. It is not just a matter of industry lobbying relentlessly or 'capturing' the regulators. Sometimes, rule-making or other policy initiatives are delegated to the private sector, which is also instrumental in monitoring the implementation of EU rules in the member states, working with the national authorities and the European Commission. The strong influence of the private sector in financial services governance has meant that some of the rules set in place were too 'market-friendly' and proved to be inadequate to safeguard financial stability, as suggested by the repercussions of the global financial crisis in Europe.

In the making of almost all the Lamfalussy directives concerning banking, securities and some post-trading activities, two main competing coalitions of public and private actors were at work, albeit other lines of division were also present, which is why coalitions were fluid and internally divided. On the one side there was the 'Northern' market-making coalition, led by the UK, and comprising the Netherlands and the Nordic countries. On the other side there was the 'Southern' market-shaping coalition, led by France and comprising Italy, Spain, other Mediterranean countries and Belgium. Germany shifted from one coalition to the other, depending on the specific issue being discussed. The new member states either had not yet joined or had only recently joined when the vast majority of financial services rules were negotiated and agreed upon during the first five years of the twenty-first century. The Commission tended to side with either coalition depending on the issue being discussed and the time frame, in that the change of the College of Commissioners in 2004 moved it closer to the 'market-making' coalition.

This line of division was because of the different configuration of the national financial systems (Story and Walter 1997; Underhill 1997), such as the presence or absence of small and medium-sized banks and investment firms without a banking licence; the presence or absence of SMEs and links between banks and industry; the degree of openness of the national financial system; the presence or absence of foreign-owned financial institutions; and the competitiveness of national financial industry (hence, 'interests'). However, paraphrasing Story and Walter (1997), it was not only 'the battle of the systems', it was also 'the battle of ideas' between different, at times competing, 'policy paradigms' (Hall 1993) concerning financial services regulation, in particular its objectives and instruments. On the one hand, the structure of national markets influenced the prevailing regulatory philosophy (or paradigm) in the member states. On the other hand, regulatory paradigms influenced market structure across the EU, in a circular process.

To put it crudely, the Northern 'market-making' approach privileged the objectives of competition and market efficiency, whereas the Southern 'market-shaping' one privileged the objectives of financial stability and consumer protection, as well as the protection of national industry. As for instruments, the 'Anglo-Saxon' approach relies on light touch, principle-based regulation, rooted in a common law legal system. There is also considerable reliance on input from the private sector and close interaction between the public authorities and industry. The 'continental' approach makes use of prescriptive, rule-based regulation, based on Roman law. The interaction between the public authorities and industry is limited and emphasis is placed on the steering action of the former. These competing paradigms are informed by different attitudes to risk and ontological outlooks concerning the functioning of the market – basically, market trust and market distrust, respectively.

Plan of the book

The book is organised as follows. Chapter 2 elucidates the research design: the theoretical framework, operationalisation and sources.

Chapter 3 accounts for the difficult process of establishing a Single Market in financial services in the EU, beginning from the early decades of European integration up to the present, focusing the analysis on the period from the late 1990s onwards. Two milestones discussed in depth are the FSAP and the setting up of the Lamfalussy framework. The chapter highlights the hindrances to and the catalysers of financial market integration, and how these factors played out across the various segments of the financial sector. A more detailed analysis is conducted in the subsequent chapters.

Chapters 4, 5 and 6 deal respectively with the governance of banking and financial conglomerates; securities markets; and post-trading activities – namely, payment services and the clearing and settlement of securities. Each chapter begins by mapping out the institutional framework in place at the international, EU and national level in each specific segment of the financial sector. It then outlines the main policy initiatives over the period from 1999, when the FSAP was issued, to the present, analysing policy dynamics, coalitions, resources and strategies: basically, who did what, when, how and why. The concluding part of each chapter tests the hypotheses put forward in Chapter 2, assessing under what conditions one set of hypotheses prevails over another.

Chapter 4, on banking governance, examines the Capital Requirements Directive (2005); and the Directive on Financial Conglomerates (2002). Reference is also made to the Basel II Accord (2004), which has largely been incorporated into the Capital Requirements Directive.

Chapter 5, on the governance of securities markets, examines the four so-called Lamfalussy directives: the Market Abuse Directive (2002), the Prospectuses Directive (2003), the Transparency Directive (2004) and the Markets in Financial Instruments Directive (MiFID) (2004).

Chapter 6, on the governance of payments services and the clearing and settlement of securities, examines: the Payment Services Directive (2007); the Single Euro Payments Area (2008); the Code of Conduct on Clearing and Settlement (2006) and the decision not to propose a directive; and the project Target 2 Securities (T2S) (ongoing). In practice, payment services and clearing and settlement are parts of banking and securities markets, respectively. They are, however, dealt with together in a separate chapter and not in Chapters 4 and 5 for two reasons. From a practical point of view, this choice was made in order not to make the preceding chapters excessively long. In terms of subject matter, these (often overlooked) financial services constitute the 'plumbing' of financial market (Norman 2007), and the policy instruments used are often very different from the 'traditional' directives that regulate banking activities and securities trading. Furthermore, certain policy stakeholders are also specific to these post-trading services. Hence, payment services and clearing and settlement are better dealt with in a chapter on their own.

Chapter 7 compares the main findings of the empirical chapters, highlighting similarities and differences across the various financial services, all of which are to a different extent interconnected. It also touches upon the theme of democracy and accountability in financial services governance in the EU.

Chapter 8, which was written last, when the global financial crisis hit with full force in the autumn 2008, provides an overall picture of the institutional arrangements for financial stability in the EU, some of which are discussed in various parts of the previous chapters. In addition it discusses the EU response to the global financial upheaval.

Chapter 9 draws some general conclusions, speculating on the evolution of financial services governance in Europe.

2   The research design

This chapter elucidates the research design: the *explanandum*, including some definitions drawn from the literature on regulation; the theoretical framework, which integrates the governance literature with traditional EU integration theories and with the political economy literature on EU financial market integration; the operationalisation of the research; and the sources for data gathering. The design outlined here is applied in a systematic manner to the empirical record in the following chapters.

The explanandum and some definitions

The dependent variable of this study is financial services governance – more precisely, the transformation of the governance of banking, securities markets and post-trading activities in the EU. Financial services governance comprises 1) market regulation (rule-setting), including de-regulation, generally taking place at the national level, and re-regulation, at the EU level; and 2) supervision (rule implementation) – that is, the monitoring and enforcement of regulation as well as the practical cooperation between supervisory authorities in various segments of the financial sector in the EU. The focus of the research, however, is on EU regulation, because supervision is still performed at the national level, even though there are EU fora for the coordination of supervisory activities that will be discussed in the following chapters. The 'disjuncture' between EU-level regulation and national supervision came to the fore when the global financial crisis hit Europe in 2007–9 and is discussed further in Chapter 8.

At this stage, it is useful to review some terms and concepts used in the literature on regulation with a view to clarifying how they have been employed (or not) in the context of this research. Regulatory reforms are often a combination of de-regulation and re-regulation (Majone 1996: 2). 'De-regulation' means the downsizing or the elimination of public authorities' rules, reducing their control in the economy or in a specific sector. 'Re-regulation' means the reformulation of old rules and the introduction of new ones. 'Liberalisation' means the injection of more competition in the economy or in a given sector (these definitions are derived from Vogel 1996: 3).

Re-regulation can be pro-competitive, with an emphasis on liberalisation, or emphasis can be placed on complementing the liberalisation process.

I do not employ this terminology here, preferring instead the concepts of market-making and market-shaping regulation, which are borrowed from the literature on regulation in the EU. 'Market-making' measures define conditions for market access and operation in order to secure the opening and proper functioning of markets (Knill and Lehmkuhl 1999). In the context of this book, these measures are directed towards the liberalisation of financial services, stimulating competition and market efficiency. 'Market-shaping' measures pursue policy objectives other than market liberalisation, such as consumer protection and financial stability, with a view to complementing the liberalisation process. Although several policy measures can be both market-making and market-shaping, they tend to be predominantly one or the other. Moreover, these two definitions – market-making and market-shaping – are useful in order to characterise the competing regulatory approaches to financial services governance in the EU.

Financial sector 'integration' in the EU refers to the removal of barriers of various types to the free circulation of financial services, coupled with mutual recognition of national legislation and some degree of harmonisation. Usually, a distinction is made between 'minimum harmonisation' and 'maximum harmonisation'. Financial 'regulation' concerns the legal framework governing market entry and market activities in the financial sector. Financial market regulation pursues several objectives: macro- and micro-stability, consumer protection, competition and efficiency (see Di Giorgio and Di Noia 2007). Regulation can also constitute a means of trade protectionism (Gowland 1990) to exploit specific comparative advantages and to reduce adjustment costs to the new rules set in place. Indeed, the content of EU regulation produces different adjustment costs for different countries and industries, and it can substantially affect their competitiveness (Egan 2001).

Financial 'supervision' refers to monitoring the application of regulation in the EU, overseeing the activities of various categories of financial actors (banks, securities firms, financial conglomerates, etc.). 'Prudential supervision' is concerned with ensuring the adherence of individual financial entities, such as banks, to prudential regulatory standards with a view to maintaining financial stability (Oosterloo and de Haan 2004). The economic literature generally distinguishes between 'macro' and 'micro' prudential supervision (Borio 2003), which have two specific objectives, namely, 'macro' and 'micro' financial stability. Macro-stability pertains to the stability of the entire financial system and of the key institutions and markets that are part of the financial system. Micro-stability involves the stability (i.e. solvency) of intermediaries, viewed from the perspective of the users of the system (Gowland 1990). Moreover (non-prudential) supervision concerns the monitoring of the application of rules of conduct and market behaviour.

'Financial services' is a term used to refer to the services provided by the finance industry. A broad classification of financial services consists of banking, securities, insurance, financial conglomerates, payments services and post-trading activities, corporate finance, accounting and auditing. A narrow categorisation of financial services focuses on the three main segments into which the financial sector is traditionally divided: banking, securities and insurance. As explained in the previous chapter, for reasons of space and scope, this analysis covers the governance of banking (including financial conglomerates), securities markets and post-trading activities.

In recent decades, market segmentation has tended to disappear, following a growing interpenetration between the various segments. In other words, there has been an increase in the blurring of boundaries between banking, securities and insurance (CEC 2002c; Group of Ten 2001). Nonetheless, important differences across the main sectors remain and certain policy dynamics are sector specific. For this reason, the dependent variable, namely financial services governance in the EU, could be decomposed into three sub-components: governance of the banking sector, including financial conglomerates; governance of the securities markets; and governance of payments services and post-trading activities. Indeed, this is the structure according to which the empirical chapters are organised.

Governance debates in the EU literature

There are numerous and often quite different definitions of governance (for a review, see Kjaer 2004; Pierre and Peters 2000; Rhodes 1997; van Kersbergen and van Waarden 2004) and, indeed, this term has been criticised for being too vague (Rhodes 1996: 652). The literature on governance is vast, ranging from international relations and international political economy, to comparative politics and political economy, to public policy and business studies. This section examines concisely three different perspectives that can be taken on governance in the EU, echoing some of the main governance debates in other disciplines.

The first approach associates governance with the fading away of the nation state, which has shrunk in size and has lost (or is in the process of abandoning) core competences. A number of policies are no longer decided and implemented at the national level by state authorities. Instead, these policy-making functions are shifted downwards, to the sub-national level, or upwards, to the international level – that is, to international organisations (or international regimes) and the EU (Peters and Pierre 1998), originating a process of 'multi-level governance'. This term describes the 'dispersion of authoritative decision making across multiple territorial levels' (Hooghe and Marks 2001: 1; see also Hooghe and Marks 2003), and the EU is a noticeable example (but not the only one) of this approach to governance (Bache and Flinders 2004; Scharpf 1997; Kohler-Koch 2003).

The member states and national governments are no longer exclusive or even privileged channels through which domestic groups can attempt to influence EU and international policy-making, and the national authorities are no longer able to perform gate-keeping functions between the national, EU and international arenas. These arenas are interconnected rather than nested (see Tsebelis 1990), because often there is no clear hierarchy, and the national authorities – but also the supranational authorities and private interests – are players in a multidimensional game, where different resources and constraints are available.

The second approach considers governance as a way of conceptualising the relation between the state and the market – that is, between the public authorities and the private sector (Knill 2001; Kohler-Koch 1999; Héritier 2002). In modern societies, functions traditionally performed by the state have been transferred to, or taken over by, the private sector, or are jointly performed by the public authorities and private agents. The public authorities are no longer in a position of command; they are simply a set of actors, among many, in the policy-making process, even though they might still possess or control important resources. So, the key issue is no longer states versus markets, but rather states and markets.

This approach often draws on the concept of policy network to describe the policy interaction and the exchange of resources between a variety of public and private actors (Peters and Pierre 1998). It can be defined as governance through networks (Rhodes 1997) and is often applied to the study of the EU (see Kohler-Koch 1999), where policy networks tend to be multi-level or multidimensional. In practice, the first and second approaches to governance discussed so far often overlap, and they can share some similarities with the networks of regulators approach discussed below. Another variation of this literature is the private-sector governance approach (Knill 2001), which echoes a broader debate in the discipline (Knill and Lehmkuhl 2002; Hall and Biersteker 2002). This approach stresses the increased reliance of the public authorities on the private sector for the provision of information and expertise and the making, monitoring and enforcement of 'soft' law, agreed by industry.

The third approach links governance to the rise of the regulatory state (Majone 1996; Moran 2002, 2000), as opposed to the traditional (interventionist) state, which used to engage not only in regulatory policies but also in distributive and redistributive ones. The regulatory state, as the name suggests, uses mainly regulation, rather than other policy instruments, to achieve certain public objectives. This inherently limits the types of public policies still performed by the state.

The EU is an example of a regulatory state (Caporaso 1996; Majone 1996), or at least a 'patchwork' of national regulatory styles (Héritier 1996: 149). Moreover, given the limited size of the EU budget, the vast majority of EU policies are regulative rather than distributive or redistributive, using regulation to make policy. This approach to governance brings to the fore the role of independent regulatory agencies or non-majoritarian regulators (Coen and Thatcher 2005; Thatcher and Stone Sweet 2002), which take over functions and policies previously performed by the state and interact with other public authorities as well as with the private sector.

It should also be noted that, after the 'governance turn' in EU studies (Hix 1998; Kohler-Koch and Rittberger 2006; Jachtenfuchs 2001; Eberlein and Kerwer 2004; Christiansen and Piattoni 2004), there is a growing literature on 'new modes of governance' in the EU (Citi and Rhodes 2006; Treib *et al.* 2007). This expression is used mainly to describe the open method of coordination, 'soft law', benchmarking and the promotion of best practice, the policy-making activities of networks of experts and regulatory agencies, etc.

Finally, there is a flourishing literature on committee governance in the EU, which can be grouped into two main streams (for a review, see Quaglia *et al.* 2008). First, there are scholarly works that are interested primarily in the role of committees in EU policy-making and more generally in EU governance (see Christiansen and Larsson 2007). Second, there are scholarly works that are concerned principally with the members of the committees and their interaction, especially the socialisation process that might take place (Beyers 2005; Egeberg 1999; Trondal and Veggeland 2003). Committees are crucial for a for policy-making and policy implementation in the EU, especially whenever 'technical' issues are concerned.

Three critiques of the governance literature in the EU can be put forward, as they contribute to informing the analytical approach used in this study. First, the governance literature tends to underplay, or at least to underinvestigate, politics (i.e. conflicts of interest) and power – to put it crudely, 'who win' and 'who lose' from a certain mode of governance, which is related to the question of 'who govern' (i.e. which are the most influential actors in the policy process). Second, it seldom generates testable (i.e. empirically falsifiable) hypotheses, as it is a heuristic device rather than a fully fledged theory. Third, although the 'governance turn in EU studies' (Kohler-Koch and Rittberger 2006; Hix 1998) has been discussed, there has been no systematic attempt to integrated the governance literature with previous theoretical approaches to European integration and with competing understandings of political economy.

In order to address these critiques, this research combines the theoretical literature on governance in the EU with the literature on theories of European integration and the political economy literature on financial market integration. In so doing, it teases out some guiding hypotheses that inform the research and speak directly to two governance approaches reviewed in this section: the multi-level governance approach and the state and market approach.

The theoretical framework

The analytical framework employed here combines the perspectives on governance mentioned above with traditional theories of European integration and with competing political economy understandings of financial market integration and regulation in the EU, as exposed in the subject-specific literature reviewed in Chapter 1. These are the intergovernmental 'battle of the system' approach (Josselin 1997; Story and Walter 1997; Underhill 1997; Coleman and Underhill 1998), the supranational entrepreneurship of the European Commission (Jabko 2006; Posner 2005, 2009a), and the role of transnational capital (Apeldoorn 2002; Mügge 2006; Bieling 2003, 2006; Macartney forthcoming).

The two main theories of European integration overlap quite nicely with these competing understandings of the political economy of financial market integration and regulation. Moreover, although theories of European integration are designed by definition to explain the process of integration, they can fruitfully be applied to shed light on the EU rule-making process because they theorise about the influence of various types of actors located at different levels of governance.

The first approach, *supranational governance*, privileges the influence of EU-level actors or forces (Sandholtz and Stone Sweet 1998). According to this approach, which to a large extent subsumed the *neo-functionalist* theory (Haas 1968), the 'push factors' in the process of integration are transnational exchange; legal provisions framing integration; and the entrepreneurship of well-resourced supranational institutions, which are the 'pull factors' of integration (Sandholtz and Stone Sweet 1998; for a critique, see Branch and Ohrgaard 1999; Moravcsik 1998, 1993).

This approach, as initially formulated, does not take sufficiently into account the fact that, on certain policies or specific issues, the EU supranational bodies and transnational industry might have different preferences, which are indeed left unexplored by this line of enquiry. Second, it does not devote attention to the negotiations among EU supranational authorities, such as the EP, the Commission and the European Central Bank (ECB), which can be seen as a revised version of the bureaucratic politics approach (for an overview, see Peters 2004) applied to the EU level. Finally, it does not investigate how (i.e. the mechanisms through which) transnational forces exert influence in the EU policy process. The literature on lobbying and participation in the EU (Bouwen 2004, 2002; Beyers 2002; Grossman 2004; Knill 2001) can contribute towards doing this. However, with a few exceptions (Wallace and Young 1997), these studies are interested more in interest group representation in the EU than in specifically investigating their influence in policy-making across various sectors and issues.

The second approach, *intergovernmentalism*, considers the member states (to be precise, some of them) as the main players – hence, the explanatory variables are located at the national level. A distinction can be made between traditional intergovernmentalism (Hoffman 1966), which takes national preferences as given and as articulated in EU fora,[1] and liberal intergovernmentalism (Moravcsik 1998, 1993; Moravcsik and Nicolaides 1999; for a critique, see Wincott 1995; Wallace 1999; Caporaso 1999), which explores the origins of national preferences.

Liberal intergovernmentalism may be presented in three main steps, whereby the second and third coincide largely with traditional intergovernmentalism. First, there is the domestic process of *national preference* formation, whereby national executives aggregate domestic preferences determined by comparative advantages and articulate them in EU fora (Moravcsik 1998: 3–5; Fioretos 1997: 293). Second, *intergovernmental bargaining* takes place in the EU arenas, using diplomatic techniques and tools. The final distributive outcome of negotiations depends on the power and resources available to the member states, the size and strength of competing coalitions of states, and patterns of asymmetric interdependence (Moravcsik and Nicolaides 1999: 73–6). Third, there is the creation and delegation of authority to *EU institutions*, acting as agents of the member states and operating to reduce coordination and commitment problems (Moravcsik 1998: 24).

A critique of both forms of intergovernmentalism is that, within a member state, different national authorities might have different preferences, which means that the member states do not necessarily act in a unitary manner – bureaucratic politics might play a role (although liberal intergovernmentalism considers this possibility; see Moravcsik 1998). Moreover, national interest groups and some national technical authorities might attempt to bypass the national governments, liaising directly with EU bodies. At the same time, in order to further their goals national industries can lobby in Brussels or access specific EU technical committees.

An important issue that is transversal to the theories reviewed above concerns the definition of actors' policy preferences – to put it crudely, whether they are interest-based (i.e. rooted in political economy and derived straight from the structural economic context) or whether they have to be interpreted, in which case non-material, socially constructed factors, such as policy paradigms (Hall 1993, 1989), can play a role. This is the rationalist–constructivist debate in EU studies (Checkel 1997; Jupille *et al.* 2003; Pollack 2001). In certain technical and/or highly complex policy areas, such as financial services, the interests of policy-makers and stakeholders are not self-evident; they need to be defined, and policy paradigms provide the 'lenses' to do this.

A policy paradigm can be defined as a shared body of causal ideas concerning a certain policy area. A useful distinction can be made between the most normative, almost ontological part of the paradigm and ideas about the main policy objectives, instruments and strategies (Hall 1993). With specific reference to market regulation, Vogel (1996: 20) highlights the importance of ideas or 'regimes orientation', defined as 'state actors' beliefs about the proper scope, goals, and methods of government intervention in the economy, and about how this intervention affects economic performance'. However, it is not only state actors who are involved in this process, which affects also private actors (industry). Hancher and Moran (1989: 4) use the broader expression of regulatory 'culture' about 'the rules of the regulatory game' – that is, the 'purpose of regulation', 'legitimate participants and their relations with each other'. Such culture tends to be context specific, as it varies across time, countries and sector (Hancher and Moran 1989). Because

EU regulation is an arena where different regulatory approaches come to the fore and confront each other, it is often a 'patchwork' of national regulatory styles (Héritier 1996: 149).

Depending on the policy area, there can be a prevailing policy paradigm, at least among certain sets of actors (e.g. the stability-oriented paradigm that predominates among central bankers and other macro-economic policy-makers; see Dyson 1994; McNamara 1998). At other times there are competing paradigms (for example, the Keynesian–monetarist debate explored in Hall 1989), which can be more or less well defined, and in some instances there is either no policy paradigm at all or it has only an embryonic form. For example, Busch (2004) notes that, unlike in the monetary policy field, there is not a widely shared paradigm or a best model concerning financial supervision in Europe and worldwide.

Sometimes 'ideas' are used for political purposes, to promote focal points of agreement (Garrett and Weingast 1993), or for advocacy purposes, to form coalitions (see Sabatier 1998 on 'advocacy coalitions' and Radaelli 1999 on 'policy narratives'). Yet it is difficult to separate interests and ideas, especially in the economic field (for an overview of the role of ideas in economic policy, see Blyth 1997; Finnemore and Sikkink 2001).[2] Economic ideas matter because they are 'clusters of ideas/interests' (Jacobsen 1995: 309) that help actors to define their objective. Within the context of this book, on the one hand, 'interests', as determined by the structure of national markets and competitive positions, influence the prevailing regulatory paradigm (ideas about financial services regulation). On the other hand, regulatory paradigms influence market structure in a circular process, as elaborated in Chapter 7.

This issue, which feeds into the broader debate on interests versus ideas and the theoretical discussion on rationalism versus constructivism, is not specifically explored here, as it would have led to an excessive number of hypotheses to be tested. However, this study leaves open venues to explore ideational politics, with a view to identifying a shared (or prevailing) policy paradigm or competing paradigms in financial regulation in the EU. The issue of preference formation and coalition formation is thus revisited towards the end of the book, feeding into the interests *and* ideas debate.

Theoretically-derived hypotheses about influence in EU governance

From the theoretical literature reviewed above, the following hypotheses can be teased out for a first-cut analysis of the empirical record. The arguments they encapsulate are oversimplified and are elaborated in more detail in the following chapters. The first set of hypotheses refers to two aspects of the supranational governance/neo-functionalist approach, emphasizing the role, respectively, of the state (in this case, the EU public authorities) and of the market (transnational industry). The second set of hypotheses pertains to two features of the liberal intergovernmentalist approach, emphasising the role of the state (national governments and supervisors) and of the market (national industry).

These hypotheses are also in line with expectations derived from previous political economy research on financial market integration and regulation in the EU, which identifies the main member states, the Commission and transnational capital as the main drivers of the process. It should be noted that, for a thorough test of the theories of European integration discussed above – which is not the purpose of this research – additional hypotheses would need to be included. Most notably, in the case of liberal intergovernmentalism, there should be a specific hypothesis concerning the creation of EU institutions in order to ensure compliance.

H1a: Financial services governance is steered by supranational authorities
According to this hypothesis, the Commission, the European Parliament (EP), and, to a much lesser extent, the European Central Bank (ECB), which does not have specific competence in this field, are the most powerful institutional actors in the making of financial regulation in the EU. The policy preferences of these bodies need to be explored, as they may truly be the preferences of those bodies or they may be influenced, in turn, by the preferences of transnational industry (thus falling under H1b), the member states (H2a) or national industry (H2b). These supranational bodies can be assumed to be in favour of further market integration. Concerning the specific content of EU rules, they may also be keen to safeguard their institutional prerogatives.

H1b: Financial services governance is steered by transnational companies
Transnational actors are companies that operate through branches and subsidiaries in member states other than the 'home' member state in which they are headquartered, as well as companies that provide financial services in other member states, even if they are not physically located in their territory. According to this hypothesis, transnational companies are the main players in financial services regulation in the EU. It is important to investigate how (i.e. through which channels) they articulate their preferences and how such preferences are defined. If the supranational authorities play a crucial role in this process, this would fall under H1a.

The preferences of transnational actors about the specific content of EU rules are determined primarily by interest-based political economy considerations – namely, the adjustment costs to and competitive implications of EU regulation. Hence, such preferences might vary from case to case and need to be empirically investigated. Transnational forces are inclined to support further market integration through de-regulation and (limited) re-regulation at the EU level. They are also likely to be in favour of EU-level supervision, or at least greater coordination among national supervisors, as this would reduce their compliance costs.

H2a: Financial services governance is steered by the national authorities of member states

According to this hypothesis, national governments (or, to be precise, the national authorities, including supervisory bodies) exert paramount influence on financial market regulation in the EU. The most powerful member states and coalitions of states are likely to carry most weight. It is important to get a sense of how national governments form their preferences and whether different intragovernmental preferences might be at play, with the caveat mentioned below concerning the limited focus of the research at the national level. If governmental preferences are defined by national industry, transnational business or EU bodies, this would fall under hypotheses H2b, H1b and H1a respectively. Alternatively, national regulators might define their preferences as to the content of EU rules and the degree of market integration either on the basis of the regulatory paradigm to which they subscribe or according to their own bureaucratic preferences – these instances need to be investigated empirically.

H2b: Financial services governance is steered by the national market players

National market players are companies that operate mainly within national borders, hence they do not have branches or subsidiaries in other member states and do not provide financial services across borders. According to this hypothesis, national market forces are the most influential players in financial regulation in the EU and the national authorities largely accommodate the preferences of national industry. As in the case of H1b, it is important to investigate how (i.e. through which channels) national companies articulate their preferences in the policy-making process, as they might attempt to bypass their national governments, and how such preferences are defined. If the national governments play a crucial role in this process, this would fall under hypothesis H2a.

The policy preferences of national financial companies about the specific content of EU rules are determined primarily by interest-based political economy considerations, namely, the adjustment costs to and competitive implications of EU regulation. These might vary from case to case and need to be empirically investigated. The assumption is that national companies are not in favour of further market integration. On the one hand, competitiveness might play a role, in that the most competitive national players might support further market integration. On the other hand, financial operators that are competitive in the market have generally managed to expand across borders, at least in the provision of financial services; hence they are likely to be transnational actors.

Across the wide range of case studies examined in this research, or even in one such study, there may be some positive evidence for more than one hypothesis, in which case it is important to evaluate their respective explanatory power, defining the scope conditions under which each theoretical approach has more analytical leverage. The ultimate goal is to devise an integrated theoretical framework that thoughtfully combines various theories (or parts of them). This is done through an inventive *sequencing* of different theories (see Jupille *et al.* 2003 on sequencing theories in the study of the EU) according to criteria that evaluate the explanatory power of each theory at different stages of the policy-making process (for a review of this literature, see DeLeon 1999), in particular 'agenda-setting', 'decision-making' and 'implementation'.

There is significant explanatory value added in a less parsimonious and less monolithic theoretical framework, which takes into account the scope and domain of application of different theories. Peterson (1995) implicitly highlights the scope conditions of various theories in the EU context by suggesting the application of different theories to different types of policy development: 'super systemic' ('history-making'), 'systemic' ('policy-setting') and 'subsystemic' ('policy-shaping'). In this work, it is instead postulated that the scope conditions of the main theories examined have to do with the stages of the regulatory process.

Operationalisation

Since this research investigates the policy preferences, the influence and the interaction between policy-makers and policy stakeholders, suitable operationalisation needs to be devised, because these are all abstract concepts, not easy to gauge.

Measuring preferences, influence and interaction

The preferences of the main public policy-makers and private stakeholders are extrapolated in an inductive way by examining the position papers and consultation documents they produced; by conducting a systematic survey of the press coverage of the main policy initiatives; and by carrying out more than eighty semi-structured elite interviews (additional information concerning sources is provided below). The initial assumption is that policy preferences are determined by conventional interest-based political economy considerations – namely, the adjustment costs to and competitive implications of EU regulation. The following chapters explain the political economy aspects of some of the most controversial issues that emerged in the EU rule-making process, even though, for reasons of space, it is not possible to delve into the details. The chapter that conducts an overall cross-sectoral assessment revisits this assumption, teasing out other factors, notably regulatory paradigms, that might play a role in the formation of policy preferences and coalitions.

There are three main complementary ways of measuring the influence in the policy process. The first is to examine whether and how the policy preferences of the various actors, as derived above, affected the policy outcome –

for example, whether these were incorporated (or not) in the legislation or 'soft' law. The second way, which also permits us to gauge interaction among actors, is to ask policy-makers, stakeholders and qualified observers who were the most influential forces in the policy process, how and why. The third is to ask industry whom they lobbied or had contact with, to ask the public authorities the reverse question, and triangulate the interviews.

This operationalisation applies to each of the policy areas covered (banking and financial conglomerates; securities; payments and post-trading activities) and each of the main policy initiatives discussed, albeit trying to avoid excessive repetition in the empirical chapters. There are obvious limitations in conducting research in this way, first and foremost concerning the reliability of the data gathered, which need to be treated with a pinch of salt. However, during fieldwork, it was rather surprising to see how the picture painted by the various actors and the information they provided was complementary rather than contradictory. Where contrasting views on issues were expressed by several participants, this is made clear in the text, and specific pieces of information gathered through interviews are flagged.

Sources

Extensive fieldwork based on access to primary policy documents and interviews was essential in order to gather an accurate understanding of financial services governance in the EU, given the paucity of academic literature on this topic. A wealth of information was available in primary documents produced or made public by the European Commission and, to a lesser extent, the EP; the Council of Economic and Finance Ministers (ECOFIN Council); the ECB; international organisations and fora; the national authorities; international, European and national financial sector associations; large firms (e.g. Deutsche Bank); NGOs and think tanks (e.g. Centre for European Policy Studies); and academic and non-academic experts. The website of the Commission was consulted extensively, in particular to reconstruct the policy-making process of the main pieces of legislation and other policy measures concerning financial services. The website of the CEBS and CESR were also useful sources of policy documents.

This material was complemented by more than eighty semi-structured elite interviews conducted specifically for this project and comprising a cross-section of policy-makers and market participants. The vast majority of these took place at the EU level, including that of the Commission, the EP, the ECB, all the so-called Lamfalussy committees, other (mainly advisory) committees linked to the Directorare General (DG) Internal Market, and all the main financial-sector associations, such as the European Banking Federation (EBF) and the European Saving Banks Group (ESBG). Interviews were also conducted in several permanent representations in Brussels and, at the national level, in seven member states (the UK, Germany, France, Italy, Belgium, Spain and Portugal) at the Treasury (or equivalent ministry), financial services authorities, central banks, national financial associations, and individual companies. The main purpose of the interviews was to gain a better understanding of the preferences of policy-makers and stakeholders, the policy-making process and the formal and informal rules governing it, the interactions between various types of policy-makers and stakeholders, the resources at their disposal, and their influence. All the interviews were confidential, triangulated and checked against primary documents and press coverage.

In the following chapters, systematic reference has been made to the interviews when presenting the empirical material, indicating place and date, but giving no names or institutional affiliations, as all discussions were held on a non-attributable basis. Points made by several interviewees are not attributed to all of them. Whenever data gathered through interviews confirmed information given in policy documents and newspaper articles, sources publicly available are quoted. There are several instances of this in the text, as the interviews were conducted with those who were involved in drafting key policy documents and industry representatives who took part in consultations for the preparation of those documents – though, of course, the unofficial views given during interviews did not always coincide with the official ones expressed in public documents.

Timeframe

The timeframe of this research spans from the preparation of the FSAP (1999), which gave new impetus to financial services regulation in the EU, to the end of 2008, so as to take in the EU response to the global financial crisis. The preparation of the FSAP has been chosen as the starting point because the Commission's document provided new impetus to and a clear road map for the relaunch of the Single Market in financial services. However, Chapter 3 provides an overview of financial market integration, regulation and supervision in the EU over the past four decades, setting the background for understanding the developments that took place from the late 1990s onwards.

3 The making of the Single Market in financial services

This chapter analyses the making of the Single Market in financial services, focusing on the period from the publication of the FSAP in 1999 to the establishment of the Lamfalussy architecture. This analysis is preceded by a brief historical overview of the first four decades of European financial integration, tracing the policy trajectory and institutional evolution over time, and identifying the main factors that explain the developments (or setbacks) that took place at various stages. The chapter begins by outlining the broad institutional framework for financial services regulation and supervision in the EU. Its purpose is to set the background for the more detailed analysis that is offered in the following chapters, which focus on the policy evolution from 1999 onwards and give a detailed description of the specific institutions governing each of the financial services examined.

In the making of a Single Market in financial services, three main stages can be detected. The first extends from the signing of the Treaty of Rome in 1957 to the mid-1980s, when the Single Market programme was relaunched. This period was characterised by slow progress in financial integration in Europe. The second stage is from the agreement on the Single European Act (SEA) to the date set for the completion of the Single Market in 1992. During this decade, market integration gained momentum in Europe and, even though it was far from being completed in the financial sector by 1992, important measures of de-regulation and re-regulation were passed in the late 1980s and early 1990s. The third period comprises the run-up to and the first decade of Economic and Monetary Union (EMU), when the pace of financial market integration quickened and financial services governance underwent significant changes.

Overall, financial market integration, regulation and supervision moved slowly in until the very end of the 1990s, despite the new momentum given to it by the Single Market programme in the mid-1980s. From the late 1990s onwards, the FSAP and the Lamfalussy framework represent milestones in the reshaping of financial services governance in the EU.

The institutional framework for governing financial services in the EU

The institutions reviewed in this section are involved in the governance of all financial services in the EU. Hence, they are outlined here and will not be discussed again in the following chapters, which will, however, tease out their role and their interaction in the policy process concerning the regulation of the financial services. In the subsequent chapters, particular attention will be devoted to the sector-specific committees and groups set up as part of the Lamfalussy framework.

The European Council is the highest political body of the EU and is usually involved in the most important political decisions concerning the Union, its policies and institutions (on the functioning of the Council of Ministers and the European Council, see Hayes-Renshaw and Wallace 2006; Westlake and Galloway 2004). Thus, the European Council decides on the most significant (or contentious) changes in the institutional setting or policy framework of financial services governance. For example, the FSAP and the Lamfalussy framework were discussed and endorsed by the European Council in 2001. Another example is the Council's endorsement of the European Recovery Plan in order to counteract the economic recession that followed the global financial crisis (European Council 2008).

The ECOFIN Council is composed of the economic and finance ministers of the member states. It meets formally on average once a month in Brussels, and informally once every six months in the country holding the EU presidency. The so-called informal ECOFIN also includes national central bank governors. The Council deals with economic policy coordination, the euro, the EU budget, and financial markets integration. For example, it was one of the main decision-makers in the reform of financial services regulation and supervision that led to the establishment of the Lamfalussy architecture. Similarly, it oversaw the negotiations of the Basel II Accord, and in particular the transposition of this non-legally binding international agreement into legally binding EU legislation. All the legislation in banking, payments and securities markets is co-decided by the Council and the EP. The Council is by its very nature an intergovernmental arena, where the national representatives of the member states negotiate legislation using mainly 'traditional' diplomatic techniques, such as compromises, trade-offs and coalition building.

The second body of the legislative triangle of the EU is the EP (on the EP, see Judge and Earnshaw 2003; Smith 1999; Jacobs *et al.* 2007). Within it, the Committee on Economic and Monetary Affairs is responsible for EMU issues, rules on competition and public aid, tax provisions, corporate governance, and the regulation and supervision of financial services. Generally, the committee examines proposed legislation concerning financial services, the rapporteur produces a report, and a vote is then taken in the plenary session. The EP co-decides all level 1 legislation in financial services. Since the revision of the comitology decision in 2006, it has also been fully involved in adopting level 2 legislation. The EP is a supranational body. However, its members, unlike the Commission's officials, are elected and represent their national constituencies (on socialisation effects in the EP, see Scully 2005; on voting in the EP, see Hix *et al.* 2007). The EP is often described as a pro-integration force, open to interaction with stakeholders, but also eager to defend its institutional prerogatives.

The Commission has the 'power of proposal', by formulating legislation after consultation with industry and the national authorities (on the Commission, see Cini 2007; Dimitrakopoulos 2004; Nugent 2001). It was the Commission that in 2001 gave new momentum to financial integration in Europe by issuing the FSAP, as explained below. The DG Internal Market is the main policy actor within the Commission, even though DG Competition has an input on issues related to banking and financial services competition policy, including the mergers and acquisition of banks, and in the arrangement for clearing and settlement of securities, as explained in Chapter 6. The Commission is a supranational institution (on socialisation effects in the Commission, see Hooghe 2001) whose officials are not supposed to represent the interests of the member state from which they come, albeit this is not always the case. It is also a powerful bureaucracy with its own prerogatives to defend. The Commission has been a motor of financial market integration in the EU, seen as an economic project in the completion of the Single Market, and as a political one in fostering closer political integration in Europe (Jabko 2006).

The European System of Central Banks (ESCB) and the European Central Bank (ECB) have no direct responsibility for banking supervision (on the ECB and the ESCB, see Dyson 2000; Dyson and Marcussen 2009; Howarth and Loedel 2005; Kaltenthaler 2006; Padoa-Schioppa 2004a; Quaglia 2008a). However, Article 105.5 of the Treaty on European Union (TEU) states that 'the ESCB shall contribute to the smooth conduct of policies pursued by the competent authorities relating to the prudential supervision of credit institutions and the stability of the financial system.' The ECB has some regulatory power in the banking field, and it is involved in a number of working groups in areas such as financial market integration (e.g. the so-called Giovannini Group) and prudential supervision, such as the Committee of European Banking Supervisors (CEBS) and the Banking Supervision Committee of the ESCB. Moreover, according to Article 105.6,

> the Council may, acting unanimously on a proposal from the Commission and after consulting the ECB and after receiving the assent of the EP, confer upon the ECB specific tasks concerning policies relating to the prudential supervision of credit institutions and other financial institutions with the exception of insurance undertakings.

Since its creation, the ECB has tried to expand its supervisory tasks, but has met with the resistance of the national central banks, the national supervisory authorities and the governments of the member states. Moreover, the ECB itself, even its executive board, seems to have been in two minds on this issue: whereas some members of the board, such as Tommaso Padoa-Schioppa, who was also responsible for banking supervision, and to some extent Wim Duisenberg, the bank's first president, were keen to expand the ECB's supervisory responsibilities (Duisenberg 2002; Padoa-Schioppa 2002, 1999a), other members were not (interview, London, November 2005). It is a not only a disagreement rooted in bureaucratic politics – power distribution between those at the 'centre', that is, the ECB and the national central banks, and between the central banks and the supervisory agencies – but it is also a matter of dissimilar policy paradigms, rooted in different national institutional arrangements (for a review, see Masciandaro 2005). Whereas some central banks perform supervisory functions at the national level, and the prevailing policy paradigm in those countries considers the central banks as the most suitable institutions to perform these tasks, others do not have supervisory competences, and the prevailing policy paradigm in those countries prescribes the separation of monetary policy and banking supervision (Quaglia 2008a). The ECB is also an important player concerning the clearing and settlement of securities, as explained in Chapter 6, which exposes different central banking schools of thought concerning the control of central bank money (Norman 2007).

Besides the main EU institutions, there are a variety of committees with different status and functions active in financial services governance in the EU. First, there are committees that have some decision-making functions: these are the Economic and Financial Committee (EFC) and the Lamfalussy committees, whose members are national representatives. A second type of committees or groups are those which have mainly advisory functions and might include representatives from the private sector, think tanks and independent experts. Sometimes the members of these consultative groups come from the supervisory or regulatory institutions of the member states, but they are not supposed to represent their countries, and they act in a personal capacity.

The EFC is the successor of the Monetary Committee (see Verdun 2000) established by the Treaty of Rome in 1957. Since the 2004 enlargement the committee has generally been restricted in size, with only one official (usually from the finance ministry or the treasury) per member state (Scheller 2004). The Commission (DG Economic and Financial Affairs) and the ECB appoint one member each. The EFC is chaired by one member state representative appointed by the members of the committee, and the secretariat is provided by the Commission. The committee's tasks are to prepare the groundwork for the ECOFIN Council and Eurogroup meetings; to provide a forum for dialogue at senior level between central banks and finance ministries; and to oversee the management of Exchange Rate Mechanism 2. An important EFC subcommittee is the one dealing with financial stability, which produced two landmark reports on financial supervision in the EU (EFC 2000, 2001, also known as Brouwer Report I and II).

In the field of financial services regulation, a key committee providing strategic direction is the the Financial Services Committee (FSC), which is chaired by a member state representative and consists of senior finance ministry officials, with a secretariat provided by the Council. The FSC is the successor of the Financial Service Policy Group, which was chaired by the Commission and had been created to develop and implement the FSAP. The mandate of the FSC is to provide advice for ECOFIN and the Commission on the oversight of financial integration; clearing and settlement; corporate governance, in so far as this relates to financial markets; and procedures for cooperation among national regulators on financial stability and crisis management. The FSC reports to the EFC, which reports to the ECOFIN Council.

The overall institutional framework for financial services regulation in the EU is outlined in Table 3.1. The so-called Lamfalussy committees are discussed in the second part of this chapter.

Hindrances to financial integration in the EU

Compared to market integration in other areas, for example the trade of goods, financial market integration in the EU proved to be very difficult to achieve (Story and Walter 1997). It was piecemeal, incremental and politically controversial. Whereas the customs union was completed in the 1960s, financial market integration was still in the making in the twenty-first century (for a historical overview of financial market integration in Europe from the 1960s onwards, see Maes 2007; for the period of the late 1980s and early 1990s, see Underhill 1997; for the last decade, see Posner 2007). There are several political and economic reasons that can explain the delay in developing an internal market in financial services, some of which also account for the asymmetric development patterns.

Politically, the financial sector has been considered a fundamental part of the national economy, having far-reaching repercussions on all the other economic sectors (Zysman 1983). This has particularly been the case in countries, such as France, Italy and Germany, characterised in the past by a high degree of state intervention in the economy, especially in the banking sector. In some member states, financial services, first and foremost banking, have experienced a high level of state intervention in the form of regulation and direct ownership. This trend has to some extent faded away in the last two decades, though convergence has been partial. For example, in Germany approximately half of the banking sector is publicly owned, whereas in Italy most of it has been privatised.

Furthermore, as Moran (1991) noted with reference to the UK, possessing a vibrant financial centre, such as the City of London, has always been regarded by the national authorities as a significant economic asset. The wave of financial market integration from the late 1990s onwards has made this goal all the more important for the countries that have large financial

Table 3.1 The general institutional framework for financial services regulation in the EU

Institution/body	Date of establishment	Membership/composition	Functions/tasks in financial services regulation
European Commission	1958	Commissioners appointed by member states; civil servants in the services of the Commission	To initiate legislation To adopt implementing measures (comitology) To monitor implementation
European Central Bank (ECB)/Eurosystem	1999	ECB and national central banks in the eurozone	To promote smooth operation of payment systems To advise on EU legislation To contribute to the smooth conduct of national prudential supervision and the stability of the financial system
European Parliament (EP)	1958	MEPs elected in the member states	To co-decide legislation
European Council	1974 (formalised)	Heads of state and government	To take high-level strategic decisions
ECOFIN council	1958	Economic and finance ministers; informal ECOFIN also includes central bank governors	To co-decide legislation
Economic and Financial Committee (EFC)	1958 (Monetary Committee), renamed in 1999 and reshaped in 2004	Senior national civil servants from economic and finance ministries; enlarged composition includes senior central bankers	To prepare work for ECOFIN Council
Financial Services Committee (FSC)	2002	Senior national civil servants from economic and finance ministries; observers from Commission, ECB and level 3 committees	To provide strategic guidance and political advice on financial services issues
Lamfalussy committees Level 2	2004	Senior national civil servants from economic and finance ministries	To assist the Commission in adopting level 2 implementing legislation (comitology)
Lamfalussy committees Level 3	2004	Senior national civil servants from supervisory authorities	To advise the Commission on EU legislation To adopt level 3 measures To strengthen cooperation between national regulators

centres. It has, for example, become a priority for the German authorities (the project *Finanzplatz Deutschland*) (Deeg and Lütz 2000). At the same time, protectionist tendencies, especially in the countries that do not have a competitive financial sector, have been resilient (Coleman and Underhill 1998; Underhill 1997; Brown 1997).

National, EU and international regulations represent not only instruments through which to ensure financial stability, to pursue financial market integration, to promote economic efficiency and competition, and to safeguard investor protection. They are also instruments to boost the comparative advantages of a country or the advantages of specific parts of an industry (Mügge 2006). Indeed, the choice of one model or another for EU regulation has different adjustment costs for different countries and can substantially affect the competitiveness of national industry (Egan 2001).

Moreover, financial regulation is a very sensitive issue because financial instability and other types of policy failure in this area have high political costs, as the British government experienced with the Northern Rock crisis. In this respect, one should note the importance of the distinctive national policy paradigms that come into play in financial services governance, as emerged during interviews with several policy-makers (practitioners generally prefer the expression 'regulatory philosophies'). For example, as far as objectives are concerned, some countries privilege consumer protection over competition – or vice versa – or value financial stability more than market efficiency. They may also prefer different types of instruments, such as soft law or binding rules, rule-based or principle-based legislation, and so on (see Fonteyne and van der Vossen 2007 with specific reference to the absence of a 'common philosophy' on financial stability).

From an economic point of view, national financial structures across Europe display important differences and constitute core features of varieties of capitalism (Albert 1993; Hall and Soskice 2001). The main distinction concerning financial systems is between banking-oriented and market-oriented financial systems (Allen and Gale 2000). Moreover, the relationships between the financial sector and the rest of the economy, especially the manufacturing sector, vary across the EU. In some countries, such as Germany, before the reform introduced in 2000, there used to be strong links to the bank industry through cross-shareholdings (Deeg 2005). In other countries, such as Italy, this was forbidden until the 1990s, but banks lent to a large number of SMEs. In the UK, industry has arm's-length relations with the City (Kynaston 2001; Reid 1988).

Last but not least, financial services regulation is a political issue with a technical content. Thus, it requires a substantive input from the technical authorities (supervisory bodies and central banks), some of which are independent and powerful actors in their own right. On the one hand, national policy-makers are keen to safeguard the national interest (for example, the competitiveness of national financial centres or the protection of national consumers) and/or their bureaucratic interest (the prerogatives or powers of their organisations). On the other hand, they are aware of the need to cooperate at the EU and the international level (Kapstein 1989). This is particularly important in the case of mobile capital and transantional companies that might escape regulation, or 'shop around' across national jurisdictions (i.e. regulatory frameworks) for lighter regulatory standards, with the risk of a race to the bottom.

Hence, the national regulatory and supervisory authorities sometimes play against each other in EU fora in defending the 'national interest' (to be defined), at times pressurised to do so by their respective governments or by industry. At other times they employ 'collusive action' to push through their policy preferences (Kapstein 1992), which can be originated by bureaucratic politics (Peters 2004), such as the defence of their own prerogatives, but also by their view of the public interest, which is also informed by the policy paradigm to which they subscribe, as well as by the structural context in which they operate. At yet other times, they act as international technocrats by engaging in cross-border cooperation to prevent policy failures (Kapstein 1989; Underhill 1991).

Partly because of the substantive differences of national economic structures and partly because of the diversity of domestic preferences, regulatory and supervisory frameworks have retained distinctive features across the EU, even though some convergence has taken place. If the three main segments of the financial sector are compared, it is clear that the progress towards market integration, regulation and supervision varied over time until the late 1990s: it has been more advanced in banking and less so in insurance and securities markets (Story and Walter 1997).

Drivers of financial market integration in the EU

There were two main waves of financial integration in the EU: the period from the mid-1980s to 1992, which was driven by the Single Market programme, and the period from the late 1990s onwards, which was driven by the effects of EMU and the FSAP. In both cases, the driving factors share some similarities.

The factors underpinning the relaunch of the Single Market in financial services from the mid-1980s onwards are part of a broader set of external and internal factors that stimulated the Single Market programme. First, competition from the US and Japan called for increased efficiency in the European economy by creating a larger internal market (on the 'costs of non-Europe', see Cecchini *et al.* 1988). Second, this objective had the full support of the Commission, which regarded it not only as an economic goal but as a means to further European integration *tout court* (Jabko 2006). Third, the Single Market programme and the Commission that relaunched it had the support of the business community, at least the most internationalised and competitive part of it (Cowles 1995; Apeldoorn 2002).

Finally, there was the agreement of member states, whose national governments were sympathetic to the creation of the Single Market, albeit for different reasons (Moravcsik 1993, 1998). The the British Conservative government, for example, considered it mainly as an economic project, whereas the German and French governments saw it as an economic and political project. Moreover, even the economic approach to the Single Market varied across countries, in that the UK regarded it as leading towards economic liberalisation, while France and Germany were also aware of the social dimensions.

In the second period of financial market integration that followed the 1992 project, and in particular the period in the run-up to EMU and afterwards, many of the driving factors towards financial market integration in the EU resembled those at play in the making of the 1992 project. The main difference was EMU and the introduction of the single currency. First, echoing the so-called Cecchini Report (Cecchini *et al.* 1988), there were the 'expected economic benefits' deriving from a single, more competitive financial market, which would strengthen the EU economy and which would bring benefits for consumers (e.g. higher pension returns), SMEs and larger companies (lower cost of capital) (Committee of Wise Men 2000: 4–8; see also *Financial Times*, 10 November 2000).

In addition there were expected 'costs of non-reform', because the existing system was too slow and rigid, and therefore it constituted a burden for the EU in the global economy, especially when competing with the US. It should also be said that the creation of a Single Market in financial services was seen as instrumental in strengthening the EU's voice in international financial fora. Indeed, the communication *Financial Services: Building a Framework for Action* (CEC 1998) made clear that the Commission's objective was for the EU to take a leading role in the international discussions to maintain a level playing field both within and beyond its borders, precisely at a time when the Basel II agreement was being negotiated (as discussed in the following chapter), and a similar argument was repeated when the FSAP was proposed.

Second, as had been the case in the mid-1980s, the Commission was one of the main actors in the relaunch of the Single Market in financial services in the late 1990s (Jabko 2006; Posner 2005, 2009b). The FSAP was indeed prepared by the Commission, which consulted with the business community, and the plan was eventually endorsed by the member states. Besides the economic objective of boosting market efficiency and the competitiveness of the European economy, it was clear to the Commission that this was an area where the main member states, including the UK, traditionally an 'awkward partner' in the process of European integration (George 1998), were willing to integrate further, supporting the proactive stance of the Commission. The UK, Germany and France, in that specific order, were certainly among the main allies of the Commission in several initiatives designed to facilitate financial services integration in the EU – for example, in the making of the Capital Adequacy Directive and the Investment Service Directive (see Brown 1997; Coleman and Underhill 1998; Underhill 1997).

Third, there was the support of part of the business (financial) community, at least the most internationalised part of it, which was likely to have the most to gain from a truly integrated market in financial services (Apeldoorn 2002; Bieling 2003, 2006; Mügge 2006). The Single Market and EMU increased the interpenetration of financial markets and cross-border financial flows, triggering the formation of large-scale financial investors. The investment horizons of several funds and private investors became more European, the volume and number of cross-border transactions increased, and the same investment firms constituted the membership of different exchanges and served multiple national client bases (Committee of Wise Men 2000).

However, the nationally based financial groups and the less competitive part of the financial services sector tended to be lukewarm towards further integration (Grossman 2004; Lütz 2004; Mügge 2006; Jabko 2006). After all, national borders represented a protective barrier in their favour. Although these companies or groups tended to be concentrated in Mediterranean member states, the picture is more fine-grained and there are several exceptions (first and foremost, Germany), which will be discussed in the following chapters. For example, the Spanish banking sector (to be precise, large private Spanish banks) is competitive and the largest Spanish banks are expanding rapidly in the European market, as are the two biggest Italian banking groups, which are also some of the largest in the eurozone (for an overview of the competitiveness of the banking sector of the main EU countries, see Deutsche Bank 2004a, 2004b, 2004c, 2005b).

Fourth, technological innovation, which increased the speed and flow of information, and the spread of new financial instruments such as securities, meant that financial markets changed rapidly (Maes 2007), and the EU regulatory framework was unable to cope with this speed (Committee of Wise Men 2000: 9). Moreover the transantionalisation of financial services in the EU challenged the traditional mode of regulation and supervision of these activities in Europe, and the Single Currency triggered the restructuring of the banking system, further stimulated by the enlargement of the EU in 2004 and 2007 (ECB 2004a, 2003c). These changes increased the pressure to update the arrangements for prudential regulation and supervision. Hence, the member states, including the national regulatory and supervisory authorities that had most to lose in terms of renouncing their prerogatives, came to terms with the need for further regulation and supervisory cooperation (Jabko 2006).

As far as the content of the legislation passed in the first four decades is concerned, the directives issued in the 1970s sanctioned the right of establishment, subject to host country control. In the 1980s, the 'home country' principle was introduced into EU legislation, meaning that financial firms could operate across the Union on the basis of rules set by the country where their headquarters were located. After the relaunch of the Single Market in the mid-1980s, and before 1999, the policy was based on three core principles. The first was national regulation, coupled with 'mutual recognition' and the 'minimal harmonisation' of national rules through EU rules, even though EU regulation was more developed in the banking sector than in other financial services (Lastra 2003; Padoa-Schioppa 1999a). The second principle was the national execution of supervision with cooperation either bilaterally, on the basis of memoranda of understanding between regulators, or multilaterally, in the form of 'technical' committees. Third, there were non-legally binding international rules, such as the standards set by the BCBS. In addition, the so-called Basel I agreement in 1988 on the 'International Convergence of Capital Measurement and Capital Standards' was transposed into an EU directive, which was legally binding upon all member states. These arrangements were substantially changed in the 2000s, as explained below.

The quickening pace of financial integration in the EU from the late 1990s onwards

The relaunch of the Single Market in financial services gained momentum at the Cardiff European Council in June 1998, which established the Cardiff process for product and capital market reform. This was a system of multilateral surveillance of structural reforms on the basis of an annual report from the member states and the Commission. An overall framework for the integration of financial services was seen as necessary for the achievement of the EU's economic potential following the introduction of the euro (Council, Presidency Conclusion, 15 June 1998).

Financial Services Action Plan (FSAP) 1999

Financial market integration in Europe was a priority for the British presidency in the first semester of 1998 (Mügge 2006). With EMU looming ahead, the Directorate General Internal Market of the Commission began working on a policy document that was eventually published in October 1998 as a communication, entitled *Financial Services: Building a Framework for Action*, setting out a framework for action on financial services (CEC 1998). Following the suggestion of the Commission, the Financial Services Policy Group was established to identify priorities among the measures outlined in the communication. It was composed of representatives of the national governments, the ECB and the Council, and it was chaired by the Internal Market commissioner (first by Mario Monti, then by Fritz Bolkestain). The Financial Service Policy Group was asked by the Council to examine four areas: where new legal initiatives were required; where existing provisions had to be adapted to new developments; where existing provisions needed to be simplified; and where these should be made more coherent. The Policy Group met repeatedly to review progress on the implementation of the FSAP. In 2005 it was transformed into the Financial Services Committee (FSC) and was chaired no longer by the Commission, but by a member state representative. The FSC advises the Commission and the Council on financial market matters (Lannoo 2005).

The FSAP was issued by the European Commission in 1999 (CEC 1999) and it was endorsed by the European Council in Cologne that same year. At the European Council in Lisbon, it was agreed that it should be completed by the end of 2005, with the first stage, the integration of the securities markets, being in place by the end of 2003. The FSAP, a five-year plan that contained a set of forty-two legislative measures, was part of what has come to be known as the 'Lisbon Agenda', a plan to make the EU 'the most dynamic, innovative, knowledge-based economy in the world by 2010'. On the wholesale side, which was its main focus, it included rules concerning securities and derivatives in order to raise capital on a EU-wide basis. On the retail side, the emphasis was on information and transparency, eliminating charges for cross-border transactions. The FSAP also incorporated a number of measures on streamlining financial supervision performed by the national authorities, supplemented by multilateral and bilateral ad hoc cooperation. Finally, it embraced measures on taxation and corporate governance, which were indirectly linked with financial markets. The most important measures put forward in the FSAP will be discussed in the following chapters.

In October 2003, the Commission set up four expert groups to report on the success of the FSAP in promoting integration in banking, insurance, asset management and securities trading. After a consultation process, the reports concluded that the FSAP had been successful not only in the adoption of legislation but also in fostering cooperation between the public authorities and market participants (Expert Group on Banking 2004; Expert Group on Securities 2004). The plan was completed at the end of 2004. In its tenth progress report on the FSAP in June of that year, the Commission indicated that, from 2005 onwards, its focus would be on ensuring implementation and monitoring the effectiveness of the plan (CEC 2004a). Thus, there would be a 'regulatory pause'.

A new financial services architecture in the EU for the twenty-first century[1]

The so-called Lamfalussy architecture is particularly important because it revised the overall framework for financial services regulation and supervision in the EU. In other words, it was not a specific directive concerning one or a limited number of aspects, but rather a change in how to make and implement rules and coordinate supervision.

In July 2000, the ECOFIN appointed an ad hoc Committee of Wise Men, led by Alexandre Lamfalussy, to discuss the best means to adopt the Commission's FSAP and adapt EU regulation to a changing financial marketplace.[2] The mandate consisted of three main elements: to assess the current conditions for implementing the regulation of the securities markets in the Union; to assess how the mechanism for regulating the securities markets can best respond to developments already under way; and to propose scenarios for adapting current practices in order to ensure greater convergence and cooperation in day-to-day implementation (Committee of Wise Men 2000: 29). It was clearly established that the committee would not deal with prudential supervision.

The working method of the committee was to elicit opinions from a variety of policy actors in an open way. It met officials from the Commission and the ECB, and Baron Lamfalussy appeared before the Economic and Monetary Affairs Committee of the European Parliament. It invited the member states, regulatory authorities and the industry itself to submit contributions. It also invited leading representatives of the major constituencies of European securities markets, trade unions and several personalities from the financial world to confidential hearings in Brussels (Committee of Wise Men 2000: 32–5).

The report was completed in December 2000 and proposed the framework described below, albeit only with reference to securities. Reportedly, the Wise Men had considered the proposal of a single European regulator for the financial sector, but quickly concluded that creating such an agency would require years of intergovernmental negotiation, and that any such agency would be hampered by the continuing diversity of national regulations in the area (Committee of Wise Men 2000: 26).

The EP endorsed the goal of the report but, in order to increase the accountability of the Commission in the level 2 committee and at the same time to safeguard its legislative powers, revived an earlier demand for a 'call-back' mechanism, which had been rejected during the negotiation of the 1999 Comitology Decision (*Financial Times*, 28 February 2001, 7 March 2001). The EP proposal was dismissed by the final report of the Committee of Wise Men, and the large majority of governments subsequently rejected it in March 2001 during the Stockholm European Council.

The question of parliamentary scrutiny was resolved in February 2002 on the basis of a compromise between the EP and the Commission, in which the former renounced its demand for a call-back mechanism in return for a statement from the Commission president, Romano Prodi, assuring the parliament that the Securities Committee would operate with 'full transparency vis-à-vis the EP' (Prodi 2002). In addition, the Commission agreed to accept the inclusion by the EP of 'sunset clauses', limiting the delegation of implementing powers to a four-year period, after which parliamentary approval would be required for renewal. Comitology was reported in 2006 (see Christiansen and Vaccari 2006).

Rather unexpectedly, the proposed level 2 Securities Committee also raised objections from Germany in the days before the planned adoption of the Lamfalussy Report by the Stockholm European Council in March 2001. Within the ECOFIN Council that preceded it, the German finance minister, Hans Eichel, sought additional guarantees that the Commission would not use its newly gained powers under the reformed regulatory committee procedure to push through legislation opposed by a simple majority of member governments (*Financial Times*, 22 March 2001, 23 March 2001). Eichel demanded a commitment that the Commission would not go against the 'predominant views that might emerge in the Council', in effect attempting to reintroduce the old safety-net mechanism whereby a simple majority could block a Commission decision. Such a commitment had already been made by the Commission as part of the 1999 Comitology Decision, and this deliberate ambiguity was preserved in the final text prepared for Stockholm (Pollack 2003: 151). Reportedly, Eichel feared that the Commission, especially DG Internal Market, would push through securities legislation that would favour London over Frankfurt as a centre for securities trading (*Financial Times*, 27 March 2001).

The Lamfalussy Report, the final version of which was issued in 2001 (Committee of Wise Men 2001), was the real trigger for the debate on financial regulation and supervision concerning the whole financial sector. In May 2002 ECOFIN, following the proposal by Hans Eichel and the British chancellor, Gordon Brown, decided in favour of extending the fast-track procedure of the report to banking and insurance (*Financial Times*, 15 April 2002). The ECB initially opposed the extension of the Lamfalussy framework from securities to other financial sectors, especially banking (Duisenberg 2002; Padoa-Schioppa 2002). However, once the proposal gained momentum, the ECB engaged in a rearguard action, calling for the inclusion of the ECB and national central banks in the new committees being created. The issue was negotiated throughout 2002, and in December the ECOFIN Council approved a proposal from the Economic and Financial Committee for the extension of the Lamfalussy framework to other sectors, namely, banking and insurance. It also took on board the ECB's request for involvement (EFC 2002). The new framework was set in place throughout 2003 and 2004. Special provisions concerning the committees on financial conglomerates are discussed in Chapter 4.

The EU policy framework established in 2004 is based on a complex multilevel system of EU rule-making and enhanced cooperation between national supervisory authorities, underpinned by newly created EU committees (such as the European Securities Committee, set up in 2001) and re-formed committees (such as the Banking Advisory Committee, which dated back to 1977 and was renamed the European Banking Committee, and the Insurance Committee, dating back to 1992). The functional division between banking, securities and insurance is maintained.

As far as regulation is concerned, the 'first level' consists of the traditional Community method, whereby the Commission drafts legislation after consulting the so-called level 3 advisory committees. The Commission's proposal is then co-decided by the ECOFIN Council and the EP, laying out common EU rules and principles in the form of either directives or regulations. These general rules are supplemented by 'technical' regulations and implementing measures produced through 'comitology', the so-called level 2 regulatory committee, in which the Commission's proposals are voted upon and the Qualify Majority Voting (QMV) applies.[3] These committees also provide advice to the Commission on draft level 1 legislation, based on the input provided by level 3 committees. Each level 2 committee has one voting national representative and one technical expert per member state nominated by the relevant ministry. The Commission service chairs and provides the secretariat.

At the third level, the advisory committees must ensure the consistent implementation of the measures agreed, by coordinating the execution of national supervision and advising the Commission on the drafting of level 2 measures. The level 2 committees can request advice from the level 3 committees. In level 3 committees, each member state has a vote allocated to the supervisory authority. The Commission has observer status. Both national central banks, with and without supervisory responsibility, and the ECB take part in the level 3 banking committee, but only the supervisory authorities possess a vote. The fourth level consists of national implementation, with an important monitoring role for the Commission.

The working in practice of the Lamfalussy architecture and the reform proposals put forward in the wake of the global financial crisis in 2009 will be discussed in the following chapters. Here, it is important to mention that, at least in theory, the Commission has an influential position: it drafts legislation at levels 1 and 2, it chairs the level 2 committees, and it participates in level 3 committees that advise on the legislation to be drafted for levels 1 and 2. Yet member state representatives sit on level 2 and 3 committees.

An overall assessment

Supranational actors were crucial at the agenda-setting stage of the process of financial market integration relaunched by the Commission's action plan in 1999 and further advanced by the Lamfalussy Report in 2001. Both the Commission and the Committee of Wise Men acted as 'policy entrepreneurs' (Laffan 1997), namely as agents that invest resources to engineer policy and institutional changes, by defining problems, such as the lack of a fully integrated and properly regulated Single Market in financial services, and by proposing concrete solutions. To be sure, the Commission had been trying to further financial services integration in this area since the 1960s (Maes 2007); however, the limited level of transnational exchange and the attitudes of the member states posed major obstacles to this. It was able to do so in the late 1990s because it had the support of the member states, which feeds into an intergovernmentalist account, as elaborated below.

Although it was not a supranational agency, the Committee of Wise Men was beyond the direct control of the national governments. It deliberately and strategically elicited the input of a vast array of non-governmental actors, first and foremost financial companies and independent experts (Committee of Wise Men 2000). It is also worth noting that when Baron

Lamfalussy, a former president of the European Monetary Institute (the predecessor of the ECB, 1994–8) and a former senior official at the Bank for International Settlements, was appointed as the chairperson of the committee, the German and British governments expressed some reservations because they regarded him as a person 'too committed' to European integration (*Financial Times*, 12 July 2000).

The EP, which was not directly involved in the agenda-setting stage, endorsed the FSAP and participated in the co-decision procedure with the Council on the setting up of the Lamfalussy framework.[4] Whereas the EP supported the plan for a Single Market for financial services and for more efficient and timely EU regulation, the accountability of the level 2 committees remained a concern, with the main bone of contention being the procedures and extent of comitology. In this respect, the EP was also keen to safeguard its institutional powers (or prerogatives) in the policy-making process, which prior to the 2006 comitology decision, involved co-decision between it and the Council at level 1 but excluded the parliament at level 2 (interview, Brussels, 29 June 2006).

The third supranational agency, the ECB, broadly endorsed the FSAP but initially did not welcome the formation of the many committees foreseen by the Lamfalussy Report. It unsuccessfully attempted to reshape the agenda for reform, making the case for enhancing the role of central banks in prudential supervision on two grounds (ECB 2001a, 2001b). The ECB argued that, since it was responsible for stability in case of a systemic crisis in the banking system, the insurance sector or pension funds, it would be the first institution to which the market would look in such a situation. It also pointed out that any potential conflict of interest between the conduct of monetary policy and banking supervision – an argument often used to prevent central banks from being active in prudential supervision – was ruled out in the EMU policy framework because monetary policy decisions were outside the exclusive control of national central banks (ECB 2003b; Padoa-Schioppa 2002; *Financial Times*, 23 March 2001, 15 April 2002, 11 July 2002, 30 January 2003). However, once it became clear that the Lamfalussy model had gathered enough support in the EU, the ECB engaged in a rearguard action so as to ensure that both it and the national central banks would be present on the relevant committees (Duisenberg 2002). One explanation for the stance of the ECB is that, once they lost their role in setting monetary policy, the national central banks that constitute the bulk of its decision-making body were eager to increase their role in banking supervision (*Financial Times*, 30 January 2003).

Transnational industry supported the FSAP and the institutional framework necessary to underpin it (the Lamfalussy framework), providing an important backing to the work of the Commission (Mügge 2006; Bieling 2003). On the whole, there are historical similarities between the Single Market in financial services and the 1992 Single Market project, and there is an interesting parallel between the European Commission's FSAP in 1999 and the Commission's White Paper in 1985. Moreover, in 2001, the European Round Table of Financial Services set up a specialist group to conduct a study on the economic costs of failure to complete the Single Market in that area. The group was chaired by Paolo Cecchini, whose report on the potential benefits of non-Europe had made him one of the most powerful architects of the relaunch of the Single Market in the 1980s (Cecchini *et al.* 2003; Heinemann and Jopp 2002). The main EU banking associations expressed their support for the extension of the Lamfalussy framework to banking, as reported in several statements issued at that time.

Some of the main market players put forward innovative proposals that went beyond what was eventually agreed upon. For example, Deutsche Bank proposed the creation of a European System of Supervisory Authorities (similar to the European System of Central Banks, ESCB), which would include but not be limited to a European Financial Service Authority (Deutsche Bank 2000; see also EUROFI 2002a, 2002b). Moreover, in 2002, EUROFI, an association of officials and market participants based in Paris, published a document arguing that, building on the Lamfalussy process, a European regulatory and supervisory system should be established following the ESCB model. Indeed, transnational business was in favour of greater institutionalised cooperation among supervisory authorities for an obvious reason: it would simplify their cross-border operations, an issue that re-emerged forcefully in the review of the Lamfalussy framework in 2007. National supervisors were reluctant to endorse this solution, though proposals moving in this direction were put forward following the global financial crisis, as explained in Chapter 8.

Transnational companies pursued their policy agenda mainly by supporting the activity of the Commission, but also, given the fact that many of them had headquarters in certain member states, by lobbying national governments – namely, the UK, Germany and France – which feeds into an intergovernmentalist explanation. Indeed, these governments were strongly supportive of the FSAP and the Lamfalussy process, but also wary of moving towards anything resembling a European regulator (interviews, Rome, 23 June 2006; London, 20 April 2006).

Because the Council endorsed both the FSAP and the setting up of the Lamfalussy framework, which constituted a substantial boost to the proposed action plan, the outcome of the policy reform is compatible with the preferences of the Commission (interviews, Brussels 29 June 2006, 27 June 2007). By initially limiting the time period for the delegation of powers for the adoption of technical rules until 2004, the preferences of the EP were also taken into account, although not entirely accommodated (e.g. no call-back clause was agreed). Similarly, although the ECB was less successful in pursuing its preferences (Engelen 2002), it managed to secure the participation of central banks in the relevant committees. It should also be noted that an outcome more in line with a supranational governance explanation, especially with the preferences of transnational financial groups, would have been the creation of a system of European regulatory and supervisory agencies or a single (supranational) European regulator.

To summarise, the hypotheses derived from supranational governance are supported by empirical record, with some important qualifications. The influence of supranational actors was greater at the agenda-setting stage and minimal, with some exception for the EP, during the decision-making stage. The policy outcome accords largely with the preferences of the Commission and the EP as well as of transnational industry. Finally, previous integration and increased economic interdependence strengthened the activities of transnational business, providing the background for the reform.

Although the decision on the composition and mandate of the Group of Wise Men was taken by the national governments gathered in ECOFIN, the role of national governments was limited in the agenda-setting phase, which largely coincided with the Commission's action plan in 1999 and the drafting of the Lamfalussy Report. However, while the Commission consulted with the national governments before putting forward the FSAP, it is not easy to gauge to what extent the member states (and which ones) were influential at that stage. Reportedly, those with the largest financial markets were strongly supportive of the policy agenda elaborated by the Commission, and the British presidency was influential in pushing through the FSAP (interview, Brussels, 29 June 2006).

National governments in ECOFIN Council meetings and European Council sessions were predominant at the decision-making phase, and this was characterized mainly by interstate bargaining, with the largest member states at centre-stage. To begin with, the ECOFIN Council approved the FSAP and the final version of the report of the Committee of the Wise Men, and also its implementation, once the EP gave its assent. It was also the ECOFIN Council, hence national finance ministers, which decided to extend the Lamfalussy framework to the whole financial sector in May 2002. Within the ECOFIN Council, the British and German finance ministers engineered such a proposal and formed the political driving force for its approval, with the active support of the French government and no noticeable opposition from other governments (*Financial Times*, 11 July 2002). This indicates the convergence, or at least the congruence, of the preferences of the member states. Although the French treasury minister, Laurent Fabius, had initially proposed a plan for the creation of a European super-regulator based in Paris – which would have greatly benefited the financial centre of the city – he scaled back the plan once lack of support for it became clear (*Financial Times*, 12 July 2000).

Several other features of the process fit well with liberal intergovernmentalist assumptions, such as the concern of national governments about the loss of sovereignty and the reluctance to delegate decision-making powers. The extension of the framework to banking and insurance can be seen as an attempt by the national governments, first and foremost the British and the Germans, to prevent the expansion of the ECB's competencies (Lannoo

2005) or the creation of a European (supranational) regulator. Another indicator of the intergovernmental logic was the proposal by Eichel and Brown to create an (intergovernmental) European Stability Forum, which was opposed by the ECB on the grounds that the Frankfurt-based Banking Supervisory Committee was the appropriate forum to discuss the financial stability of the system (*Financial Times*, 15 April 2002). Similarly, the proposal to reconfigure the Financial Services Policy Group into the FSC with a member state chair, which was intended to provide political oversight on financial market issues for the benefit of ECOFIN, also has a strong intergovernmental flavour. Indeed, this body comprises one high-level representative of the relevant ministry per member state and one alternate; the Commission has one member, ensuring the representation of the chair of the level 2 committees and the ECB and level 3 chairs have observer status.

The 'liberal' hypothesis, which also highlights the relations between states and markets, is that the national preferences articulated in the intergovernmental negotiations were the aggregated preferences of powerful domestic economic interest groups. The financial service sectors in Britain, Germany and, to a lesser extent, France were in favour of the FSAP because their leading financial investors were efficient and competitive, and hence well positioned to compete successfully in a single European financial market (Pagoulatos 2003). Furthermore, financial operators in these countries already had a trans-European dimension and were therefore expected to benefit from access to a continental Single Market for financial services, regulated by efficient and timely legislation and coordinated supervision, to be ensured by the Lamfalussy framework (interviews, Frankfurt, 17 January 2006; London, 20 April 2006). The banking sector in Germany was, however, divided in terms of policy preferences; whereas the large private banks supported the reform, the regional public banks, which tend to be inward-oriented, did not (on the traditional divide between these two categories of bank, see Deeg 1999; Lütz 2004).

Previous research indicates that the financial sectors in Britain, Germany and, to a lesser extent, France represent influential lobbies in their national setting, and that they have an important role in informing the negotiating position of their national governments in EU fora (Coleman 1996, 1994; Josselin 1997; Moran 1994). However, as revealed by national policy-makers and industry representatives, the intensive and extensive consultations that took place with reference to other policy episodes discussed in the following chapters (e.g. the Basel II Accord and, especially, the Capital Requirements Directive; see Chapter 4) did not take place at the national level in relation to the Lamfalussy process. As explained in Quaglia (2008b), the Lamfalussy process did not elicit a high degree of direct involvement from interest groups because it had the characteristics of a public good, which meant that financial associations and private companies had limited incentive to lobby on this issue: the specific costs of doing so outweighed the diffuse potential benefits.

Moreover, the implications of the new framework for the activity of interest groups were highly uncertain.

The most important caveat is that the interest groups and companies that were expected to benefit most from the reform were actually transnational actors with substantial shares in activities in more than one EU country, as opposed to purely domestic actors (Mügge 2006). The investment horizons of funds and private investors had become more European, and so had their lobbying, as suggested by the activities of the European Financial Services Round Table. Furthermore, at times they tried to bypass the national governments, acting directly at the EU level. The dynamics of the reform process, at least at certain stages, such as the preparation of the Commission's proposals or the drafting of the Lamfalussy Report, deliberately encouraged input from financial market operators, which feeds into the supranational governance explanation.

The public authorities (primarily the treasury ministries and to some extent the supervisory authorities, namely, the Financial Services Authority in the UK and the Bundesanstalt für Finanzdienstleistungsaufsicht in Germany) largely defined national preference in accordance with their own priorities, opposing any extension of the ECB's supervisory competences as well as the creation of a single European regulator (Engelen 2002), two options which were welcomed by parts of the banking sector that had contributed to the debate (see Deutsche Bank 2000; EUROFI 2002a, 2002b). Furthermore, while it is certainly true that the industry's drive for the establishment of a fully integrated and better regulated Single Market in financial services provided the trigger for the reform, it is also the case that this goal was supported by the authorities in both the UK and Germany, home to the two largest (and possibly expanding) financial centres and financial markets in Europe. The British authorities have always been quite outspoken regarding their objective of maintaining the City of London's position as the leading financial centre in Europe (Moran 1991; interview, London, December 2005), and towards the end of the 1990s the German government had also taken a similar approach to the Frankfurt *Finanzplatz* (Lütz 2004; interview, Frankfurt, 16 January 2006).

Overall, the hypothesis that the final outcome reflected the preferences of the main member states and was acceptable to all the national governments is supported by the empirical record. Germany and the UK were the main proponents of the Lamfalussy framework for the whole financial sector, France supported it, and Italy did not have any strong preferences. The discussions preceding and surrounding the FSAP and the Lamfalussy framework suggest that, among the member states, there was basic agreement on the need for further financial market integration, moving towards EU regulation and supervision of these activities, without creating a European super-regulator or increasing the supervisory competences of the ECB. Obviously, some divergences remained, but the policy history indicates that no government opposed the core of the FSAP or the Lamfalussy process.

On the whole, the hypotheses derived from intergovernmentalism are confirmed, subject to some qualifications. The national executives were the main actors in the decision-making stage of the project, though they were only by the Commission and the Committee of Wise Men consulted at the agenda-setting stage. The policy outcome is located within the Pareto frontier of the member states, and it reflects especially the preferences of the main players, namely, the British and German governments. In the formation of national preferences, the financial sectors and large companies took the lion's share, though it is questionable to what extent they can be regarded as domestic actors, for they tend to be transnational forces, also directly engaged in lobbying activities in Brussels.

Conclusions

This chapter outlined the institutional framework for financial services governance in the EU. It also discussed the making of the Single Market in financial services – the background trends and the specific factors that initially slowed down and subsequently gave new momentum to the process of financial integration. Particular attention was devoted to the formulation of the FSAP, although its implementation and measures concerning specific financial services will be discussed in the following chapters, which will also explain the main similarities and differences across the main segments of the financial sector. Finally, this chapter examined the establishment of the Lamfalussy architecture, identifying the key issues, the institutional actors, and their preferences and interactions.

4   Governing banking in the EU

This chapter analyses the governance of the banking sector in the EU. It first maps the institutional framework for banking regulation and supervision in the EU and globally, given the fact that international regulation has an established tradition in this sector in comparison with the less developed international regulatory framework in place in other financial services. The institutional arrangements for financial stability and the EU policy response to the financial turmoil are examined in Chapter 8 because, even though the latter involved primarily the banking sector, its effects extended to all financial services. From a chronological and thematic point of view, it also makes sense to deal with the issues raised by the financial crisis towards the end of the book.

The second part of the chapter examines the main policy initiatives that took place in the governance of the banking sector in the EU, from the issuing of the FSAP in 1999 up to the present. These are the Basel II Accord, an international agreement that was subsequently transposed into the Capital Requirements Directive, and the Capital Requirements Directive itself. Finally, this chapter examines the policy-making process of the Financial Conglomerates Directive, which had implications for governance of the banking sector both in and outside the EU. This section also provides a useful bridge to the following chapters, dealing with securities markets and investment firms.

It is argued in this chapter that the Basel II Accord and the Capital Requirements Directive were instrumental in solving the problems of setting adequate capital requirements for credit institutions internationally and in the EU. Hence, the negotiations of the new rules were based largely on a 'cooperative game' between national regulators. However, the Basel II Accord and the Capital Requirements Directive also provide clear instances of economic diplomacy – a 'regulatory game' – whereby national authorities and industry attempted to gain comparative advantages or to limit the adjustment costs resulting from the rules set in place.

In the EU there was, on the one hand, a coalition of countries, led by Germany, France and Italy, which were concerned about the effects of the new rules on SMEs and small and medium-sized banks. On the other hand, there were countries, principally the UK, which were concerned about the effects of the regulation on non-bank financial firms. This division largely reflected domestic political economy structures: the configuration of the national financial system and the links between banks and industry.

The institutional framework for governing banking

This section first reviews the main international institutions dealing with banking governance and then focuses on the regulatory institutions in the EU. A short reference is also made to regulatory and supervisory arrangements at the national level, so as to give the flavour of how the three levels of governance interact in the banking sector.

The international institutions for governing banking

The Basel Committee on Banking Supervision (BCBS) was established by the central bank governors of the Group of Ten countries in 1974 (for an in-depth analysis of the BCBS, see Wood 2005). Initially, the committee was designed to promote international cooperation in order to close gaps in supervision, and two basic principles informed its work: no banks should escape supervision, and supervision should be adequate. Besides providing a forum for regular cooperation on supervisory matters, over time the BCBS developed into a standard-setting body on all aspects of banking supervision, including capital requirements.[1] Countries are represented in the committee by their central bank and, whenever this is not the central bank, by the authority with formal responsibility for the prudential supervision of banking activities. The committee's members come from Belgium, Canada, France, Germany, Italy, Japan, Luxembourg, the Netherlands, Spain, Sweden, Switzerland, the United Kingdom and the United States.

The BCBS can be seen as an international forum where central banks and banking regulators cooperate in the setting up of international regulatory standards in the banking sector, with a view to fostering financial stability and preventing market failures. It is also a competitive arena in which the national authorities negotiate, under the pressure of domestic politics, in order to protect national comparative advantages (Singer 2004). This is the 'regulators' dilemma' (Kapstein 1989: 323), which is conducive to a form of 'redistributive cooperation' (Oatley and Nabors 1998: 35): national regulators cooperate, but they are mindful of the costs and the benefits of doing so.

The main formal channel of coordination between banking supervisors and the supervisors of non-bank financial institutions is the Joint Forum, for which the secretariat of the BCBS provides the secretariat. The Joint Forum was established in 1996 under the aegis of the BCBS, the International Organization of Securities Commissions (IOSCO) and the International Association of Insurance Supervisors (IAIS). The decision to establish this body was taken as a response to the increasing de-segmentation of financial services and the expanding number of financial conglomerates (Porter 2005). 'It represented an initial response to the dichotomy of fragmented supervisory structures and increasingly integrated markets' (Tietmayer 1999). The Joint Forum is comprised of an equal number of senior bank, insurance and securities supervisors.[2] Its main task is to address policy issues common to the banking, securities and insurance sectors, including the regulation of financial conglomerates. In 1999 the Joint Forum released a set of documents on the supervision of financial conglomerates, developed in consultation with industry and supervisory authorities worldwide.[3] These documents, or, to be precise, some of the principles they outlined, informed the drafting of the first EU directive on financial conglomerates, issued in 2002.

The rationale behind the creation of the Joint Forum was subsequently expanded with the creation of the Financial Stability Forum (FSF), which brings together policy-makers dealing with a variety of financial activities (on the FSF, see Drezner 2007). The FSF was created by the G7 in 1999, following the proposals articulated in a report prepared by the president of the Bundesbank, Hans Tietmeyer (1999), who had been given the mandate of considering ways of strengthening financial sector surveillance.

The FSF comprises representatives from central banks, supervisory authorities and treasury ministries, senior officials from international financial institutions (the IMF, the BIS, the OECD, the World Bank) and international regulatory bodies (the BCBS, the IOSCO, the IAIS, the International Accounting Standards Board), as well as the CPSS and the ECB (Drezner 2007). Before 2009, it included representatives from G7 countries plus Hong Kong, Singapore, Australia and the Netherlands, even though in the autumn of 2008 proposals were put forward with a view to enlarging its membership. In early 2009, in the wake of the global financial crisis, it was renamed the Financial Stability Board (FSB), endowed with a more robust institutional structure and had its membership enlarged. As is the case in other international regulatory fora, there is a trade-off between 'representation' through an expansion of membership, admitting other countries, which would augment its legitimacy, and 'effectiveness', which rests partly on the limited number of participants (André Icard, quoted in Fratianni and Pattison 2001: 212).

Other activities of the G7 are not reviewed here, as they are not directly relevant to the governance of banking (for an analysis of the role of the G7 in shaping the international financial order, see Baker 2006; Porter 2005).

The EU institutions for governing banking

The five main institutions involved in financial services governance in the EU have been outlined in the previous chapter and hence are not discussed again. This section deals mainly with the committees and groups involved in banking governance that were set up as part of the Lamfalussy framework.

The European Banking Committee, which held its first formal meeting in July 2005, is the successor to the Banking Advisory Committee, set up in 1978. The European Banking Committee is composed of high-level representatives from the member states, usually from the treasury or the finance ministry, though in a few cases from the central banks and/or supervisory authorities – it is up to each member state to decide. It is chaired by a representative of the Commission, usually a senior official from Directorate General Internal Market – Financial Services, and the secretariat is also provided by the Commission. Observers from the ECB and the CEBS and representatives from both European Economic Area (EEA) countries and candidate countries are invited to attend the meetings.

Unlike the Banking Advisory Committee, which had mainly advisory powers, the European Banking Committee is a level 2 committee that fulfils comitology functions, which means that it assists the Commission in adopting implementing measures (generally directives, less frequently regulations) for level 1 framework legislation and provides advice on policy issues related to banking activities. It operates by QMV, and the voting weight is the same as in the Council of Ministers, though de facto consensus is sought (interview, Brussels, 29 March 2007).

Unlike the analogue committee in the securities sector, the European Banking Committee has not dealt with any Lamfalussy directives because it has focused on the transposition of the Basel II Accord. To date, the main comitology procedure that has gone through the committee concerned the amendment of the provisions dealing with cross-border mergers in the Banking Directive 2000/12. The committee has also discussed the reform of the supervisory arrangements in the EU, an issue on which 'passion builds up' because the member states know that they can express their views freely (interview, Brussels, 29 March 2007).

The CEBS was set up in 2004 in London (on the CEBS, see Quaglia 2008c). According to its charter, each member state designates a senior representative from the national competent supervisory authority in the banking sector, and this representative is the voting member. In addition, each member state appoints as a non-voting member a senior representative of the national central bank when the latter is not the competent authority. If the national central bank is the competent authority, the member state may designate a second representative from this institution. The ECB also designates a senior representative as a non-voting member. Representatives from countries of the EEA participate as observers, together with the European Commission and the chair of the Banking Supervision Committee of the ESCB (Article 1).[4]

The CEBS advises the Commission, either on its own initiative or at the Commission's request, in particular concerning the preparation of draft-implementing measures in the field of banking activities (level 2 measures) and in the preparation of level 1 legislation. It contributes to the consistent implementation of EU legislation by issuing 'standards' and 'guidelines' (level 3 measures) and to the convergence of member states' supervisory practices throughout the EU. Finally, it promotes supervisory cooperation through the exchange of information.

The committee aims to work on a consensus basis. If no consensus can be reached, decisions will be taken by qualified majority, whereby each member state has the same number of voting rights as in the Council of Ministers. When a decision is taken by qualified majority, the committee should identify and elaborate the opinion of individual members. In such a case, members that do not intend to apply the decisions must state their reason for not doing so – the so-called complain or explain procedure (Article 5).

The main permanent working group of the CEBS is the Groupe de Contact, a long-standing group of banking supervisors from the EEA, which dated back to 1972 and had traditionally focused on supervisory practices and the exchange of confidential and non-confidential information (CEBS 2005). Other groups were set up with a separate mandate in 2005–7. The most active have been those dealing with the implementation of the Capital Requirements Directive.

After the creation of the ECB, the Banking Supervision Committee of the ESCB with a secretariat at the ECB was established in Frankfurt, comprising banking supervisors from all EU member states and chaired by a national central bank. This committee assists the ECB in drafting banking legislation and supports the Eurosystem in the conduct of its tasks in the field of prudential supervision of credit institutions and financial stability (ex Article 105.5 of the TEU). Once the Lamfalussy framework was established, the need arose to clarify the relationship between the Banking Supervision Committee of the ESCB and the CEBS. The crucial difference is that the former deals with issues related to financial stability, whereas the latter deals with banking regulation.

After the endorsement of the Lamfalussy framework, a specific level 2 committee, the European Financial Conglomerates Committee, was created, bringing together officials from the treasuries and finance ministries of the member states. The ECB has observer status and the Commission provides the secretariat in Brussels. De jure the committee takes decisions by QMV, but de facto consensus is sought. So far it has not adopted any level 2 implementing measure – the Financial Conglomerates Directive was not a Lamfalussy directive, as it was passed before the Lamfalussy process had been set in place. It has, however, given advice to level 3, for example on equivalence, as explained towards the end of this chapter.

A corresponding level 3 committee on financial conglomerates was not created, and the CEBS, the CESR and the Committee of European Insurance and Occupational Pensions Supervisors decided to set up an informal structure called the Interim Working Committee on Financial Conglomerates, which was composed of national experts coming mainly from the CEBS and the the Committee of European Insurance and Occupational Pensions Supervisors and became operative in 2006. The existing level 3 committees felt that there was no need for a permanent separate committee for financial conglomerates, and the proposal to create one was rejected (interview, London, 17 May 2007). The level 3 committees were also concerned that a new committee on financial conglomerates would take on a life of its own (interview, Brussels, 27 May 2007). There are two representatives per member state, one from the banking supervisor and one from the insurance supervisor. Countries that have a single supervisor also have two members from the same organisation. The ECB and the Commission have observer status.

The financial conglomerates working group does not deal with cross-sectoral issues, such as the revision of the rules for cross-border mergers and acquisitions in the various segments of the financial sector. Cross-sectoral issues are dealt with using the so-called 3L3 format – that is, meetings of the chair and secretariats of the banking, securities and insurance committees.

An overview of the international and EU institutions for the governance of banking and financial conglomerates is provided in Table 4.1.

The national institutions for governing banking

Along with EU and international regulatory and supervisory institutions and fora, it is important to review the institutional framework for banking governance at the national level, at least in general terms, given the fact that specific arrangements vary from country to country (for a comprehensive overview, see Masciandaro 2005; ECB 2003b; Pagoulatos 1999). It should be noted that the national authorities surveyed in this section sit in the EU and international regulatory and supervisory fora mentioned above, though representation in such bodies varies across countries. For example, in the case of Italy and Spain, the central bank is the sole country representative on the BCBS, the CEBS and the Banking Supervision Committee; in the case of Germany and the UK, after the 2002 and 1997 reforms respectively, the financial supervisory authority sits alongside the central bank.

The political authorities, first and foremost the treasury ministry (or an equivalent, such as the Ministry of Finance in Germany and the Ministry for the Economy in Italy and France), form the regulatory body, even though in several countries the supervisory agencies have some regulatory powers. Representatives from the treasury or finance ministry usually sit on the European Banking Committee.

The 'technical' banking supervisory authorities can be the central banks (as in Italy and Spain), independent agencies separated from the treasury (the British Financial Services Authority) or semi-independent bodies, ultimately responding to the treasury or finance ministry (this last is the case of the Bundesanstalt für Finanzdienstleistungsaufsicht [BaFin] in Germany). In some countries the central bank is de facto involved in certain aspects of banking supervision, as is the case in Germany (Lütz 2004). In Ireland there is a supervisory agency that deals with the entire financial sector, but this is

Table 4.1 The institutional framework for banking governance (international bodies in shaded boxes)

Institution/body	Date of establishment	Membership/composition	Functions/tasks in financial services regulation
Basel Committee on Banking Supervision (BCBS)	1974	Central bankers and banking supervisors from thirteen developed countries	To set international standards in banking To promote cooperation on supervisory matters
Joint Forum (JF)	1996	Banking, insurance and securities supervisors from BCBS, IOSCO, IAIS	To address policy issues common to banking, securities and insurance sectors, including regulation of financial conglomerates
Financial Stability Forum (FSF)	1999	Central bankers, supervisors and treasury ministry officials (G7), senior officials from international financial institutions (IMF, BIS, OECD, World Bank) and international regulatory bodies (BCBS, IOSCO, IAIS, IASB), as well as the CPSS and the ECB	To assess vulnerabilities affecting the financial system and oversee action needed to address them To promote coordination and information exchange To collaborate with the IMF to conduct Early Warning Exercises
Financial Stability Board (FSB)	2009	FSF transformed into FSB and membership enlarged	
European Banking Committee (EBC)	2004	Senior national civil servants from economic and finance ministries in the EU; chair: Commission; observers from ECB, CEBS and EEA	To assist the Commission in adopting EU level 2 implementing legislation in banking (comitology)
Committee of European Banking Supervisors (CEBS)	2004	National banking supervisors, ECB; observers from Commission, BSC, EEA	To advise the Commission on EU legislation in banking To adopt level 3 measures To strengthen cooperation between national banking supervisors
Banking Supervision Committee (BSC)	1999	Banking supervisors from all EU member states, ECB representative	To assist the ECB in drafting banking regulation To support the Eurosystem in conducting prudential supervision
Financial Conglomerates Committee (FCC)	2004	National treasuries and finance ministries officials in the EU; chair: Commission	To assist the Commission in adopting EU level 2 implementing legislation on financial conglomerates (comitology)
Interim Working Group on Financial Conglomerates (IWGFC)	2006	Members of CEBS, CEIOPS; observer: CESR	To advise the Commission on EU legislation on financial conglomerates To adopt level 3 measures To strengthen cooperation between national regulators

located in the central bank (Westrup 2005). In the Netherlands the central bank is the prudential supervisor for the banking and insurance sectors, though there is also a supervisory authority dealing with the conduct of business. In some countries (the UK, Germany and Belgium after the reforms of 1997, 2002 and 2004, respectively) there is one supervisor for the entire financial sector. The Scandinavian countries adopted a single supervisor model in the late 1980s.

At the national level, the arrangements for the supervision of financial conglomerates vary remarkably. Where there is a single supervisor for the entire financial sector, located either within or outside the central bank, that authority supervises financial conglomerates. It is no coincidence that some of the countries with both the biggest and the highest number of financial conglomerates have adopted the model of a single financial supervisor (Quaglia 2008d). Countries that do not have a single supervisory authority, such as Italy and France, rely mainly on the cooperation between sectoral supervisors, normally with the banking supervisor in the driving seat.

The Lamfalussy framework has given more prominence in the making of EU legislation to the national supervisory authorities dealing with banking supervision, as well as securities and insurance supervision. Indeed, the national supervisory authorities sit on the level 3 committees, which have the task of monitoring the uniform implementation of EU rules at the domestic level; facilitating cooperation and exchange of information and best practices among national supervisors; and promoting the convergence of supervisory standards across the Union. Moreover, the involvement of the supervisory authorities is not limited to the implementation stage, for they advise the Commission in the drafting of level 2 legislation (implementing measures) and hence can have indirect influence at the decision-making stage.

It should be noted that national regulators and supervisors (treasuries and supervisory authorities) wear several hats at the same time, depending on the policy fora. First, they perform the functions of regulators and supervisors at the national level, with a view to providing the domestic public goods of 'good regulation' and 'financial stability'. Second, they act as policy-makers engaged in international and EU regulation and supervision, with a view to providing the international public goods of 'good regulation', 'financial stability' and 'effective cooperation'. Third, they act as national representatives negotiating in EU or international fora, protecting the 'national interest' or, to be precise, the interests or policy preferences of the national government and financial interest groups. Finally, they can act as self-interested bureaucracies, defending their prerogatives. This 'multiple-hatting' (this expression was used by a financial regulator interviewed in Frankfurt on 11 September 2007) is not new for treasuries or finance ministries, though it is somewhat more recent for some supervisory authorities.

Regulating banking in the EU

This second part of the chapter analyses policy-making in the banking sector in the EU by focusing on two main interrelated policy initiatives, namely, the Basel II Accord and the Capital Requirements Directive. The Financial Conglomerates Directive is also discussed. Other initiatives relevant to the banking sector, for example payment services and clearing and settlement of securities, are discussed in Chapter 6.

The Basel II Accord

The international standards for capital requirements that had been established by the Basel I agreement signed in 1988 were revised and integrated by the Basel II Accord, *International Convergence of Capital Measurement and Capital Standards: A Revised Framework* (BCBS 2005a). The rationale for the revision was to tailor the capital requirements of banks more closely to the actual economic risk that they faced, while also taking into account innovations in financial markets and risk management strategies. The Basel II accord based capital requirements on three pillars. Pillar 1 was concerned with the minimum capital requirements covering three types of risk: credit risk, market risk and, innovatively, operational risk. Innovations were also introduced with reference to risk measurement. 'Credit risk' is the probability of loss from a debtor's default and is the risk that a counterparty to a financial transaction will fail to fulfil their obligations. 'Market risk is defined as the risk of losses in on and off-balancesheet positions arising from movements in market prices' (BCBS 2005b: 1). 'Operational risk' is defined as 'the risk of loss resulting from inadequate or failed internal processes, people and systems or from external events' (BCBS 2005a: 140). Pillar 2 was the supervisory review process aimed at covering external factors that were not fully taken into account when computing the minimum capital requirements. Supervisors were therefore enabled to take measures which, if necessary, could go beyond the minimum capital requirements. Finally, Pillar 3 was the discipline imposed by the market, facilitated by transparency requirements.

The negotiations on Basel II gained momentum in June 1999 with the publication of the first consultative paper by the BCBS, followed by a second consultative paper in January 2001 and a third in May 2003. These documents were subject to open consultation, and the responses from industry, experts and national authorities were posted on the website of the BCBS. Further, the committee conducted four quantitative impact studies (QISs), in 2001 (QIS1), 2002 (QIS2), 2004 (QIS3) and 2005 (QIS4), concerning the implementation of the new rules. Such assessments were conducted in aggregate terms – that is, they were not country- or sector-specific. However, since not all countries were satisfied by the results of the QIS3, the US, Japan,

South Africa and Germany decided to conduct national impact studies, which became the QIS4.

During the negotiations, the Commission, which sat in the BCBS as an observer, as the ECB also did, maintained the primary objective of ensuring that the application of the Basel II rules to the EU Single Market was suitable (interview, Brussels, 27 June 2007). The Commission's service review of capital requirements took place in parallel with the activities of the BCBS.[5] The issue of the transposition of the Basel II Accord into EU legislation also informed the attitudes of the member states negotiating in Basel. It should be noted that the Basel and EU processes ran for five years and, throughout this period, the BCBS, the Commission and the national authorities maintained a constant policy of industry consultation on the proposals formulated, even though this varied from country to country.

The Basel II Accord was agreed in June 2004. In July 2005, in close cooperation with the IOSCO, the international body of securities supervisors that monitors the activities of securities firms and investment houses, the committee published a document on the treatment of banks' 'trading books'. This text was subsequently integrated with the June 2004 text in a document released in June 2006. According to the BCBS (2005b: 55), 'A trading book consists of positions in financial instruments and commodities held either with trading intent or in order to hedge other elements of the trading book.' It is different from the 'banking book', where securities are meant to be held until maturity and are not actively traded. It was therefore very important for investment banks and investment firms, whose main-line business concerns the trading book, whereas commercial banks have most or part of their business in the 'banking book'.

The national authorities in the G10 countries sitting on the BCBS subsequently adopted the Basel II text through domestic rule-making and approval processes. Indeed, the committee does not possess any formal supranational supervisory authority and its conclusions do not have legal force – they have to be implemented (statutorily or by other ways) by the participating countries.

The following account, though incomplete, focuses on the main issues that were raised during the negotiations of the Basel II Accord. Some of these issues, which concerned both pillar 1 and pillar 2, such as the use of internal rather than external rating, the need to counteract the pro-cyclical effects of the accord and the potential negative effects for SMEs and mortgage lenders, were partly addressed throughout the negotiations in Basel (interview, London, 19 May 2006). Others, such as the 'solo' or 'consolidated' model of supervision, the role of 'consolidating supervisor' and the risk weighting for 'intragroup exposure', featured more prominently during the discussions regarding the transposition of the accord into the Capital Requirements Directive, examined below.

An important issue, settled early on in the negotiations, concerned the initial US-led proposal to use external rating in order to assess the credit risk that is part of the first pillar (Wood 2005: 130). The European members of the BCBS suggested instead the use of internal rating, which was regarded as more reliable and also less disadvantageous for European banks that lend extensively to unrated companies (interviews, London, 19 May 2006; Frankfurt, 17 January 2006; Rome, 23 June 2006). This proposal was endorsed by the BCBS, and it was thus included in the second consultative paper (BCBS 2001).

A key issue in shaping the Basel II Accord concerned the implications of the new capital rules relating to the terms of, and access to, bank credit for SMEs. During the negotiations towards the proposed accord, a concern was voiced that the risk weighting for SMEs would remain the same as that used when lending to large unrated corporates, on account of the fact that most small and medium-sized borrowers do not have external credit ratings. This was a prominent issue for SMEs in Germany (see Bundesverband deutscher Banken 2003; European Savings Banks Group 2003; *The Economist*, 10 November 2001), the *Mittelstand*, which rely largely on bank loans for their funding, as is also the case in Italy (see Associazione Bancaria Italiana 2003) and France. The German authorities were so concerned about the domestic impact of Basel II that they decided to conduct a quantitative impact study of their own (BCBS 2005c).

The changes that were subsequently made to the rules of Basel II regarding these issues can be ascribed largely to the activity of the German representatives, which joined forces with the Italian and French authorities, also worried about the implications for SMEs (interviews, Frankfurt 17 January 2006; Rome, 23 June 2006). It should also be noted that, because of its domestic importance, the German chancellor and the economics minister went public in October 2001, criticising the accord for being detrimental to SMEs (Wood 2005: 141). It was one of the few instances of direct political interference in the process, even though there were several other instances of indirect pressure, such as that exerted by the US Congress on American negotiators and evidenced in several congressional hearings (House Committee on Financial Services 2003a, 2003b).

As part of pillar 1, the newly introduced operational risk charges were criticised by banks: US-based banks and the Institute of International Finance were particularly vocal on this issue (Wood 2005: 129, 140). They admitted that this type of risk existed – for example, the risk of disruption to banks' operations through staff fraud or natural calamities – but that it was better dealt with internally by banks (House Committee on Financial Services 2003a, 2003b). Provisions concerning operational risk were watered down in the final version of the accord.

Another issue was the risk weighting of commercial mortgages, which in the Basel I Accord were granted special treatment. German policy-makers were keen to preserve a lower risk weighting for commercial mortgages in Basel II because, domestically, German rules allowed banks to hold commercial mortgages at 50 per cent risk weighting, a special treatment that in other countries is given only to residential mortgages (see Zentraler Kredit Ausschuss 2003). Moreover, German mortgage banks issue the *Pfandbriefe*, a special bond with only 10 per cent risk weighting. The other countries, principally the UK, Italy, France and Spain, led by the US, complained that this gave German banks a competitive advantage. In the end, the Germans seemed to have lost the battle, even though some ambiguity was preserved in the relevant article (Wood 2005: 133).

Among the overarching regulatory and competition issues, there was a concern that inconsistent implementation across countries would distort competition and could significantly increase regulatory burdens for those banks operating in more than one country. This was a real issue for the large banks in Germany and Britain and operating in several countries. Finally, there were issues such as the inherent pro-cyclicality induced by the content of the agreement, its negative effects on developing countries (Claessens *et al.* 2008; Griffith-Jones 2003) and its excessive complexity (500 pages). On these issues EU countries did not have different preferences.

The Capital Requirements Directive[6]

Capital requirements were already regulated by EU legislation that had been issued throughout the 1990s and largely incorporated the Basel I Accord. When negotiations on the Basel II agreement began, the member states agreed that the new capital requirements framework agreed in Basel II would be incorporated into EU legislation by the amendment through the recasting procedure of the existing directives, the Codified Banking Directive 2000/12/EC and the Capital Adequacy Directive 93/6/EC. The Capital Requirements Directive comprises Directive 2006/48/EC, relating to the taking up and pursuit of the business of credit institutions, and Directive 2006/49/EC, on the capital adequacy of investment firms and credit institutions. Though it possessed the same rationale at Basel II, the Capital Requirements Directive had a wider scope of application.

The intention of the directive was to ensure a level playing field between firms competing within the same EU markets, and thus it applied to all credit institutions and investment firms as defined by the Investment Services Directive (see Chapter 5). In common with the Basel II agreement, the Capital Requirements Directive was articulated on three pillars: requirements for an internal capital assessment by financial institutions (exposure to credit, market and operational risks); a supervisory review process to evaluate the risk profile of each institution; and market discipline.

However, there were three main differences between Basel II and the Capital Requirements Directive. Basel II was an international agreement, signed by thirteen countries, including the US, Japan and Switzerland, and de facto extending worldwide (for example, Basel I was applied by most banks in more than 100 countries). In contrast, the Capital Requirements Directive applied to only the twenty-seven (then twenty-five) EU member states.

Second, Basel I and II were so-called gentleman's agreements, that is, they were not legally binding, whereas the Capital Requirements Directive is a legally binding instrument. Third, Basel II related only to credit institutions (banks), whereas the Capital Requirements Directive related also to investment firms; the former applied only to internationally active banks (for example, it was estimated that in the US only up to a dozen internationally active banks would be affected; *Financial Times*, 8 October 2004), whereas the latter applied to all banks and investment firms, even if their activities were purely domestic. On some more specific points, the Capital Requirements Directive made a number of adaptations of the Basel II rules.[7]

In addition to the issues raised in the context of the Basel process, a number of concerns directly relevant to industry were raised over the EU's implementation of the Basel II Accord through the Capital Requirements Directive. The following account is by no means exhaustive. The Capital Requirements Directive enhanced the role of the *consolidating supervisor* for the supervision of EU cross-border groups – namely, the national supervisor in the member state where the group's parent firm is authorised. The consolidating supervisor is in charge of coordinating the treatment of an application that such a group may make for the approval necessary to use the more sophisticated capital calculation rules. All supervisors concerned are expected to reach an agreed decision on such an application within six months, and, in the event of a failure to do so, the consolidating supervisor is empowered to make a decision in order not to impose extra burdens on firms dealing with multiple supervisors.

Banks undertaking cross-border activities (mainly British-based banks and large private German banks) were largely in favour of the establishment of a 'lead supervisor' (British Bankers' Association and London Investment Banking Association 2003: 11; British Bankers' Association 2003: 9) with greater decision-making powers rather than what was proposed for the consolidating supervisor. Cross-border banking groups pointed out the disadvantage of duplicating compliance costs, owing to the fact that under the consolidating supervisor their activities would still be subject to somewhat different national systems of supervision (British Bankers' Association 2003: 8). The concept of leading supervisor was ultimately successfully opposed by the national supervisors, who were eager not to see their supervisory power diluted (interview, London, 8 December 2005; Frankfurt, 17 January 2006).

The Basel II Accord was designed for internationally active banks, while the Capital Requirements Directive was created to be applied also to *investment firms*. However, the wider scope of the directive raised the issue of whether the calibration of specific parts of Basel II was appropriate for firms whose sole business lay in these areas (HM Treasury 2003a, 2003b). This was the issue of the trading book, which introduced specific rules concerning the capital requirements for trading activities. It was one of the main priorities of the associations of international securities dealers and investment banks (see the joint letter to the BCBS by the European Banking Federation, the Institute of International Finance, the International Swaps and Derivatives Association, the London Investment Banking Association and the Bond Market Association 2004) and the British authorities (*European Voice*, 9 June 2005). Indeed, the structure of the UK investment sector differs from that in much of continental Europe, where firms offering investment services are required to hold banking licenses and the business lines of investment services are often integrated into the commercial activities of major banking groups. There is no such requirement in the UK for those firms to hold banking licenses, and Britain has a very high number of specialised investment firms (Association of Private Client Investment Managers and Stockbrokers 2003).

A specific concern of the British Bankers' Association and the London Investment Banking Association related to the initial Commission proposal requiring the calculation of capital requirements at a 'solo' and 'sub-consolidated' level, as well as at the 'aggregate' holding company level (British Bankers' Association 2003, 2004a). Fundamentally, the 'solo' model insulated the principal regulated entity from other members of its group, whereas the 'consolidated' model allowed regulation and supervision to be applied to the top tier (i.e. parent or holding companies) of the group, covering all members that provided financial services. British banks, in conjunction with the British authorities, wanted the application of the 'solo' model to remain a possibility in the UK by virtue of the EU legislation, and this was achieved after an intensive period of lobbying aimed at both the Commission and the EP (interview, London, 8 December 2005).

Another relatively minor, yet extremely controversial issue was the *treatment of intragroup exposure*. The German savings and cooperative banks wanted zero risk weighting for this kind of exposure within their sub-sector, and directed intense lobbying at the EP in order to achieve this objective (interviews, London, 8 December 2005; Frankfurt, 17 January 2006). The zero risk weighting would have lowered the capital requirements for savings and cooperative banks, giving them a competitive advantage. Thus it was challenged by private banks in the UK and especially in Germany (British Bankers' Association 2003; interviews, Berlin, April 2008, Brussels, March 2007). Moreover, the ECB considered a zero weighting for internal group lending to be generally inadequate in terms of risk assessment, and therefore unreliable (ECB 2003a). In the end, a compromise solution of zero risk weighting was achieved in the event that certain conditions were met.

Finally, there was the concern that, if the implementation of Basel II and the Capital Requirements Directive was not simultaneous, compliance and operation costs for international banks would increase, particularly if they had to run different systems for their EU and non-EU operations. The formal adoption of the Capital Requirements Directive by Council and the European Parliament took place in June 2006 (Council of the EU and EP 2006). The Capital Requirements Directive came into force at the beginning of 2007, with the most sophisticated approaches available from 2008, in line with the introduction of Basel II rules. In light of the global financial crisis, which gained full force in 2008, the Basel II Accord and the Capital Requirements Directive are in the process of being revised, as explained in Chapter 8. In both cases, the policy debate has focused on the revision of risk weighting for securitised products, the trading book review and new rules for liquidity risk management.

An overall assessment

The Commission's role at the agenda-setting stage of the Capital Requirements Directive, unlike other EU legislation on financial services, was very limited, as the draft largely incorporated the content of the Basel II Accord, to the formation of which the Commission and the ECB had participated as observers. However, the fact that the Capital Requirements Directive transposed into EU legislation the Basel II Accord also limited the Council's room for manoeuvre.

The ECB was keen to keep at arm's-length distance from the industry and the national authorities on this matter. Deliberately, given its very limited competence on supervisory issues, as well as the political salience (especially in some countries) and the different national preferences and policy positions concerning certain points of the accord, the ECB kept a low key and impartial stance, being concerned mainly with the overall implication of both the accord and the directive for the stability of the financial system in the eurozone and in the EU more broadly, since 'financial instability does not stop at the eurozone borders' (interview, Frankfurt, 20 January 2006). However, there were instances in which the ECB directly intervened to comment on specific points, for example, criticising the excessively low level of capital requirements that would have resulted from certain provisions on intra-group exposure (ECB 2003a).

The EP was involved early on in the process, while the Commission was still consulting on the draft directive, and so managed to have significant amendments made to the final draft (interview, London, 2 April 2007). The parliament was a responsive target for lobbying by both industry (European and national associations, individual firms) and some national governments. For example, the European Banking Federation and the association of German private banks interacted with MEPs (at least with some of them) to prevent the inclusion of intra-group exposure rules. Similarly, the European Savings Banks Group, the European Association of Public Banks and the German saving banks association interacted closely with some (mainly German) MEPs to maintain the provisions for intra-group exposure. The British Bankers' Association, the London Investment Banking Association and the UK Treasury interacted with some (mainly British) MEPs on the issue of the solo model, which was a priority for British industry (interviews, London, 8 December 2005; Frankfurt, 17 January 2006). It was therefore not only industry that lobbied MEPs; the national governments engaged in this activity under specific circumstances, and in these instances the member states teamed up in the parliament and the Council.

In the negotiations of the Basel II Accord and the Capital Requirements Directive there was agreement on the need to update and fine-tune capital requirements. However, on the specific content of the new legislation there were two main coalitions, comprising national governments and national industry. On the one hand, there were member states, such as Germany, France and Italy, particularly concerned about the effects of capital requirements for small and medium-sized banks and the credit to SMEs. On the other hand, the UK, given its limited number of SMEs and small banks, did not share these concerns. The priority of British policy-makers was to set adequate capital requirements for non-bank investment firms, to maintain the solo model of supervision used in the UK, and to define the power and tasks of the consolidating supervisor and the host authorities, for the UK hosts, and is home to, several cross-border banking groups (interviews, London, 2 April 2007, 8 December 2005).

The large number of national discretions left in the level 1 legislation, which partly determined the complexity of the level 3 implementing measures, as well as the limited convergence of supervisory practices can be explained by different configurations of the national financial system and its ties with other parts of the national economy. They are also the result of different regulatory approaches in the member states, such as rule-based versus principle-based regulation; reliance on on-site inspections or off-site supervision; reliance on external auditors; and informal tools based on dialogue versus more formal administrative tools (CEBS 2007b: 6).

As for the role of industry, it is clear that the private sector was more important in the making of the Basel II than in the making of Basel I (Speyer 2006; Underhill and Zhang 2008). A similar observation applies to the Capital Requirements Directive, the successor of the Capital Adequacy Directive agreed in 1993. Not only was the Institute of International Finance one of the main industry interlocutors for the BCBS (Wood 2005), but the BCBS also held open consultations with industry and the national authorities on various drafts of the agreement, as well as conducting several quantitative impact studies. For example, the first consultative paper received 200 sets of comments and the second received 250 comments. The Commission and the EP sought interaction with industry, and industry sought interaction with them. In addition, the national authorities consulted with their national banking industry, more or less extensively and intensively, depending on the salience of the Basel II Accord for domestic audiences and the established national practices of consultation by the public authorities.

For example, because of the implications that the content of the Basel II Accord and Capital Requirements Directive could have for the country's large number of SMEs, it was also an important issue outside the banking community in Germany. Germany also has a corporatist tradition of interaction between the public sector and industry (Grossman 2006) and hence the involvement of industry was intense (interviews, Frankfurt, 17 January 2006). Consultation with industry was less concentrated in Italy and France, despite the fact that the issue was important domestically in these two countries, because the national authorities are less used to interacting with industry and industry is less used to being consulted by the authorities (interview, Rome, 23 June 2006).

The intensity of preferences and the involvement of policy actors on Basel II varied across countries. For example, in the UK, direct input was provided mainly by a few internationally active banks, those to which Basel II applies. Salience was high in Germany, where interest groups mobilised intensively and extensively, in particular with regard to the issue of the implications for SMEs. The national authorities in Germany not only engaged in an in-depth consultation process, they also received a great deal of position papers from the public.[8] While the Bundesbank took part in several hearings before the federal parliament, political pressure was exerted upon it, along with the German financial services authority, the Bundesanstalt für Finanzdienstleistungsaufsicht, both at the *Land* and the federal level, accompanied by the lobbying activities of various sectors of society (interview, Frankfurt, 17 January 2006).

In lobbying, there was an implicit division of competences, whereby national associations and individual companies expressed their policy preferences mainly to the national authorities, which negotiated in Brussels and Basel, whereas EU-level associations liaised principally with the EP and the Commission. There were, however, exceptions. For example, the British Bankers' Association liaised with (mainly British) MEPs and German associations liaised with (primarily German) MEPs. Moreover, whenever an issue was particularly important for an interest group and the latter had the necessary resources to influence those outside its borders, national lines were also crossed during lobbying activities. In the final phase of the negotiations, the German private banks association wrote to all national representations in Brussels concerning the abolition of the intra-group exposure that was a priority for the private banks, as it would make them more competitive vis-à-vis public banks (interview, Brussels, 28 March 2007). This was also a case in which domestic political economy conflicts played out in EU policy-making.

In looking at the positions papers of these associations on the Capital Requirements Directive (as well as on other financial issues), it is noteworthy that there is a remarkable similarity of views between the positions expressed by the British Bankers' Association, the London Investment Banking Association, the German private banks association and the European Banking Federation, on the one hand, and the German savings banks and the European Savings Banks Group, on the other. Indeed, the British Bankers' Association and the German private banks association are important players in the European Banking Federation, as are German savings banks in the European Savings Banks Group. The German public banks and the European Association of Public Banks share the same office, even though there are two entrances and some of the senior official at the European Association of Public Banks come from the German public banks association.

The Financial Conglomerates Directive

Financial conglomerates cross the milieu between banking, securities and insurance, as they are large groups active in different segments of the financial sector, offering a range of services, such as banking, insurance and securities, often across national borders. These groups constitute an increasingly important part of the financial sector, especially in some countries, notably the UK and the Netherlands. Overall, financial conglomerates groups hold about one-third of European bank deposits and a quarter of Europe's life assurers (*The Economist*, 19 October 2002).

The 'Directive on the Supplementary Supervision of Credit Institutions, Insurance Undertakings and Investment Firms in a Financial Conglomerate 2002/87/EC' (Council of the EU and EP 2002), better known as the Financial Conglomerates Directive, implemented the international recommendations on the supervision of financial conglomerates agreed in 1999 by the Joint Forum of financial conglomerates in the framework of the G10, under the auspices of the BIS. The directive also addressed some of the recommendations of the first 'Brouwer group' Report (EFC 2000) on stability in the financial sector (Lannoo 2005), subsequently endorsed by the ECOFIN Council in Lisbon.

The Financial Conglomerates Directive was designed to enhance the prudential soundness and the effective supervision of financial conglomerates; to promote convergence in national supervisory approaches and across sectors; and to enhance financial stability and the protection of depositors, insurance policy holders and investors (CEC 2000a). The rationale was to ensure adequate supervision of the increasing number of financial conglomerates resulting from the consolidation taking place in the financial sector, a financial trend that provided the background to the directive. Financial conglomerates are often systemically important, either in the member states or for the EU as a whole, because they hold a substantial share of the domestic financial markets in some countries and their number has increased remarkably over the last decade.

The main shortcomings of the regulatory environment before the introduction of the Financial Conglomerates Directive were identified by the Commission as follows. Certain types of financial groups were not covered by the existing directives, and important prudential issues that were regulated by sectoral directives – concerning banking groups, investment firms and insurance groups – were not regulated at the level of financial conglomerates. Hence, there were inconsistencies in the treatment of similar prudential questions, and the same financial group could be covered by different sectoral directives (CEC 2000a: 4). Finally, impetus to the directive, which some dubbed the post-Enron directive (see, for example, *The Economist*,

19 October 2002), was also given by US corporate scandals, such as the Enron case, which highlighted the need to provide adequate supervision of financial conglomerates.

The directive contained measures to align the rules for financial conglomerates with those for homogeneous financial groups with a view to ensuring equivalent treatment and a level playing field. The rules prevented the same capital being counted twice over in different entities in the same financial conglomerate – the so-called multiple gearing of own funds. The directive also introduced methods for calculating a conglomerate's overall solvency position and to deal with the issues of intra-group transactions, risk exposure and suitability of management. The parent firm was prevented from issuing loans to finance its subsidiaries – the so-called excessive leveraging. Finally, the directive introduced group-wide supervision of financial conglomerates, requiring closer cooperation and information sharing among supervisory authorities across sectors – the so-called coordinating supervisor, which is very similar to the concept of the 'consolidating supervisor' under the Capital Requirements Directive.

Before proposing the directive in April 2001, the Commission launched consultations on the regulation of financial conglomerates in December 2000, the responses to which suggested overall support for a directive on financial conglomerates. In March 2002, the European Parliament in plenary session adopted the report prepared by Alain Lipietz supporting the broad thrust of the proposed directive, which had previously been discussed by the Committee on Economic and Financial Affairs (EP 2002a, 2002b). In May 2002 the Council reached a political agreement on the proposed directive, which returned to the parliament for a second reading under the co-decision procedure. In November 2002 the European Parliament agreed on the directive, which was formally adopted in December 2002. The existing directives on insurance, banking and investment services were also amended to prevent clashes with the directive on financial conglomerates.

During the negotiations, on the one hand, there was consensus that the directive should be comprehensive, filling the regulatory gap. On the other hand, the national supervisors felt that the solutions should not radically change the existing practices and instruments in the various sectors. Hence, for example, insurance supervisors did not want to have a directive that would force them to adopt banking supervision techniques, and vice versa (interview, Brussels, 27 June 2007). The member states that had separate supervisory authorities for various segments of the financial sectors – these were all the Mediterranean countries and some new member states – were also worried that the directive would force them to move towards a single supervisory authority, similar to the British Financial Services Authority. Basically, they were concerned that the directive would impact on the structure of supervision (interview, Brussels, 27 June 2007). Some member states, such as the UK, Germany, France, Spain and Portugal, were also keen to include waivers based on the small-size criteria, as these countries have several relatively small financial conglomerates. Finally, the very definition of financial conglomerate was problematic.

Unlike other directives in the financial sector, some of the main issues in the negotiations of the directive concerned the impact that the legislation would have on non-EU (especially US-based) companies – that is, the 'extra-territorial impact' of the directive (*The Economist*, 19 October 2002). It was the issue of 'equivalence'. Had the EU decided that the supervision of US firms was not equivalent to EU standards, forcing US companies to adapt to EU rules would have increased the costs of their operations in Europe, generating a competitive disadvantage vis-à-vis EU-based conglomerates (Dür 2008; Posner 2009b).

A related point of friction was the role of the consolidated supervisor. The directive required that any financial conglomerate that was not already subject to group-wide oversight should come under the supervision of a single consolidated supervisor. Whereas European groups were already subject to consolidated supervision, big financial firms in the United States were supervised by a variety of authorities. For instance, the US Securities and Exchange Commission was responsible for monitoring firms' broker–dealer operations; the Federal Reserve supervised its banking arm; and state regulators oversaw its insurance ventures (*Financial Times*, 27 October 2003).

In this respect, US supervisory standards were considered too lax by many EU member states, and this was a problem for the US companies operating in Europe whose parent company was located in America. The UK was particularly keen to have equivalence with the US, hence upgrading US standards, because there are many US financial conglomerates operating in London (CEC 2002b). In the end, the Securities and Exchange Commission had to amend US legislation because it did not fulfil the requirements of the EU Financial Conglomerates Directive (interview, Brussels, 27 June 2007).

The transatlantic disagreement between the EU and the US also involved the extra-territorial impact of the Sarbanes–Oxley Act (formally, the Public Company Accounting Reform and Investor Protection Act of 2002) passed by the US Congress. The main point of dispute concerned the control of auditors of foreign companies listed on US stock exchanges (*The Economist*, 19 October 2002) and, precisely, the need for auditor firms to register with the US authorities (the Public Company Accounting Oversight Board). This would have given the Public Company Accounting Oversight Board the right to inspect European auditors if, for example, they audited a US subsidiary (*Financial Times*, 23 April 2004). The Commission, on behalf of the EU and its member states, negotiated with the respective US regulatory agencies (the Securities and Exchange Commission and the Public Company Accounting Oversight Board). During these negotiations, a link was made between the auditor oversight provisions of the Sarbanes–Oxley Act and the 'reciprocity' in the treatment of US financial conglomerates operating in Europe and subject to the Financial Conglomerates Directive (Ferran 2004).

In the end a compromise was reached, which involved mutual concessions concerning the treatment of US financial conglomerates (as explained above) and the EU commitments to change certain provision of EU laws on auditors, after which reciprocal registration requirements would apply (Ferran 2004). Proposals subsequently set out by the Commission replicated several provisions of the Sarbanes–Oxley Act – which represented the US regulatory response to major corporate and accounting scandals, one of the most prominent being the Enron affair – so as to reduce the regulatory distance between the EU and the US (*Financial Times*, 23 April 2004).

In this episode, the EU, negotiating as a united block represented by the Commission, was able to 'punch its weight', acting as a counter-power to the US, most likely achieving a more satisfactory outcome than would have been the case had bilateral negotiations taken place between the US and the member states (interview, Brussels, 27 June 2007). Indeed, the ECOFIN ministers explicitly requested the Commission to act on their behalf, though the Public Company Accounting Oversight Board also collaborated closely with the competent authorities of some member states, principally the UK, followed by France and Germany (Ferran 2004).

Before 2002, financial services were not seen as a major issue in EU–US relations. However, the extra-territorial effects of the Financial Conglomerates Directive and the Sarbanes–Oxley Act prompted EU and US regulators to meet and discuss practical solutions to regulatory differences and potential 'spillovers' – the expression preferred by the Commission in its official documents. The discussions on accounting standards and the implementation of the Basel II Accord heightened the need for systematic consultation and cooperation between the US and the EU. Hence, the Financial Markets Regulatory Dialogue was established in 2002 (on the cooperation between the EU and the US, see Dür 2008; Posner 2009b). Since then, meetings between the US authorities and the Commission have taken place approximately every six months and have been complemented by ongoing cooperation on a technical basis.[9]

An overview of the main regulatory measures concerning banks and financial conglomerates adopted by the EU over the last decade is provided in Table 4.2.

Conclusion

The decision-making power of the national authorities was paramount in the making of the Basel II Accord compared with the role of the Commission and the ECB, which participated in the BCBS simply as observers, with the caveats mentioned above, and did not have a vote. By contrast, the transposition of the international agreement into a EU directive brought supranational bodies squarely into the picture. It also intensified the direct involvement and lobbying of industry. Even though the substance of the

Table 4.2 The main regulatory measures in the banking sector over the last decade (international rules in shaded boxes)

Regulation	Date of adoption	Institutions/bodies	Scope/objectives
Basel II Accord	2005	BCBS	To set minimum capital requirements for banks; 3-pillar structure
Capital Requirements Directive	2006	EU (Commission proposes, co-decision Ecofin Council, EP)	To set minimum capital requirements for banks; 3-pillar structure
Risk Concentration Principles	1999	JF, BCBS, IOSCO, IAIS	To ensure adequate supervision of financial conglomerates To promote convergence in national supervisory approaches and across sectors
Financial Conglomerates Directive	2002	EU (Commission proposes, co-decision Ecofin Council, EP)	To ensure adequate supervision of financial conglomerates To promote convergence in national supervisory approaches and across sectors Group-wide supervision

directive was basically predetermined by the provisions of the Basel II Accord, some room for manoeuvre remained in the process of its transposition into EU legislation.

Thus, the post-Basel II phase of the making of the Capital Requirements Directive largely resembled the traditional EU legislative process, even though it was not a Lamfalussy directive. This means that there were no level 2 implementing legislative measures to be adopted, which also explains why the text of the Capital Requirements Directive was rather long and detailed. However, the level 3 committee, the CEBS, was involved in issues concerning the practical implementation of the directive – the level 3 measures.

The Financial Conglomerates Directive was a cross-sectoral issue in which the Lamfalussy committees were not involved, as they had not been set up at that time. With the exception of the Capital Requirements Directive, this was the directive on which the impact of factors outside the EU was greater, both in setting the rationale for the legislation and in the negotiations of its specific content and scope of application.

The discussions of the Basel II Accord, the Capital Requirements Directive and the Financial Conglomerates Directive highlight the strong links between international and EU rule-making in banking governance, which is characterised by a multiplicity of regulatory arenas. Finally, the investigation of the governance of financial conglomerates stresses the interpenetration of the main segments of the financial sector and the regulatory difficulties that this poses in the EU and internationally, as well as the effects of EU rule-making outside the EU and vice versa.

5 Governing securities markets in the EU

This chapter analyses the governance of securities markets in the EU from the drafting of the FSAP in 1999 onwards. It first maps the institutional framework for the regulation and supervision of securities trading, both in the EU and internationally, arguing that the latter is less developed than the former. It should, however, be noted that, until the late 1990s, the EU framework was not particularly robust, though it underwent a significant reform following intense legislative activity in the early 2000s. The second part of the chapter analyses the functioning of the Lamfalussy framework and the policy-making processes of the four so-called Lamfalussy directives – named after the framework through which they were agreed and implemented – the Prospectus Directive (2003), the Market Abuse Directive (2003), the Transparency Directive (2004) and the Markets in Financial Instruments Directive (MiFID) (2004).

These framework directives, which contained (or, in principle, were suppose to contain) only the key principles of legislation, were agreed through co-decision between the Council and the EP (the so-called level 1 of the Lamfalussy process). The level 1 directives were complemented by implementing measures (mainly directives and some regulations) agreed through comitology – that is, proposed and adopted by the Commission, assisted by the European Securities Committee (level 2) and advised by the CESR (level 3). To these legislative measures concerning securities trading, one should add the policy initiatives concerning post-trading activities, such as the clearing and settlement of securities, discussed in Chapter 6.

It is argued in this chapter that the negotiations of the most important directives concerning securities trading involved two competing coalitions of public and private actors: the Northern European market-making coalition and the Southern European market-shaping coalition. These were primarily coalitions of interests rooted in domestic political economy, namely different financial market structures across countries. However, the division into competing coalitions was reinforced by different policy paradigms – 'ideas' about financial services regulation, its objectives and instruments. Regulatory paradigms are strictly interconnected with and partly informed by the configuration of national financial systems and the institutional arrangements for regulation and supervision. However, the opposite is also true, in that the configuration of national financial markets is influenced by the 'ideas' (or policy paradigms) that the national authorities have about financial services regulations, its objectives and instruments. On certain issues, the division cut across national lines, hence the coalitions were fluid and internally fragmented.

The institutional framework for governing securities markets

This section begins by reviewing the main institutions and bodies active in the governance of securities markets internationally, in the EU and in the member states.

The international institutions governing securities markets

As explained in Chapter 3, international regulatory and supervisory fora dealing with securities markets are less developed than those active in the banking sector. First, securities markets, and hence securities regulation and supervision, developed relatively recently in some countries. For example, the federal securities supervisor in Germany, the Bundesaufsichtsamt für das Kreditwesen, was set up in the 1990s (Lütz 1998). In 2002, it was replaced by a single authority for the entire financial sector, the Bundesanstalt für Finanzdienstleistungsaufsicht (Quaglia 2008d; Westrup 2007). Until the 1990s, the traditional juxtaposition was between the bank-oriented financial systems, such as in France, Germany and Italy, and the market-oriented (or securities-based) financial systems, such as in the UK and the US (Allen and Gale 2000).

Second, banking activity, for its very nature and its potential to trigger systemic crises, has traditionally been heavily regulated and supervised, whereas in securities dealing the risk of systemic crises is limited. While supervision in the banking sector focuses on institutions (banks or financial entities carrying out banking activities), in the securities markets it concentrates on transactions (Joint Forum 2001). Furthermore, the need for consumer protection is perceived differently, being more intense in the banking sector, albeit this varies from country to country. The assumption is that investors dealing with securities are equipped with the technical knowledge necessary to make informed investment decisions, though such investors need to have access to relevant information – hence the importance of disclosure rules, which informed the content of several Lamfalussy directives (Ferran 2004).

Third, the supervisory agencies involved in banking supervision tend to be the central banks, even though this has partly changed since the reforms that have taken place in several countries over the last two decades. Central banks have a long-lasting tradition for cooperation in established fora, first and foremost the BIS (Toniolo 2005), which was created in the interwar period, and the BCBS, which was set up in the mid-1970s. There are no comparably robust international institutions in the securities sector, even though there are international standard setters.

The International Organisation of Securities Commissions (IOSCO), an international cooperative forum for regulatory agencies, is the international standard setter for securities markets (on the politics of the IOSCO, see Coleman and Underhill 1998; Porter 2005; Simmons 2001; Singer 2004; Underhill 1995). It is composed of more than 100 national securities markets regulators. Some self-regulatory organisations, such as national stock exchanges, are affiliate members without voting power. The function of the IOSCO, which was established in 1983, is to promote cooperation and adequate standards of regulation among its members; to facilitate the exchange of information; and to promote the development of domestic markets and effective surveillance of international securities transactions.

One of the most important documents produced by the IOSCO was a comprehensive set of 'Objectives and Principles of Securities Regulation' (1998), which are recognized as the international regulatory benchmarks for all securities markets. The IOSCO also cooperates with central banking bodies, such as the Committee on Payment and Settlement Systems (CPSS) of the central banks of the G10 countries, based in Basel. In the 2000s, the IOSCO and the CPSS issued a series of recommendations concerning securities settlement, discussed in Chapter 6. In 2005 it also cooperated with the BCBS to draft the trading book review that became part of the Basel II Accord.

The EU institutions governing securities markets

The main EU institutions that are active in the regulation of the securities markets are the same as those that take part in policy-making in the banking and insurance sectors: the Commission, especially DG Internal Market, and, within it, the directorate dealing with financial services; the EP and, within it, the Committee on Economic and Monetary Affairs; and the ECOFIN Council, whose groundwork is prepared by the EFC and the FSC. The ECB does not have any specific competence in this field, though it is generally consulted because many banks trade in securities. As discussed in Chapter 6, in 2007 the ECB decided to expand its role in the clearing and settlement of securities in the euro area by proposing the setting up of TARGET 2 securities.

Besides these EU institutions, there is a plethora of other bodies (mainly committees or 'groups') active in policy-making in the securities sector. The most important committees (i.e. those with some decision-making power) are relatively recent in origin, as they were set up (or reshaped) with the establishment of the Lamfalussy framework. It should, however, be noted that, even before the agreement on the Lamfalussy architecture was reached, the FSAP had already given new momentum to the creation of several consultative and advisory groups active in securities markets governance in the EU.

The European Securities Committee was established in 2001 and was explicitly mentioned in the *Report of the Committee of Wise Men on the Regulation of Securities Markets*, chaired by Baron Alexandre Lamfalussy. The committee is composed of high-level representatives from the national treasury or finance ministry or, in some cases, from the central bank and/or the supervisory authority – it is up to each member state to decide. There is one delegate per member state, one or two alternates, and occasionally one or two experts depending on the topics dealt with in the meeting.[1] Observers from the ECB, the CESR (see below) and the EEA countries are invited to attend. The European Securities Committee is chaired by a senior official from DG Internal Market – Financial Services, which also hosts the secretariat.

Like the European Banking Committee in the banking sector, the European Securities Committee is a level 2 committee in the securities sector. It fulfils comitology and advisory functions, in that it assists the Commission in the adoption of level 2 implementing measures for EU directives agreed at level 1 and provides advice on policy issues concerning securities markets. It operates by QMV, and the voting weight is the same as in the Council of Ministers, even though votes are not often taken (interview, Brussels, 28 March 2007).

The CESR was established in 2001 and, together with the European Securities Committee, was explicitly envisaged in the *Final Report of the Committee of Wise Men* (on the CESR, see De Visscher *et al.* 2008; Coen and Thatcher 2008; Quaglia 2008c). Its predecessor was the Forum of European Securities Commissions, which had no official status and was described by one of its senior members (who subsequently sat on the CESR) as 'a club of nice persons working together' (interview, Paris, 25 April 2007). The CESR is based in Paris and has a secretary general, whereas the chair and the vice chair are elected among the members for a period of two years. There is one seat per member state – the members are usually the chairpersons of national securities regulators – but they may be accompanied by experts. A representative of the Commission is entitled to participate unless there are confidential discussions related to individuals and/or firms.

The CESR is involved in levels 2 and 3 of the Lamfalussy process. At level 2, it advises the Commission in the drafting of implementing measures voted upon by the European Securities Committee. At level 3, it monitors the implementation of EU legislation across the Union; it facilitates the cooperation and the exchange of views and best practices between supervisory authorities (regulatory convergence); and it promotes the convergence of supervisory standards and requirements (supervisory convergence). Decisions by the committee are taken by consensus – consensus being understood as all members concurring, with one or two exceptions. If consensus cannot be reached, decisions are taken by qualified majority. In such a case, members that do not intend to apply the decisions must state the reason for not doing so – the so-called complain or explain procedure (Article 5).

The CESR cooperates with the other level 3 committees established as part of the Lamfalussy process. It also has close contacts with the ECB and the ESCB, particularly in the field of securities clearing and settlement, where a joint group was established by the CESR and the ESCB, as explained in Chapter 6. As far as accountability is concerned, the committee submits an annual report to the Commission, the EP and the Council. The chair of the committee reports to the EP periodically and when requested, and maintains strong links with the European Securities Committee (Article 6).

It is not feasible to review all the consultative and advisory committees, groups, and fora dealing with securities governance in the EU. The vast majority of these are expert groups advising the Commission generally in the pre-legislative stage and during implementation and are composed of experts from the member states or from industry; however, they act in a personal capacity only and are not supposed to represent either their member state or their company. The Commission often chairs the meetings and provides some secretarial support.

One of the most influential expert fora was the Giovannini Group, which brought together financial market participants under the chairmanship of Alberto Giovannini to advise the Commission on financial market issues. DG Economic and Financial Affairs provided the secretariat for the group and officials from DG Internal Market and the ECB also participated. The group was formed in 1996 and was organised in three working groups (equities, bonds and derivatives). Its work was focused mainly on identifying inefficiencies in EU financial markets and proposing practical solutions to improve market integration. The group produced five reports. The first report, on the impact of the introduction of the euro on capital markets, was published in July 1997, followed by a report on the EU repo market, a report on coordinated public debt issuance in the euro area, and two reports on EU cross-border clearing and settlement of securities in 2001 and 2003, respectively (Giovannini Group 2001, 2003). The importance of these reports is discussed in Chapter 6. The group concluded that clearing and settlement processes in the EU could be improved by market-led initiatives designed to promote convergence, such as providing inter-operability in technical requirements and in market practices across national systems. However, the group recognised that the removal of barriers related to taxation and legal certainty was the responsibility of the public authorities, and two specialised groups were set up to deal with these issues.

The Clearing and Settlement Advisory and Monitoring Expert Group was established in July 2004, following the second report of the Giovannini Group on clearing and settlement. It is composed of approximately twenty high-level representatives of various mainly private bodies involved in clearing and settlement, along with four observers from the public authorities, with Alberto Giovannini as principal policy adviser and a chairperson from the Commission. The group advises the Commission on market-led initiatives to promote the integration of EU securities clearing and settlement systems, with a view to eliminating the barriers to integration identified in the previous reports of the Giovannini Group (Giovannini Group 2001, 2003). It also advises the Commission on the coordination of action between the public and the private sectors. Its activities are discussed further in Chapter 6. Table 5.1 provides an overview of the international and EU institutions for the governance of securities markets.

The national institutions governing securities markets

It is important to review the institutional framework for securities markets governance at the national level, at least in general terms, given the fact that specific arrangements vary from country to country (for an overview, see Masciandaro 2005; ECB 2003b). It should be noted that the national authorities examined in this section sit in the EU and international regulatory and supervisory fora mentioned in the previous sections, though representation in such bodies varies. For example, Ireland, the UK and Germany are represented in the IOSCO by single regulators – respectively the Central Bank and Financial Services Authority, the Financial Services Authority and the BaFin – whereas France and Italy are represented by sectoral regulators, the Autorité des Marchés Financiers and the Commissione Nazionale per le Società e la Borsa.

To begin with, there are the political authorities, first and foremost the treasury ministry (or an equivalent, such as the Ministry of Finance in Germany or the Ministry for the Economy in Italy and France), which generally forms the regulatory body, even though supervisory agencies have regulatory powers in several countries. Usually, representatives from the treasury or finance ministry sit on the European Securities Committee, albeit there are exceptions.

Second, there are the 'technical' supervisory authorities, which can be independent agencies separate from the treasury (such as the UK's Financial Services Authority) or semi-independent bodies, ultimately responding to the treasury or finance ministry (the latter is the case of BaFin in Germany) (see Masciandaro and Quintyn 2007). In some countries the central bank is involved in certain aspects of securities supervision, as is the case in Italy, where it is responsible for the macro-supervision of banks and investment firms, whereas the Commissione Nazionale per le Società e la Borsa deals with the conduct of business and consumer protection. In Ireland there is a supervisory agency that deals with the entire financial sector, but this is located in the central bank. In the Netherlands the central bank is the supervisor for banking and insurance, the Financial Markets Authority oversees securities markets, and there is also a supervisory authority dealing with the conduct of business.

In some countries, such as in the UK, Germany and Belgium after the reforms of 1997, 2002, and 2004, respectively, there is one supervisor for the entire financial sector outside the central bank. In the Scandinavian countries

Table 5.1 The institutional framework for securities markets governance (international bodies in shaded box)

Institution/body	Date of establishment	Membership/composition	Functions/tasks
International Organization of Securities Commissions (IOSCO)	1983	Securities regulators worldwide	To set international standards in securities market To promote cooperation and exchange of information
European Securities Committee (ESC)	2004	Senior national civil servants from economic and finance ministries; observers from ECB, CESR and EEA countries	To assist the Commission in adopting EU level 2 implementing legislation in securities trading (comitology)
Committee of European Securities Regulators (CESR)	2004	National securities regulators in the EU; observers from Commission and EEA	To advise the Commission on EU securities legislation To adopt level 3 measures To strengthen cooperation between national securities supervisors
Clearing and Settlement Advisory and Monitoring Expert Group (CESAME)	2004	Representatives from industry; observers from public authorities	To advise the Commission and to promote the integration of securities clearing and settlement

a single supervisor for the entire financial sector was set up in the late 1980s. In several countries there is a specific authority supervising securities markets, as was the case in Germany and the UK before the 2002[2] and 1997 reforms, respectively, and as is the situation in France and the Netherlands. When there are different supervisory authorities dealing with securities, there can be instances of turf wars or uneasy relations. For example, in Italy, where the central bank and the Commissione Nazionale per le Società e la Borsa are involved in different aspects of securities markets supervision, some tension surfaced in the case of the Parmalat bankruptcy and the ill-fated Cirio bonds, two financial scandals that occurred in the early 2000s.

The Lamfalussy framework has given more prominence to the national supervisory authorities overseeing securities markets in the making of EU legislation. Overall, the membership of the CESR has strengthened securities supervisors in the domestic arena – that is, vis-à-vis the national political authorities (first and foremost, the government) – which is particularly important whenever the supervisor has relatively weak institutional capabilities and/or faces an 'intrusive' government prepared to get involved in supervisory matters. Indeed, one member of the CESR referred to this committee as 'the trade union of securities supervisors' (interview, Paris, 25 April 2007). Of course, contacts – and, at times, pressure – between the political authorities and the supervisors remain at the domestic level and can influence the functioning of the CESR, given the fact that, as one member observed, some supervisors are better able than others to maintain arm's-length relations with their respective governments. Some instances of political dynamics affecting the functioning of the CESR are reported below.

Regulating securities markets in the EU

This second part of the chapter analyses policy-making concerning the regulation of securities markets in the EU by focusing on the four so-called Lamfalussy directives agreed in the early 2000s and their implementing measures. The Prospectus Directive concerned the documents required to accompany the sale of new securities, which help investors to assess issuers trying to raise capital and to have their securities traded. The Market Abuse Directive dealt with issues such as insider dealing (using information that has not been made public to one's advantage), and market manipulation (spreading misleading information), which distort the price-setting mechanism of financial instruments. The Transparency Directive set requirements with regard to information on issuers whose securities are admitted to trading on a regulated market. The MiFID, also referred to as the Investment Service Directive 2 (following the first Investment Service Directive, issued in 1993), gave investment firms a 'single passport', allowing them to operate throughout the EU on the basis of authorisation in their home member state. Other initiatives that are relevant to securities markets, such as the clearing and settlement system, are discussed in Chapter 6.

The Prospectus Directive and the Market Abuse Directive were drafted by the Commission in 2000–1 and involved limited consultation with stakeholders, even though, according to the Commission and some securities regulators, the industry was given the opportunity to comment on the legislation in the making (interviews, Brussels, 27–30 March 2007). An important reason for this limited consultation is that work on these two directives began before the publication of the Lamfalussy Report that prescribed extensive consultation with industry in the policy process.

Thus, when the proposals for these two directives were sent to the EP for the first reading as part of the co-decision procedure, they were subject to many amendments by the MEPs sitting on the Committee on Economic and Monetary Affairs, which, in turn, was lobbied by industry. The amendments, initially passed in the committee, were subsequently voted on by the plenary session, after which the Commission redrafted several parts of the directives, both of which were eventually approved at the second reading. Having learned from this experience, the MiFID underwent extensive consultation before it appeared in official draft form. However, given the complexity of the issues dealt with and the last-minute changes to the official draft produced by the Commission, it had to go through a second reading. The Transparency Directive had been the subject of two Commission's consultations before it appeared in its official draft, and the EP and the Council were able to reach an agreement on it at the first reading.

The Market Abuse Directive (2002)

The Market Abuse Directive was designed to promote market integrity in the field of financial instruments and to contribute to harmonising the provisions concerning market abuse in the EU. It was also intended to ensure equal treatment of market participants and cooperation among the national authorities. In fact, each member state was required to appoint a single authority to deal with market abuse issues. The directive and the implementing measures distinguished two categories of market abuse: insider dealing and market manipulation.

The Market Abuse Directive was the first framework directive adopted using the Lamfalussy process, even though it was partly drafted before the Lamfalussy Report was published. Hence it did not undergo extensive consultation as prescribed by the Lamfalussy framework, even though the Forum of European Securities Commissions (the predecessor of the CESR) provided some technical advice to the Commission. The draft directive was officially proposed by the Commission in May 2001 and a final agreement by the ECOFIN Council was reached in June 2002. Given that during the first reading in March 2002 the EP proposed several amendments, a second reading was necessary, and the proposed directive was approved by the EP in October 2002. The ECOFIN Council accepted the parliament's amendments and the directive was adopted in December 2002. It contained general principles and procedural norms for the exercise of implementing powers by the Commission as well as a sunset clause whereby such power would need to be renewed after four years. This technique was subsequently applied in other Lamfalussy directives (Ferran 2004).

Three main features of the policy-making process concerning the Market Abuse Directive are important, and two of them also apply to the Prospectus Directive. First, the initial Commission drafts had to be substantially reworked and required a second reading – partially on account of the limited consultation with industry that had taken place. Industry consequently lobbied the Council and the EP, which proved receptive to the preferences of stakeholders and asked the Commission to amend its proposals.

Second, stakeholders were consulted both by the Commission and by the CESR. This process of 'double consultation' was repeated for the adoption of the implementing measures of other Lamfalussy directives, raising criticism from industry, which pointed out the duplication. On the Market Abuse Directive, the responses came mainly from EU-level banking associations, some German, French and Italian banking and securities dealers associations, and some international associations, such as the International Swap and Derivatives Association.[3] Compared with other directives, where the vast majority of responses came from British-based companies, there was not a substantial engagement by British associations, despite the size of the securities markets in the UK. The explanation is that market abuse rules were already relatively strict in the UK, but less so in Germany, Italy and France, which therefore were more concerned about the content of the directive.

Third, a couple of broad issues were particularly controversial in the negotiations. The Market Abuse Directive did not consider either the way in which investment banks addressed internal conflicts of interest – with Chinese walls, for instance – or the sophistication of many investors, who did not need costly protection from abuse (*The Economist*, 9 March 2002*)*. This was an issue for the many international investment banks and securities dealers located in the City of London (see International Swaps and Derivatives Association 2001).

Furthermore, the Market Abuse Directive was seen by some stakeholders as too broadly phrased and as covering too wide a range of markets and products, and some associations argued against its extension beyond securities markets (see International Swaps and Derivatives Association 2001). Moreover, as initially drafted, it would have included securities analysts and financial journalists providing misleading information in bona fide (*The Economist*, 16 June 2001). Especially as a result of the amendments proposed by the EP, which had been lobbied intensively by the journalists' and publishers' associations (the British press was reportedly particularly vocal on this), the final text limited the obligations placed on financial journalists.

The Prospectus Directive (2003)

The directive on the prospectus to be published when securities are offered to the public or admitted to trading allowed capital to be raised throughout the EU on the basis of one set of documents – the prospectus – and gave bond issuers a choice of regulator. It enhanced investor protection by strengthening the disclosure requirements for issuers and introduced a harmonised definition of 'qualified investor'. Exemptions from the obligation to publish a prospectus were clearly defined. Finally, the directive gave competence to a single authority in the member state to supervise compliance with the provisions. It also provided the opportunity for some countries to 'clean up' their own legislation (interview, Brussels, 16 June 2007).

The rationale of the directive was to encourage cross-border competition and promote market access, given the fact that the pre-existing rules concerning the mutual recognition of prospectuses were largely ineffective in practice, as different versions of the prospectus had to be prepared for each member state (Deutsche Bank 2002). In order to facilitate passporting, the issuer can publish its prospectus in 'a sphere customary of international finance' (a politically correct way of indicating the English language). The only extra requirement that can be imposed by the host member state is, if securities are to be offered to retail investors, for the summary to be translated into the official language/s (Ferran 2004). However, this is unlikely to impose an extra burden because it would be done anyway, as part of the marketing exercise.

The Prospectus Directive and its implementing measures outline a disclosure regime to be applied uniformly across the EU: member states cannot impose additional requirements on issuers. However, for specific issuers, such as start-up companies, the relevant authorities in the member states can modify the information required, even though the Commission has been keen to stress the 'restrictive character of this derogation' (Ferran 2004: 140). The disclosure requirements are largely informed by the IOSCO international disclosure standards, mentioned above, with a view to simplifying the activity of securities issuers engaged in cross-border operations and European issuers active in the US markets (Ferran 2004).

Some preliminary work on the issue was carried out by the Forum of European Securities Commissions (the predecessor of the CESR) in 2000. The directive was first proposed by the Commission in May 2001, incorporating many of the suggestions made by the Forum of European Securities Commissions. Nevertheless, the Commission's proposal was criticised by industry, which lamented that the draft had not be subject to a consultation procedure before being formally adopted (*Financial Times*, 16 June 2001, 7 September 2001), as pointed out in the joint response of several banking associations and stock exchanges (see European Banking Federation *et al.* 2002). Reportedly, the initial draft produced by the Commission was close to the preferences of the Mediterranean member states (in particular, Italy and France).

The main criticisms from industry, which were taken on board by the EP, were as follows. The crucial bone of contention was 'the home country principle' to determine the competent authority for the approval of the prospectus, whereas industry wanted to be given a choice (*Financial Times*, 22 November 2001). The Commission, backed by France, Italy and Spain, had initially proposed that all equity and most debt issuers could go for approval only to their national regulator, which would thus enjoy a sort of monopoly. The EP, industry, the UK and the Northern states wanted the freedom for issuers to use whichever market in the Union they preferred, seeking the approval of any EU regulator. This issue was particularly important for participants in the Eurobonds market, who opposed the principle that future prospectuses should be vetted by the competent authorities of the country where the issuer was based and not where the bonds would be listed – generally, London or Luxembourg (Deutsche Bank 2002). It was also important for the big investment banks, such as Goldman Sachs, ABN Ambro and Deutsche Bank, which formed part of an informal group against a 'heavy' prospectus (interview, London, 12 May 2007). Because it has one of the largest derivatives markets in Europe, Germany wanted a choice of regulator for bonds and derivatives. It did not support the choice of regulators for shares, arguing that country- and company-specific knowledge was required for this supervisory activity (interview, Berlin, 24 April 2008).

On the one hand, the concern was that some regulators – in particular those from the Mediterranean countries with France as part of the coalition – might insist on the use of the national market as a condition of approval (Huhne 2002). It was also pointed out during interviews that other parts of the financial industry, such as legal and financial consultants, also benefit from having the prospectus approved by the national supervisor (interview, Berlin, 23 April 2008). On the other hand, the concern of Southern regulators and the Commission was that the freedom for issuers to choose the regulator from which to seek approval might trigger a 'race to the bottom', as issuers would shop for easy approvals. Besides being a clash of national interests – the national governments were keen to set in place rules that were most advantageous for their own financial centres – it was also a matter of different economic philosophies, the 'market-making' versus 'market-shaping' paradigm, as elaborated below.

A second concern that emerged in the drafting of the directive was that it could have negative repercussions on the smaller unregulated markets, such as the Alternative Investment Market and Ofex (Association of Private Client Investment Managers and Stockbrokers 2001). This was on account of the 'one size fits all' approach, which treated all types of securities, both debt and equity, as coming from the same type of issuer, whether they were multinational corporations issuing bonds or companies on Ofex issuing a limited number of shares (*Financial Times*, 25 October 2001). Since the directive imposed extra burdens on quoted companies, these extra costs and the added management time would be disadvantageous for small companies. Because of the EP's insistence, a compromise was reached on the ability of national authorities to delegate approval of prospectuses to stock exchanges and other bodies, such as the nominated advisers in the Alternative Investment Market. This issue was particularly important for the UK, which hosts several of these markets.

The third issue was the designation of one competent authority per member state, because in some countries there was more than one authority. Germany was keen to prevent a single authority being designated, as this would have meant changing established practices and institutional arrangements in Germany (Deutsche Bank 2002). It was perhaps for this reason that the German authorities, rather surprisingly, put forward the proposal for the creation of an EU agency for the approval of prospectuses, but this was not supported by the other member states.

A fourth issue was the scope of the directive, whereby industry highlighted the insufficient number of exemptions that were included, an issue linked to the definition of 'qualified investors'. Industry wanted a broader definition, for example including certain private investors. This is because less burdensome provisions for the issuer usually apply whenever the investor is a 'qualified investor', requiring less legal protection than a non-qualified investor. Industry also wanted the duration of the vetting period to be as limited as possible. Finally, there were issues concerning certain features of the prospectus content, cross-border use and updating (Deutsche Bank 2002).

A final criticism concerning the directive was that it tried to achieve too much in one piece of legislation, as it sought to match the objectives of greater competition, wider access and transparency with greater investor protection (*Financial Times*, 25 October 2001). This was partly because of the clash of different regulatory paradigms, as explained below. For example, whereas the obligation to publish a prospectus did not apply to securities offered only to qualified investors, Mediterranean countries insisted on having detailed information provided for retailers, arguing that the latter need greater protection than wholesale professional investors.

The EP, which received intense lobbying from industry, asked for significant amendments concerning the points mentioned above in the first reading in February 2002. The socialist MEPs mostly lined up with the approach preferred by the Southern countries (France, Italy and Spain), whereas the conservatives and liberals mostly took on board the requests put forward by the Northern Europeans (the UK, the Netherlands, Luxembourg and the Scandinavian countries), even though there was also to some extent a split along national lines (interviews, Brussels, 13 June 2007).

The Council, under the Belgian and Spanish presidencies, reached an agreement on the distinction between equities and bonds, whereby under certain conditions bond issuers would be able to choose the competent authorities for the approval of the prospectus. In August 2002, the Commission presented a revised proposal incorporating some, but not all, of the amendments suggested by the EP, the Council Working Group, some member states and industry. One of the most important changes was the retention of the home country principle in determining the competent authority, but with free choice for issuers of non-equity securities (bonds) with a denomination of at least €50,000.

Reportedly, the Danish presidency, with its liberal democrat prime minister, was instrumental in promoting the cause of the Northern front in the second semester of 2002 (interview, London, 5 July 2007). In July 2003, the EP approved the proposal at the second reading, and the Prospectus Directive was subsequently officially adopted on the basis of several compromises. In the end, companies that issued bonds above €1,000 were granted a choice of regulator, which de facto gave freedom of choice to the vast majority of issuers (*Financial Times*, 1 July 2003). Exemptions related to qualified investors were extended to certain private investors with relevant expertise. The single competent authority per member state was retained, and Germany was granted a five-year transition period in order to bring its domestic arrangements into line with the directive. A compromise was also reached on the duration of the vetting period.

The issue of the treatment of SMEs and start-up companies, which had already surfaced at the level 1 discussion, emerged prominently in the adoption of implementing measures, exposing different regulatory approaches and economic structures in the EU. A similar debate took place also in the negotiation of the Capital Requirements Directive, as explained in Chapter 4. One view, expressed mainly by the continental coalition, considered SMEs as having lower capital requirement and default risk. Therefore, the argument went, they should be subject to 'light touch' regulation, so as not to overburden them. The opposite approach, taken mainly by the Northern coalition, regarded them as potentially risky, and therefore to be subject to ordinary rules (Ferran 2004).

These competing views came to the fore in the making of the level 2 implementing regulation. The Commission, advised by the CESR, did not initially envisage a special treatment for SMEs, despite the fact that the level 1 directive stated that the size of issuers should be taken into account (Ferran 2004). One explanation is that the consultation conducted by the CESR received responses principally from the main market players, whereas SMEs were underrepresented. Hence, it is not surprising that the responses did not consider a special (lightened) set of rules for SMEs to be necessary. As mentioned above and elaborated further in Chapter 7, the limited influence of small market players in the consultation process is a recurrent critique. Their treatment was particularly important for countries that have many SMEs, such as Germany, France and Italy, as it came to the fore in the negotiations of the Capital Requirements Directive.

What is rather distinctive in the policy-making process concerning this directive is that, as Chris Huhne pointed out, it spotlighted the influence of regulators within the Lamfalussy framework, as evidenced by the first draft of the directive giving national regulators a de facto monopoly on the approval of issues:

> In theory, they [national regulators] have a mere advisory role, with ministers and officials in the driving seat. In fact, the main member state representatives on the Council's working group have been national regulators. With their supposed knowledge of the markets, they have been able to set the pace.
>
> Huhne (2002)

Besides being a clash of national interests – the national governments were keen to set in place rules that were most advantageous for their own financial centres and their regulators – it was also a matter of different policy paradigms, based on different deep normative beliefs: market trust and market distrust. In Northern European and Anglo-Saxon countries, the prospectus is considered as an information tool, not a consumer protection tool: it is 'light' and it is not vetted by regulators. In Southern Europe, including France, it is seen as a consumer protection tool: the information in it has to be detailed and is vetted by the regulators (interview, London, 12 May 2007). This also exposed different views about the role of the public authorities vis-à-vis the market.

The Transparency Directive (2004)

The directive on transparency requirements with regard to information on issuers whose securities are admitted to trading on a regulated market revised and replaced the provisions of Directive 2001/34/EC, on the admission of securities to official stock-exchange listing. The rationale was to upgrade the information available to investors, enabling them to invest their funds on the basis of a better informed assessment. It supplemented the rule of the Prospectus Directive and the Market Abuse Directive by harmonising the reporting obligations for issuers whose securities are admitted to trading on a regulated market, as defined by the MiFID, discussed below. Unlike the Prospectus Directive, which was based on maximum harmonisation, the Transparency Directive relied on minimum harmonisation, as it allowed home member states to impose extra requirements on issuers under their jurisdiction, though host member states were prevented from doing so. This was choice-informed political pragmatism, the result of different periodic disclosure requirements in place in the member states (Ferran 2004). A fully harmonised approach would not have been feasible.

The directive required issuers to publish an audited annual financial report, half-yearly financial reports, and interim management statements from those share issuers who did not publish quarterly reports. Financial information was to be drawn up according to the International Accounting

Standards (subsequently renamed International Financial Reporting Standards) or an equivalent set of accounting standards. The Prospectus Directive also left open the possibility of choosing the accounting standard, with the Commission adopting implementing measures for uniform application (Ferran 2004).

In July 2001, in the preparations for the draft directive, the Commission launched a consultation on the transparency obligations of issuers whose securities were traded on regulated markets. This was followed by a second consultation in May 2002. In March 2003, the Commission presented the official proposal for the Transparency Directive. The disclosure requirements originally proposed by the Commission were downgraded as a result of the reactions of the stakeholders who considered the proposed reporting standards to be too onerous (Ferran 2004). The proposal was subsequently submitted to the European Parliament and the Council of Ministers for adoption under the co-decision procedure.

The draft went through the first reading by the EP in March 2004, when some amendments were proposed, and the following May the Council reached political agreement on the amended draft. Given the fact that the Council agreed with the EP, there was no need for a second reading, and the Transparency Directive was adopted in December 2004. The facts that enlargement was about to take place and that parliamentary elections were forthcoming contribute to explaining why the directive was adopted after a single reading (Ferran 2004).

The main issue in the negotiations of the Transparency Directive was how to report, when and to whom. Two specific points were particularly contentious during the negotiations: the reporting requirements and the potentially negative effects on the Alternative Investment Market. The MEPs and the Council rejected the Commission's original proposal, which would have obliged companies to publish their profit and loss every three months, as is the case in the US. The Commission, supported by countries that already required companies to report on a quarterly basis, argued that this would improve investor confidence (Lannoo 2005). Some member states, particularly the UK, as well as a large part of the industry, argued that the requirements would have been expensive for business without producing proportionate benefits to investors (London Stock Exchange *et al.* 2003). Onerous reporting requirements would have been a problem, particularly for the Alternative Investment Market. Moreover, especially in the UK, this could have induced potentially adverse effects, increasing 'short termism', whereby companies would use 'quick fix' measures to keep their figures up rather than concentrating on long-term profitability (interview, Brussels, 27 March 2007).[4] In the end, the quarterly reporting requirement was deleted.

Here again, different national regulatory approaches came to the fore. The Mediterranean countries, including France, for the same reason they favoured quarterly reporting, wanted to include provisions that required several documents, especially concerning the notification process: they maintained it would improve investor protection. In order to strengthen their argument, they cited as an example US regulation in an attempt to convince the British and the Germans authorities (interview, Paris, 19 July 2007). The UK favoured the submission of fewer documents and a simplified procedure in order to notify when the percentage threshold of holding, or voting rights in a company, has been passed, pointing out the necessity of not overburdening industry (interview, Brussels, 13 June 2007). For Germany, there was the issue of transferable bonds that do not require notification, and hence the Germans supported the British approach.

The Markets in Financial Instruments Directive (MiFID) (2004)

The MiFID was a core part of the FSAP and was described by the financial press as the 'new Big Bang' in financial services (*Financial Times*, 26 October 2006). It was proposed in November 2002 to update the existing Investment Service Directive issued in 1993, which applied only to a specified number of financial instruments and investment services (for a discussion of the politics of the MiFID, see Macartney forthcoming; Macartney and Moran 2008; Mügge 2006; see also De Visscher et al. 2008; on the legal aspects, see Ferran 2004; Ferrarini and Wymeersch 2006). All the firms previously covered by the Investment Services Directive were subject to the MiFID, but new categories of firm fell within the remit of the new directive, such as investment banks, stockbrokers and broker dealers, futures and options firms, commodity firms, and portfolio managers. Moreover, retail banks and building societies were subject to the MiFID for some parts of their business, such as investment products and the sale of securities. Although targeted mainly at the wholesale market, as is the case for the vast majority of measures proposed by the FSAP, the directive also contained rules concerning investor protection (Ferran 2004).

The MiFID set common rules for securities and derivatives markets, permitting investment firms to operate throughout the EU by using a single passport, which allowed financial firms to conduct business across Europe with the approval of their home authorities. Investment firms were enabled to process client orders outside regulated exchanges (stock exchanges), which had previously been impossible in some member states. This was the so-called concentration rule, which had been one of the main bones of contention in the negotiations of the Investment Service Directive in 1993 (see Coleman and Underhill 1998; Underhill 1997; Brown 1997), as it was a priority for France and other Southern European countries which had this rule in place. Consequently, in several member states, principally France, Italy and Spain, the MiFID exposed exchanges to competition from 'multilateral trading facilities' (i.e. non-exchange trading platforms) and 'systematic internalisers' (i.e. banks or investment firms that systematically execute client orders internally on their own account, rather than sending them to exchanges). This was already the case in some member states, such as the UK and Germany.

In contrast to the Investment Service Directive, the MiFID involved greater harmonisation, setting 'pre-trade transparency' and 'post-trade transparency' requirements for equity markets in order to facilitate comparison of terms and conditions offered by regulated markets (basically, stock exchanges), multilateral trading facilities, and systematic internalisers of retail order flow in liquid equities. Multilateral trading facilities and systematic internalisers were subject to similar pre- and post-trade transparency requirements as the exchanges, ensuring a level playing field between the exchanges and their competitors. Since the directive allowed client orders to be executed in different venues, it also imposed a 'best execution' obligation for investment services providers, designed to ensure investor protection. To this end, a 'suitability and appropriateness' test of the client by the investment service providers was also required. At the same time, the directive established a category of 'execution only' services that precluded such tests.

The MiFID extended the scope of the passport to take in commodity derivatives and credit derivatives. Moreover, investment advice was covered for the first time, since retail customers increasingly invest in securities, seeking advice from their bank or their broker. It should be noted that there is a link between the Capital Requirements Directive and the MiFID, because most firms that fall within the scope of the latter also have to comply with the former, which set requirements for the regulatory capital that credit institutions must hold.

Finally, the MiFID improved the operation of the passport for investment firms by clearly delineating the allocation of responsibility between home and host country for passported branches. Basically, the directive increased the standing of the home country authorities that had the power of granting (or denying) authorisation to investor services providers with their main office located in the state territory. The home authorities remained responsible for the supervision of such providers, even when they offered services in other member states, as well as for the supervision of their branches operating in other member states. The host authorities were responsible for compliance with the rule of conduct of branches located in their territory (Ferran 2004). As in the case of the Prospectus Directive and the Market Abuse Directive, the MiFID aimed to promote the convergence of the powers of the competent authorities across the EU.

Before issuing a formal proposal, the Commission conducted open pre-legislative consultation. In November 2000, it issued a communication, *Upgrading the Investment Services Directive* (CEC 2000b), which analysed some of the main issues at stake and to which industry and regulators responded (for the Commission's response to the comments received, see CEC 2001a). The European Parliament also issued a report (EP 2001), which robustly endorsed the Commission's suggestion to end the concentration rule, which was one of the most important points raised in the document issued in 2000. The debate that unfolded at this stage, with the division into two main camps, was a forerunner of the policy debate that took place in the following years.

In July 2001, the Commission produced a second document with its preliminary views for the new directive (CEC 2001b). This was also commented upon, and in March 2002 the Commission issued a further document that contained important changes (for an in-depth discussion of these documents, see Ferrarini and Recine 2006). The most important concerned pre-trade transparency obligations and the distinction between systematic and incidental internalisers, subjecting the former to heavier post-trade transparency and best execution rules than the latter. This last document elicited a robust response by industry. On the one side, stock exchanges, in particular Euronext (2002), defended the benefits of the concentration rule. On the other, investment banks and financial intermediaries based in the City of London criticised the rule for its anti-competitive effects (Association of Private Client Investment Managers and Stockbrokers *et al.* 2002). Subsequently, when it became clear that the concentration rule would be abolished, the debate between stock exchanges and financial intermediaries focused on the transparency requirements, with the former keen to impose onerous requirements (on financial intermediaries) and the latter eager to resist them. It should, however, be noted that the two groups did not present a monolithic front.

The official proposal submitted by the Commission in November 2002 did not entirely follow the ideas articulated in earlier consultations – which also highlights the 'political' limits of the consultation process (Ferran 2004). One of the most controversial provisions on pre-trade transparency had not been subjected to pre-legislative consultation (Deutsche Bank 2003; Federation of European Stock Exchanges 2003). According to the *Financial Times* (19 November 2002), the belated insertion of this provision in the official draft was the result of political intervention by the then president of the Commission, Romano Prodi, who had been lobbied by the French and Italian stock exchanges and who interposed personally to have the provision on pre-trade transparency inserted into the text (Ferran 2004). From then onwards, the policy-makers and stakeholders who opposed it had to fight a rearguard action to have the provisions amended.

The proposed directive was subsequently amended by the European Parliament at its first reading in September 2003, and the text was further amended by the Council. Once the Council formally adopted a common position on the basis of the political agreement in October 2003, the proposal returned to the parliament for its second reading. The negotiations between the EP, the Council and the Commission before the second reading ensured that, at that stage, the parliament was able to approve a compromise text also acceptable to the Council. The directive was finally adopted in April 2004.

These were among the most controversial issues during the negotiations of the level 1 legislation, and some of them were reopened in the negotiations of the level 2 legislation. The first was the 'internalisation' of client orders by investment firms, meaning that securities trading could be dealt with internally (i.e. within an investment bank), without resorting to trading on the stock exchange, as previously prescribed by the concentration rule in some countries. As explained above, in some member states, such as France, Italy and Spain, securities dealing had to take place through the stock exchange. By contrast, the UK and Germany had no concentration rule in place, and large investment banks and financial intermediaries, which are well established in the UK, performed such operations internally.

The Commission initially presented a legislative draft that was closer to the position of the Mediterranean coalition (Ferran 2004). This raised objections among some MEPs and part of the industry, especially investment firms in the UK and the global investment banks, several of which are US-owned but based in London, where large private German banks – in particular the Deutsche bank – are also active. The Commission's draft was approved by the Council by QMV after the rather unusual decision of the Italian presidency – despite the dissent of the UK, Ireland, Luxembourg and the Nordic countries (*Financial Times*, 9–11 October 2003; *The Banker*, 1 November 2003) – to call a vote, rather than continuing negotiations with a view to reaching a consensus, as it is common practice in the Council. The presidency was criticized, as it was seen as having a vested interest in pushing through the proposal as it stood (i.e. limiting internalisation), in spite of the opposition of countries that have a large financial sector. The EP, with the backing of some member states, principally the UK and the Nordic countries, managed to have important amendments included at the second reading (Ciani 2006). In the end, the MiFID ended the concentration rule present in much of continental Europe. This issue was particularly important for the UK, which never had a concentration rule and whose internalisation business generated considerable revenue in the City of London.

The second controversial issue – related to the first – was 'pre-trade transparency', which referred to publishing the prices of securities, hence the obligation by which investment firms have to reveal to the markets details of client orders and, if the firms are trading on their own account, some indication of the terms on which they stand ready to buy or sell a specified share. This was common practice for the stock exchanges, which had price quote, but it was not done by banks dealing with securities internally. In the UK, and to a lesser extent Ireland, Scandinavia and Germany, off-exchange dealing was a major part of the trading industry, and firms would be subject to considerable risk if they were forced to be open about their trading positions.

The difficulty was to produce pre-trade transparency requirements which were workable, because, if the obligations were too onerous to comply with, investment firms would not compete with exchanges – they would not 'internalise' (i.e. execute share trades off-exchang; interviews, Frankfurt, 10 and 12 September 2007; London, 2 April and 20 April 2007; Brussels, 27 June 2007). However, without pre-trade transparency obligations, there would not be a level playing field between stock exchanges and banks (interviews, Brussels, 24 October 2007; 13–14 June and 29 June 2007; Paris, 19 July 2007).

As initially drafted, the pre-trade transparency requirements (Articles 23–8, especially Article 25) were seen as placing investment firms at a disadvantage vis-à-vis regulated markets, ultimately de facto reintroducing the pre-existing concentration rule (Deusche Bank 2003). Negotiations in the Council and the EP focused intensively on this issue. In the Council, preferences differed widely, ranging from the removal of the relevant articles to extending the provisions. Under an earlier position taken by the ECOFIN Council, stockbrokers would have had to publish in advance prices for potential trades of over €3 million, which the MEPs claimed was too risky, even though the EP was also divided on this issue.

On the issue of pre-trade transparency rules applied to internalisers, opinions divided largely on national lines within the two main groups: stock exchanges and investment intermediaries (Ferrarini and Recine 2006). So, for example, the Italian and French banking associations expressed their dissent from the position taken by the European Banking Federation (see European Banking Federation 2002), which was seen as close to the position of the British banking associations and big investment banks. The London stock exchange had a less strict position than the French, Italian and Spanish stock exchanges (*Financial Times*, 1 June 2002).

In the end, the principle of pre-trade transparency was maintained for firms with the designation 'systematic internaliser' (a firm that on a systematic, organised and frequent basis deals on its own account by executing orders outside a regulated market or multilateral trading facility; Article 20, Implementing Regulation) for 'liquid shares' and for transactions up to a certain threshold, defined as 'standard market size' – meaning that very large trading positions will not have to be divulged. It was also recognised that firms needed some flexibility so that, in certain cases, they could offer their clients better prices than they quoted publicly.

As became evident, the final deal gave a considerable (and somewhat political) role to the level 2 committee, the European Securities Committee, and the level 3 committee, the CESR, which assisted the Commission in the adoption of the implementing measures that defined 'transactions above standard market size' and 'liquid share' – two relatively elastic concepts (interview, Berlin, 23 April 2008) that should have been decided at the political level (Treasury Committee 2006: Ev 6). A notable example of the politics at play in the adoption of the level 2 measures was the definition of 'liquid share', which ended up being facetiously called 'politically liquid share', because it was agreed that national authorities could nominate which shares were considered liquid in their market.

The MiFID extended the scope of post-trade transparency requirements from regulated markets (such as stock exchanges) to multilateral trading facilities and investment firms trading outside regulated market or multilateral trading facilities. All trading venues have to make public specific information about completed transactions in shares as close to real time as possible (with delays for large risk trades) and on a reasonable and non-discriminatory commercial basis. Investment firms can choose the disclosure channel.

A third important issue was the application of the 'suitability and appropriateness test' when assessing clients' needs and interests. According to the amendments proposed by the EP, a suitability test was required only in cases where the client received investment advice, whereas 'execution only' services, where the investment firm merely carries out clients' instructions, could be provided without any need for a full test. These cheap transactions, with no advice given to customers, were quite common for British financial firms, hence it was a priority for the British authorities and some (in particular British) MEPs.

Fourth, there was the technical problem of defining 'best execution', as practices differed across countries, and changing practices would have meant additional costs for national industry. For example, in the UK 'best execution' means the best price for the customer and is based on a 'price benchmark as a minimum execution standard' (Davies *et al.* 2006: 184). In Italy best execution refers to the best possible conditions with reference to time, size and type of transaction – it is therefore more detailed than in the UK. It refers to the 'total cost of trading, which includes not only transaction price but also any other explicit and/or implicit execution costs born by the trader' (ibid.: 183). Best execution means that firms are required to take all reasonable steps to ensure that relevant factors, including the price, cost, and speed of execution and settlement, are taken into account so that the client achieves the best possible result. Industry felt that this could have serious legal implications because, in theory, someone who asks an investment house to trade for them could challenge the transaction made on their behalf if they find a better deal on another exchange or later.

Finally, two interconnected issues came to the fore after the directive was passed, affecting the policy-making process of the level 2 implementing measures and future revisions of other directives. To begin with, it was realised that there was a strong link between the MiFID and the directive on undertakings for collective investment in transferable securities. This link had initially been overlooked by policy-makers, but it became clear when implementation of the MiFID was discussed (interviews, Paris, 18 July 2007). The Undertakings for Collective Investment in Transferable Securities Directive is of particular importance for mutual funds and assets managers, represented at the EU level by the European Fund and Asset Management Association and at the national level in the UK by the Investment Management Association, in Germany by the Bundesverband Investment und Asset Management, in France by the Association Française de la Gestion Financière and in Italy by the Associazione Italiana del Risparmio Gestito. The connection between the two directives was particularly important in France, which has one of the largest industries in Europe for collective investment firms, but also in Germany and the UK.

Second, and related to this, some investment firms, especially assets managers, were torn between the two directives for similar services. This was highlighted by the main associations dealing with investment management at both the national and the EU level. The MiFID and the Undertakings for Collective Investment in Transferable Securities Directive cover different parts of the financial services industry. Article 2 of the MiFID lists fund managers among those exempted from the application of the directive, but Article 66 states that it will apply if a fund manager is undertaking portfolio management. A priority for investment funds associations was to keep the two directives apart (interview, Frankfurt, 14 September 2007; Paris, 18 July 2007). It was thought that this result had been achieved at level 1, because specific provisions on 'best execution' did not apply to fund managers. However, the level 2 implementing directive stated that assets managers also had to comply with best execution, which was a problem for fund managers because they rely largely on brokers for the execution of operations; hence, they argued that it was difficult for them to ensure best execution.

This case exemplified a negative side effect of the Lamfalussy framework: the tendency to introduce additional rules at level 2. The tendency is sometimes reinforced at level 3 by the measures adopted by regulators. In this specific instance, there was the attempt by the CESR to introduce level 3 additional rules on best execution and 'inducement' (e.g. proportionality requirements), which were strongly opposed by industry, and in the end the proposal was dropped (interview, Frankfurt, 14 September 2007).

To sum up, the directive basically pitted two coalitions against each other. This was evident in the making of the level 1 legislation, but it also surfaced in the adoption of certain level 2 measures. On the one hand, national governments and economic interests in continental Europe exposed a market-shaping approach, trying to limit the extent of market opening and, using the argument of investor protection, calling for transparency rules and best execution. However, this was also a way of protecting the national stock exchanges in continental Europe, such as Euronext, Borsa Italiana and Bolsa de Madrid, which were especially vulnerable to competition from the large (mainly British-based and German) investment banks, because the MiFID removed rules that in effect eliminated competition in their home markets (*Financial Times*, 13 March 2006).

On the other hand, the UK financial services industry and the British authorities preferred a market-making approach, promoting market access and greater competition. The investments intermediaries and their international associations based in the City of London were keen to end the concentration rule and limit pre- and post-trade rules. The London Stock Exchange and to some extent the Deutsche Börse actually expected more business as a result of the MiFID, through the extension of single passport rules that allowed more investment firms to operate on a pan-European basis (*The Economist*, 9 September 2006). These stock exchanges were already operating without the concentration rule at the national level, unlike those in France, Italy and Spain, which therefore faced greater adjustment costs and were mindful of the competitive effects resulting from the abolition of the rule. A persistent concern in the UK was gold-plating, which takes place whenever governments and regulators add their own requirements to those of a directive. The industry was outspoken on this issue, stressing the potential impact on the competitiveness of the UK (*Financial Times*, 13 March 2006). The position of the German government was unclear and unstable because there were competing domestic policy preferences. Whereas the most domestically oriented part of the banking system (the savings banks and cooperatives) shared the policy preferences of the Southern front, the large private banks shared the preferences of the Northern group (interviews, Berlin, 23 April 2008; Frankfurt 10–12 September 2007). The public banks in Germany tend to have better access to policy-makers in the *Länder*, whereas the large private banks have better access to policy-makers at the federal level.

The federal state structure, the ongoing competition among ministers and the role of party political rivalry compounded the definition of the German position on the MiFID (interview, Paris, 18 July 2007). Observers reported that its position during the negotiations very much depended on which authority (and even which individual) was representing the country. This also explains why the Germans switched position somewhat, voting against the UK, Luxembourg and the Nordic countries when the Italian presidency called a vote in 2003. The Italians reportedly made specific concessions on issues that were important for Germany in order to get the latter's vote (interview, Brussels, 14 June 2007). The position taken by German savings banks and public banks is also in line with the positions expressed by the respective EU associations (where the German component is very important) on pre-trade transparency and internalisation, which contrasted with the preferences of the British banks and global investment banks and was closer to the position of the Italian and French banks (interviews, Brussels, 28–30 March 2007, 27 June 2007).

An overview of the main regulatory measures concerning securities markets adopted by the EU over the last decade is provided in Table 5.2.

An overall assessment

The Commission was particularly influential at the agenda-setting stage, in drafting the level 1 directives, which were endorsed by the main national governments. However, whenever the draft was not in line with the policy preferences of some (big) member states, the EP and relevant interest groups, the document had to be substantially redrafted for the second reading. The Commission was also in the driving seat at the implementation stage, because, assisted by the European Securities Committee and after receiving

Table 5.2 The main EU regulatory measures in the securities sector over the last decade

Regulation	Date of adoption	Institutions/bodies	Scope/objectives
Market Abuse Directive	2002	EU (Commission proposes, co-decision ECOFIN Council, EP); comitology	To promote market integrity To harmonise provisions concerning market abuse To promote supervisory cooperation
Prospectus Directive	2003	EU (Commission proposes, co-decision ECOFIN Council, EP); comitology	To allow capital to be raised throughout the EU on the basis of one set of documents – the prospectus
Transparency Directive	2004	EU (Commission proposes, co-decision ECOFIN Council, EP); comitology	To upgrade the information available to investors To harmonise reporting obligations for issuers on a regulated market
Markets in Financial Instruments Directive (MiFID)	2004	EU (Commission proposes, co-decision ECOFIN Council, EP); comitology	To set common rules for securities and derivatives markets, creating a 'single passport' for investment firms

advice from the CESR, it drafted the level 2 measures. The level 2 process was sometimes characterised by turf wars between the Commission and the member states gathered in the committee (interviews, Brussels, 28 March 2007; Paris 25 April 2007).

The EP was an important channel through which the industry could articulate its policy preferences, especially in the making of level 1 legislation. The MEPs were both lobbied by and actively encouraged interaction with industry, seeking information and expertise, producing reports and trying to understand the issues, as highlighted by the evidence submitted by industry representatives to the Treasury Committee (2006) as well as during several interviews conducted for this project. The MEPs were accessible and willing to listen to business, working across party and national lines. A representative of one big financial group explained that they tried to be 'as tutorial as possible' in their interaction with the EP (interview, Paris, 19 July 2007).

The European Parliament was quite sympathetic to the preferences of industry and amended significantly the main directives in response to requests – for instance, reducing the regulatory burden for SMEs in the Prospectus Directive and inserting measures to facilitate the functioning of the Eurobond markets. The role of the rapporteurs proved to be pivotal in achieving these outcomes, because they steer the legislative proposals through the Committee on Economic and Financial Affairs and the plenary vote in the parliament (Ferran 2004). Examples are the part played by Chris Huhne in securing the amendments to the provisions for the Alternative Investment Market and Eurobonds markets in the Prospectus Directive and the work of Theresa Villiers in pushing through the amendments to the pre-trade transparency rules in the MiFID. The rapporteur of the Transparency Directive, Peter Skinner, was instrumental in preventing the obligation of quarterly reporting.

The EP, and particularly the relevant committee, proved to be market friendly, open to the preferences put forward by the most competitive parts of the industry, which are generally located in the UK and to some extent Germany and France. Moreover, the committee avails itself of the advice of market participants sitting on the Advisory Panel of Financial Services Experts (Ferran 2004) and the European Parliamentary Financial Services Forum (Bieling 2006). Since three out of four directives in the securities sector were adopted at the second reading, the EP was able to have many of its proposed amendments incorporated in the final draft, and some member states also supported those changes.

It should be noted that indirect 'governmental lobbying' took place in the EP. For example, the British government was seriously unhappy with the first official draft of the MiFID and approached British MEPs (interviews, Brussels, 13 June 2007, 27 March 2007). Hence, the member states sometimes teamed up in the parliament and the Council, though more often than not the MEPs voted according to party lines (see Hix *et al.* 2007). However, in the internal debate leading to a vote, whenever the matter was of domestic importance they also took into account national preferences.

At level 2, the influence of the EP was more limited, as, unlike the member states represented in the level 2 committee, it did not have formal decision-making power. However, in practice, the EP was kept closely informed, it was actively lobbied by industry, and ultimately it was able to have a number of preferences incorporated in level 2 legislation – for example, exploiting the need for renewing the securities legislation that contained a sunset clause. This technique was also used to pressure the Council to amend the co-decision procedures and, indeed, a revised decision granting equal power to the EP and Council at level 2 was issued in 2006 (see Christiansen and Vaccari 2006).

The member states (to be precise, the national governments, particularly the treasury and finance ministries) were key players in co-deciding level 1 legislation, as the ECOFIN Council, together with the EP, had ultimate decision-making power. In the negotiations, the national governments' positions reflected the preferences of powerful domestic groups, especially in countries such as the UK where there is traditionally intense and constructive interaction between public authorities and industry. Sometimes national industry had divergent preferences, as was the case with Germany and the MiFID, and the position of the German authorities shifted throughout the negotiations. In countries such as France and Italy, where the tradition is for the public authorities to take the lead, the latter expressed their own preferences, as in the case of the Prospectus Directive, even when they differed from those of industry, or part of it, as in the case of the MiFID. At levels 2 and 3, the process was less intergovernmental without being supranational – it was characterised by committee governance, and the specific dynamics that unfold in these technical committees.

The large member states, which are also those with the biggest financial sector, were the most influential in the process, followed by some of the old member states with a relatively large financial sector, and then the new member states with a smaller financial sector, which also tends to be foreign owned (interviews, Brussels, 13 June 2007; Berlin, 23 April 2008). Moreover, the directives were negotiated and agreed either before or shortly after the 2004 enlargement, when the new member states were dealing with post-accession issues.

The specific coalitions of public and private actors varied depending on the directive being negotiated, even though the traditional line of friction was between the 'market-making' states (the UK, Ireland, the Nordic countries and the Netherlands), privileging the objectives of competition and market efficiency through the instruments of light touch and principle-based regulation, and the 'market-shaping' ones (France, Italy and Spain), privileging the objectives of stability and the protection of both investors and national markets, and adopting a 'rule-based' approach which resulted in detailed prescriptive regulation. Germany switched position, and hence coalition, depending on the specific content of the legislation being negotiated.

However, such a line of attrition also ran within member states and national industries (most notably in Germany), usually between the internationalised and competitive part of the sector and the domestically oriented state-owned one (Mügge 2006). For example, there was a divide between the private banks and the public banks in Germany on the MiFID, and to a more limited extent between some large banks and the small and medium-sized banks that comprised the rest of the sector in France and Italy.

The banking federations at both the national and the EU level were important players because many banks trade in securities. Outside the banking sector, two important EU associations were the Federation of European Stock Exchanges and the European Fund and Asset Management Association (formerly the European Fund and Asset Management Association), and their equivalents at the national level. The most influential members in the Federation of European Stock Exchanges were the largest national stock exchanges – the London Stock Exchange, Deutsche Börse AG, Euronext (Brussels, Paris, Amsterdam, Luxembourg, Lisbon, London International Financial Future Exchange),[5] Borsa Italiana and Bolsa de Madrid. The national members of the European Fund and Asset Management Association most active in the EU debate were the Investment Management Association in the UK, the Bundesverband Investment und Asset Management e.V (BVA) in Germany, the Association Française de la Gestion Financière in France, Assogestioni (Associazione Italiana del Risparmio Gestito) in Italy and Iverco in Spain (interviews, Frankfurt, 14 September 2007; Paris, 18 July 2007).

The main EU umbrella associations were split on certain issues because their members (national associations) had different preferences, and some of the national associations were also split internally. In the negotiations of the MiFID, the European Banking Federation had to reconcile the different policy preferences of the French and Italian banking associations on the one hand and those of the British banking association on the other (interview, Brussels, 2 April 2007; for this difficult balancing act, see European Banking Federation 2002). The positions of the European Fund and Asset Management Association were also moderated by the need to find a compromise between the preferences of its members (i.e. national associations), and a similar conundrum was sometimes faced by national associations at the domestic level. The French and Italian banking associations represent both large banks (such as BNP Paribas, Unicredito) and small savings and cooperative banks,[6] which had different policy preferences as far as the MiFID was concerned (interviews, Brussels, 30 March 2007, 27 October 2007).

Furthermore, there were international associations, many of which were US-based but with an office in London: the International Swaps and Derivatives Association, the International Capital Market Association (formed by the merger of the International Primary Market Association and the International Securities Market Association – formerly known as the Association of International Bond Dealers), the Bond Market Association (which in 2006 merged with the Securities Industry Association, creating the Securities Industry and Financial Markets Association) and the Future and Options Association. These organisations often take joint position, or similar positions expressed individually, with a view to increasing the number of responses to consultation. The Association of Private Client Investment Managers and Stockbrokers is an association of more than 200 firms, mainly British based, which deal in stocks and shares for private investors. In 2002 it merged with the European Association of Securities Dealers, increasing the ability of the organisation to represent its members in the EU and the UK.

In the lobbying on securities markets governance in the EU, as in the banking sector, there was an implicit division of competences. National associations and individual firms interacted mainly with the national authorities, whereas the EU-level associations interacted with the EU-level authorities (the Commission, the EP). However, the most active national associations, such as the British Bankers' Association and the German private banks association (the latter has a well-staffed office in Brussels), and some international companies, which either have offices in Brussels or use the services of lobbying firms based there, also lobbied at the EU level, usually (but by no means only) the MEPs and the Commission officials of their own nationality (interviews, Brussels, 30 March 2007; London, 20 April 2007; Berlin, 23 April 2008). Other national associations that had limited experience of lobbying in Brussels preferred to rely on their public authorities (see Greenwood 2003).

At times, the presence and activity of national associations (and private companies) pursuing different policy preferences in Brussels – for example, all the German banking associations, the French banking association and the Italian banking association have representatives there – presented difficulties in coordinating the position and actions of EU associations (interview, Brussels, 27 June 2007). However, these channels have proved effective, and indeed the City of London decided to open an office in Brussels in 2004.

In some instances, the national associations or individual companies which felt that their policy preferences were not adequately represented by their national government resorted to lobbying governments other than their own, generally targeting the permanent representations in Brussels, which tend to be more 'Europeanised' than national administrations (Kassim *et al.* 2000; Lewis 2005, 2002). For example, a well-known French bank reportedly approached the UK permanent representation in Brussels on the MiFID, and a similar strategy was adopted by a familiar German bank, which at times was unhappy with the line taken by the German authorities in the negotiations (interview, Brussels 27 March 2007).

Finally, it should be noted that the level 3 committee interacted intensively and extensively with industry, which was a novel procedure for many national regulators sitting on the CESR. Indeed, whereas consultation and interaction with industry, especially in the financial sector, is quite common in the UK, it is relatively uncommon in continental Europe, especially in France, Italy and Spain, albeit this has begun to change during the last decade. An important catalyst for this change has been the principle of 'better regulation' promoted by the EU. In Italy and France, for example, this has been crucial in spearheading consultation between the private sector and the public authorities in the financial services sector, as well as in other sectors (interview, Brussels, 27 June 2007).

Policy-making was less intergovernmental at level 2 than at level 1, without being supranational, as the technical committees involved are not supranational authorities in the manner of the Commission and the EP. However, despite the fact that they are composed of representatives from the member states, they are not arenas for intergovernmental political negotiations – though there are exceptions – but rather for technical joint decision-making. This applies more to the level 3 committees, since the level 2 committees are more 'parapolitical' (interview, Brussels, 29 March 2007): the senior officials sitting at level 2 report to their ministers and interact with national industry, whereas the members of level 3 committees come from (often independent or semi-independent) supervisory authorities.

The empirical record shows that there were circumstances under which politics entered the decision-making process of these committees, when the coalitions were brought together by overlapping interests, along the lines of attrition mentioned above, rather than the process being based on technocratic consensus and expertise. Occasionally, passive trade-offs took place between the national representatives sitting on the committees because members identified which issues were important for other member states and made concessions that were reciprocated (interview, Brussels, 27 March 2007). Moreover, there were occasional turf wars between the member states and the Commission, resembling the intergovernmental versus supranational divide, though it can also be seen as a form of bureaucratic politics among technocrats.

However, even at level 2, policy-making is generally based on technical argument rather than straight intergovernmental negotiations: if a member state explains convincingly why it has a problem with a certain provision, the issue is taken on board by other member states on the committee. Most of the time it is not a matter of protecting domestic interests, strictly defined, but a question of member states doing things in different ways, thus giving rise to considerable adjustment costs for those member states required to change, as confirmed in several interviews. As one policy-maker colourfully put it: 'there are different ways to skin a cat' (interview, Brussels, 27 March 2007).

The general view is that the level 3 committees take decisions not on a political basis, especially when developing level 3 measures (e.g. standards), but on evidence (interview, Brussels, 29 March 2007). However, there have been rare instances in which the advice concerning the level 2 implementing measures given by the level 3 committees was affected by considerations as to what might be politically acceptable to the national governments (Treasury

Committee 2006: Ev 52) and national financial systems. An example of member states teaming up at levels 2 and 3 was the CESR's advice on the broad definition of 'liquid share' in the MiFID. Moreover, on issues that directly affect the tasks and the powers of the supervisory authorities, the members of the committees might be inclined to defend their bureaucratic preferences and institutional prerogatives. Some advice given by the CESR on the MiFID and the Prospectus Directive suggests this.

Given the economic significance of the issues, the focal points of agreement for the formation of coalitions in the negotiations were generally constituted by overlapping or compatible interests, though the prevailing policy paradigms in the member states also played a role. At stake were two competing market models and their underlying regulatory philosophies, which in turn both influenced and were influenced by the structure of the market. As argued in a joint paper by the British Treasury and the Financial Services Authority (see HM Treasury and FSA 2007), a regulatory approach suitable for international financial centres dominated by wholesale markets, such as the City of London, is different from a regulatory approach for retail-focused national markets, which prevail in Southern Europe.

It is difficult to separate policy paradigms (hence, ultimately, 'ideas') clearly from the features of the national financial system and regulatory issues related to the competitiveness of industry or specific preferences of market players (thus, 'interests'). British policy-makers have traditionally adopted an internationalised market-making approach, but this is also influenced by the large number of foreign-owned companies (especially from the US) located in the City of London. French, Italian and Spanish policy-makers embrace a market-shaping, inward-oriented policy paradigm, which is interconnected with the limited competitiveness and the restricted internationalisation of their financial sector. German policy-makers also subscribe to a market-shaping policy but, given the competitiveness of part of their financial sector (private investment banks and financial conglomerates), tend to be more market-oriented and competition-friendly than France, Italy and Spain, even though this also depends on the specific issues being negotiated.

The two competing paradigms are characterised as follows. The Northern approach is market-making, privileging the objectives of market efficiency and competition, even when this implies a trade-off with consumer protection. This approach relies on the instrument of light-touch, principle-based regulation and private sector governance. It is rooted in common law and is based on the ontological principle of market trust. It should, however, be noted that, as pointed out by a financial regulator, the principle-based approach in the UK is relatively recent, having been adopted only in the last decade (interview, Frankfurt, 13 September 2007). It is also incorrect to label it as 'Anglo-Saxon', because the US has a rule-based approach to financial services governance, especially on accounting and auditing standards.

The Southern or continental approach is market-shaping, privileging the protection of consumers and, at times, of national industry, even when this reduces competition and market efficiency. This approach relies on the instruments of prescriptive rule-based regulation, with a very limited role for private sector governance. It is rooted in Roman law, emphasises the role of the public authorities and is based on a distrust of the market. The governance of financial services in the EU has been moving towards principle-based, market-making regulation and private sector governance over the last decade or so, but this has created friction between the two paradigms and the coalitions subscribing to them. Moreover, as discussed in the following chapter, the global financial crisis may have halted if not reversed this trend, at least temporarily.

To sum up, intergovernmental and supranational dynamics were at work, with the former prevailing at level 1 and decreasing significantly when moving downwards to levels 2 and 3. The supranational dynamics at levels 2 and 3 took the form of committee and technocratic governance – that is, national representatives undergoing a process of socialisation through repeated interaction and making policy based primarily on technical rather than political arguments, though politics was never completely absent from the process. The influence of the Commission, a supranational body, was greater at level 2 than at level 1, while the opposite was true for the EP, even though each institution remained influential at both levels. The EP was involved in the policy-making process (and hence it was lobbied) early on, when the Commission was still in the process of drafting legislation. The Commission, in turn, remained engagaged in the process (hence it was lobbied) even after the draft directive had been presented to the parliament and the Council, as in some instances the directive had to be redrafted. The third main supranational body, the ECB/Eurosystem, was generally not involved, though it worked with the CESR to produce level 3 standards on securities settlement, as explained in the following chapter.

Industry was given extensive access to the public authorities at all the levels of the Lamfalussy framework, though in practice its influence depended on the resources (financial resources, human resources, expertise) available to market participants. Consequently, the large financial associations, global banks and investment firms had better access and were more influential (Mügge 2006). However, they sometimes had different preferences, as was the case with the MiFID. Moreover, if an issue was particularly salient, for instance, for the small banks or for SMEs, these organisations were able to have their preferences taken into account, especially if they were backed up by their national governments and/or some MEPs. Indeed, most of the rules adopted at the end of complex EU negotiations were based on compromise, and there was not one set of actors whose preferences systematically prevailed. Consumer groups were generally underrepresented, a feature that touches upon the issues of openness and democratic input, as elaborated in Chapter 7.

Conclusion

This chapter has examined the governance of securities markets in the EU, arguing that the pace of regulatory activity quickened after the FSAP and the setting up of the Lamfalussy framework. The four directives passed and their implementing measures concerning securities trading were designed to increase financial market integration in the EU substantially, through de-regulation at the national level, re-regulation at the EU level, convergence of supervisory practices and improved cooperation among national supervisors.

In the making of these directives, but especially in the Prospectus Directive and the MiFID, there were different preferences among, and in some cases within, the member states, and so there were strong intergovernmental negotiations as well as intragovernmental negotiations in some countries, first and foremost Germany. This also meant that the final outcomes were often rather 'odd' compromises (e.g. the home country supervisory approach for shares but not for bonds in the Prospectus Directive, the definition of 'liquid shares' and 'standard market size' in the MiFID), or issues were left open, to be decided later on, as the devil is in the details.

In some cases, the shortcomings of the solutions adopted became apparent only when the directives were implemented. For example, the 'simplified' 'European prospectus' that was the objective of the Prospectus Directive was not particularly simplified, because the directive was excessively convoluted. Several policy-makers and many stakeholders called for its revision shortly after it was implemented (see European Securities Markets Expert Group 2007). In other cases, the problem was the excessive use of national discretion and/or gold-plating by the national authorities. Finally, the implementation stage brought new stakeholders into the policy process (e.g. assets managers and distribution industry in the case of the MiFID). It also showed the linkage between directives, as, for instance, undertakings for collective investment in transferable securities had been overlooked during the negotiation of the MiFID and needed to be addressed in the revision of the Undertakings for Collective Investment in Transferable Securities Directive.

Securities markets regulation has been the area of most intense EU activity in the 2000s, partly because market integration had lagged behind, partly because securities dealing and technical innovation in this field have become more important. The next chapter focuses on the post-trading activities clearing and settlement of securities, as well as payments systems – the 'plumbing' of the EU financial markets – on which a large part of EU regulatory activity focused after 2004, once the main directives on securities trading had been passed.

6 Governing post-trading in the EU

The establishment of EMU and the FSAP drew attention to the governance of payment services and the clearing and settlement of securities. Although these financial services are often overlooked in the analysis of financial market integration, they underwent substantial regulatory reforms in the 2000s, which complemented the changes of banking and securities trading regulation discussed in the previous chapters.

There was legislative activity at the EU level, namely, the Payment Services Directive, and an initial attempt by the Commission to issue a directive on the clearing and settlement of securities, subsequently set aside in favour of a voluntary code of conduct. The latter was an example of market-led action, prompted by the threat of legislation. A similar approach was adopted with reference to the Single Euro Payments Area, a goal that was strongly supported by the Commission and the ECB. The ECB also decided to intervene directly in the settlement systems of the eurozone by proposing to set up the TARGET2 Securities (T2S). The main difference is that the Single Euro Payments Area applies to retail payments, whereas T2S is linked to the platform TARGET2 for large-scale payments in the euro area and concerns the wholesale settlement of securities.

It is argued in this chapter that, in the governance of the payment services and the clearing and settlement of securities, there were two competing and variable coalitions of private and public actors, which came to the fore in the discussion of the main legislative measures – the Payment Services Directive and the eventually decision to opt for a code of conduct on clearing and settlement. On one side was the Southern market-shaping coalition (better described in the case of the Payment Services Directive as the continental coalition, since Germany was a leading force), with a 'traditional' outlook concerning financial services, emphasising the objectives of systemic stability and consumer protection and preferring the instruments of hard law and prescriptive legislation. On the other side was the Northern market-making coalition, which in this case also included some of the new member states, privileging the objectives of competition and financial innovation and the instruments of soft law and market-led action. As with the governance of other financial services in the EU, these were coalitions of interests informed by domestic political economy considerations, but they also embodied different regulatory approaches. Likewise, different regulatory approaches came to the fore in the discussions on T2S. Furthermore, more than in the other case studies previously discussed, there were important 'transversal' or 'sectoral divisions' within each coalition, and the ECB was a key player in its own right in the making of T2S.

Payment services in the EU

Payment systems, which are the infrastructures through which payment services are carried out, are regulated and monitored at the international level because of their potential to trigger cross-border financial instability, for example following a gridlock in the system affecting systemically important payments. Central banks, which are primarily in charge of financial stability, have traditionally been involved in overseeing payment systems at the domestic level and have engaged in joint regulation and monitoring of this activity at the international level. In the TEU, the ECB was explicitly given the task of contributing to the smooth operation of the payment system in the euro area.

The institutional framework for governing payment services

The institutional framework outlined in the previous chapters applies also to the governance of payment services and the clearing and settlement of securities, even though for each of these activities there are specific bodies at the international, EU and national level that should be mentioned.

The Committee on Payment and Settlement Systems (CPSS) is a coordination forum for the central banks of the G10 to monitor, analyse developments and reduce risks in domestic payments and settlement and clearing systems, as well as in cross-border and multi-currency settlement schemes. It was created in 1990 – though its predecessors date back to 1980 – and is composed of senior officials responsible for payment and settlement systems in thirteen national central banks[1] and the ECB. The committee meets three times a year, but there is no public release of the agendas or discussions; regular reports are made by the chairman to the committee of the G10 central bank governors.[2] The Bank for International Settlements hosts the secretariat. Over time, the CPSS, which cooperates with the IOSCO, the BCBS and the FSF, has contributed to setting standards, codes and best practice for the sound management of the payment systems worldwide. Some of the most important documents produced were the *Core Principles for Systemically Important Payment Systems* (2001), the CPSS–IOSCO *Recommendations for Securities Settlement Systems* (2001) and the CPSS–IOSCO *Recommendations for Central Counterparties* (2004). Some of these documents were transposed into EU rules, highlighting the interconnection between international and EU rule-making. For example, the *Core Principles for*

Systemically Important Payment Systems (standards for the design and the operation of such systems in all countries), agreed after consultation with industry and under the chairmanship of a member of the ECB executive board, Tommaso Padoa-Schioppa, were adopted in 2001 by the governing council of the ECB as minimum standards for its oversight of large-value payment systems operating in euro. There was also a controversial attempt to transpose the CPSS–IOSCO *Recommendations for Central Counterparties* into EU level 3 measures, as explained below.

The ECB contributes to the smooth operation of the payment systems in the EU. The management of the payment systems in the euro area is shared between the ECB and the national central banks, the former overseeing cross-border large-value payment systems and TARGET1 and 2, the latter overseeing domestic systems. TARGET is the Trans-European Automated Real-Time Gross Settlement Express Transfer system for the euro and is used in the settlement of central bank operations, large-value euro interbank transfers and other euro payments. It was created in 1999 by interconnecting national euro real-time gross settlement systems and the ECB payment mechanism. A real-time payment system was necessary in the eurozone to provide the procedures for implementing the ECB's monetary policy and to promote sound and efficient payment mechanisms.[3] It was replaced by TARGET2 in 2007, as explained below.

As far as industry is concerned, the European Payments Council is the decision-making and coordination body of the European banking industry in relation to payments. It was established in 2002 with the purpose of promoting the creation of the Single Euro Payments Area through industry self-regulation. The European Payments Council brings together the main banking associations in the member states representing the various parts of the industry. It defines common positions for core payment services, provides guidance for standardization, encourages best practice and monitors implementation.

At the national level, the central banks are the institutions that look after the functioning of payment systems. It should be noted that, whereas only some central banks are involved in the clearing and settlements of securities, all central banks oversee the national payment systems because of the implications that this has for the conduct of monetary policy, financial stability and the functioning of the banking sector. An overview of the international and EU institutions for the governance of post-trading is provided in Table 6.1.

Regulating payment services in the EU

The SEPA

In the past, the retail payment markets across the EU varied considerably as regards technical standards, national legislation and domestic customer

Table 6.1 The institutional framework for payments, clearing and settlement governance (international bodies in shaded boxes)

Institution/ body	Date of establishment	Membership/composition	Functions/tasks
International Organization of Securities Commissions (IOSCO)	1983	Securities regulators worldwide	To set international standards in securities markets To promote cooperation and exchange of information
Committee on Payment and Settlement Systems (CPSS)	1990 (predecessor dating back to 1980)	Senior officials responsible for payment and settlement in thirteen national central banks and ECB	To set international standards on payments, clearing and settlement To monitor developments in payments, settlement and clearing systems To reduce risks in payment and settlement systems
ECB National central banks in Eurosystem	1999	Executive board and governing council	ECB to oversee cross-border large-value payment systems and to manage TARGET1/2 National central banks to oversee domestic systems
European Payments Council (EPC)	2002	Banks and banking associations across Europe	To promote the creation of the Single Euro Payment Area
Group of Thirty (G30)	1978	Bankers, central bankers and academics	Think tank on financial matters De facto standards setter

preferences for different payment instruments. In the first decade of the twenty-first century, two parallel initiatives were under way in order to promote an internal market for payments. First, the industry engaged in the design of pan-European standards and infrastructures to transform eurozone payments into domestic payments, as envisaged by the Single Euro Payments Area. The objectives of this were to remove the barriers to cross-border movement of funds and reduce the cost of euro payments to the level of domestic transfers by 2010 through the setting up of common standards and services. It involved all the countries in the euro area, for domestic as well cross-border payments to other countries.

The background to the programme and the creation of the European Payments Council was the adoption of the 'Regulation on Cross-Border Payments in Euro' issued in 2001, shortly before the physical introduction of the single currency. The regulation brought the cost of cross-border card transactions, electronic cash withdrawals and bank transfers in euro into line with the cost of national transactions. This provided an incentive for the modernisation of the payment industry, streamlining cross-border payment infrastructures.

The creation of the Single Euro Payments Area was promoted by the European Commission and the ECB working with the Eurosystem. Both the Commission and the ECB promoted the project as a means of increasing economic efficiency, completing the Single Market, and demonstrating concrete benefits ensuing from EMU (CEC and ECB 2006). The Commission did not specify how the Single Euro Payments Area was technically to be achieved because it preferred to leave it to the market. Yet the Commission itself was reportedly divided on this issue: the internal market directorate preferred a pan-European system, while the competition directorate was concerned about the potential anti-competitive repercussions (*The Economist*, 4 February 2006). The ECB held the opinion that TARGET was a pan-European wholesale payment system that was unsuitable for retail payments. Both bodies were reluctant to build a separate retail system and were eager that the banks should take it on (CEC and ECB 2006).

The Single Euro Payments Area project was led by the European Payments Council, which, however, had problems in reaching an internal consensus. On the one hand, pressure for change came from big companies, such as Royal Dutch Shell, Hewlett-Packard, General Electric and IBM, which aimed to standardise their connections to banks worldwide, rather than just in Europe. On the other hand, smaller companies were concerned about the cost and interruption that change could bring (*The Economist*, 21 May 2005).

One reason for the inertia of the banks and most of their customers (except for the biggest companies) was that, by and large, national payment systems worked well. Second, payment systems are costly to build, and small cross-border payments – i.e. of less than €50,000 – accounted for only 3 per cent of overall volume in 2004. Some bankers thought that 'building a single pan-European system makes about as much sense as buying a Rolls-Royce for monthly visits to the hairdresser' (*The Economist*, 21 May 2005). Third, payment services were more lucrative for banks if they were combined with other services such as cash management, foreign exchange or custody of securities. So banks were disinclined to consider payments as a service that could easily be switched from bank to bank. Industry's reluctance, which emerged in particular in 2004, was overcome by the strong insistence, if not outright pressure, exerted by the ECB and the Commission, which threatened legislation or other forms of public intervention if the Single Euro Payments Area was not established (CEC and ECB 2006). The ECB periodically monitored the progress towards its acheivement (see, for example, ECB 2004b).

The Payment Services Directive

The Single Euro Payments Area, which was a market-led project strongly encouraged by the public authorities, was complemented by a directive initially called the New Legal Framework for Payments in the Internal Market and subsequently renamed the Payment Services Directive. It developed a harmonised legal basis to be applied to all types of payment service providers throughout the EU, set up the legislative framework to license payment service providers and paved the way for the introduction of European-wide payment services for credit transfers and direct debits.

The rationale of the directive was to make it 'as easy, cheap and secure to make a cross-border payment by credit card, payment card, electronic bank transfer, direct debit or any other means as it was to make a payment within member states' (CEC 2003). After the creation of EMU, although the euro area member states had a single currency, there was no common legal framework for non-cash payments, which also meant that service providers were effectively blocked from competing and offering their services across the EU.

The core elements of the directive were 'enhanced competition by opening up of markets to payment services providers other than banks'; 'harmonised market access requirements for non-bank payment service providers' – the so-called payment institutions; and the 'standardisation of rights and obligations for users and providers of payment services in the EU' (CEC 2003). Unlike the Single Euro Payments Area, the directive, which amended two existing directives, applied to all member states and all EU currencies.

The opportunity (or otherwise) to legislate was considered in the early stage of the preparation of the Payment Services Directive. Indeed, the Commission released a working document for public consultation in May 2002 with a view to understanding whether action was required in this field. Given the overall positive response (CEC 2002a), in December 2003 the Commission issued the communication *A New Legal Framework for Payments in the Internal Market* (CEC 2003), inviting responses on the proposed content for the new directive. The Commission adopted a formal proposal in December 2005 (CEC 2005c).

In September 2006, the Economic and Monetary Affairs Committee of the EP adopted the report prepared by Jean-Paul Gauzès (EP 2006). In March 2007, progress was made in the ECOFIN Council, and the finance ministers unanimously adopted a general approach on a compromise text for the Payment Services Directive. In the same month, the text was examined in a trialogue with representatives of the EP, the Commission and the Council of Ministers, represented by the presidency. In April 2007, the MEPs in plenary session approved without further changes the compromise text worked out between the rapporteur and Council representatives. This already had the political support of the Council, so the legislative process was completed at the first reading.

Some of the most controversial issues that surfaced during the negotiations were the appropriate prudential framework for payment institutions; the activities that payment institutions could undertake; and the possibility of waiving the application of parts of the directive, either for certain smaller institutions and natural persons or for particular instruments used primarily for payments of small amounts. Another issue was whether the directive should apply only to payments in the EU and in euro. Finally, there was the question of consumer protection, which cut across some of the specific points mentioned above. Among these, the most controversial was the requirement for non-bank service providers, because allowing non-bank providers into the market would, for example, let consumers make payments with their mobile phones or pay their electricity bill in supermarkets.

Let us look at these issues in more detail. The directive proposed the creation of payment institutions (non-banks), raising the issue of the appropriate regulation and regulatory capital for these entities. One view, which was supported by the institutions themselves, was that, since they were not banks, they should not be subject to capital requirements. Others, principally the banks, thought that, since the payment institutions performed services provided by banks, according to the principle of 'same risks, same regulation' (Deutsche Bank 2005a), they should be subject to the same capital requirements to protect consumers and ensure a level playing field (*European Voice*, 11 May 2006). On the one hand, British officials reportedly hinted that capital requirements for payment institutions were intended to protect banks – in particular German public banks – rather than consumers (*Financial Times*, 28 February 2007). On the other hand, continental officials pointed out that they were concerned about the soundness of the system and the solvency of payments institutions, as well as the repercussions on consumers (ibid.). This view was also expressed by the ECB (2006a).

Second, and related to this, there was a discussion as to the activities that the payment institutions could or could not undertake (see ECB 2006a). According to the banks, the New Legal Framework, as initially proposed, did not distinguish adequately between payment services and 'ancillary services', such as exchange services and the storage and processing of data. They were critical of the 'broad' (according to them) list of ancillary services that the payment institutions would be able to provide and wanted these restricted (see Deutsche Bank 2005a).

The third issue was to what extent 'professionals', as opposed to 'consumers', should be subject to different treatment under the directive. In EU directives in the financial sector, consumers are usually protected by stricter rules than are professionals, the argument being that the latter have the technical competence to make informed choices. This raised the issue of how consumers should be defined in a manner consistent with other EU directives. The Payment Services Directive, as initially drafted, had a broader definition of consumers than previous directives, and this was seen as unnecessarily burdensome for banks and other payment institutions, which would be bound to apply specific (stricter) rules for consumer protection than would otherwise be the case (Deutsche Bank 2005a).

Fourth, besides intra-EU payments, the Commission initially planned to include in the scope of the New Legal Framework cases in which the payment service provider of either the payer or the beneficiary was located outside the EU, as well as payments not in euro (the so-called two-leg payment transactions). This was resisted by industry on the ground that EU legislation was applicable only inside the Union and that, from a technical and economic point of view, differences existed even between payments in euro and those in other EU currencies (*European Voice*, 11 May 2006). Eventually, the Payment Services Directive applied only to payments within the EU, though with a commitment from the Commission to review its extension to non-EU countries in the future. Finally, the industry felt that, since the objective of the directive was to legislate mostly on retail and commercial payments, it should apply only to payment transactions of up to €50,000. The proposed threshold of €50,000 was initially proposed, then taken out and eventually reinstated.

Following the amendments put forward by the EP and intense discussions among the member states in the Council, the final agreement was based on a proposal by the German presidency involving the following compromise. Capital requirements were imposed on payment institutions, but lower than those for banks, which are regulated by the Capital Requirements Directive, as explained in Chapter 4. Non-banking institutions were allowed to offer credit, but only within a limited twelve-month period. The application of certain provisions was waived in specific circumstances. Moreover, especially with reference to capital requirements, a significant degree of national discretion was retained in the directive.

Let us examine in more detail the preferences of the main players. The Commission drafted the directive after public consultation. However, many observers noticed that the proposal, as originally drafted, did not take sufficiently into account the policy preferences expressed by banks and member states with a bank-oriented financial system and a 'traditionalist' view of financial services, such as France, Italy, Spain, and also Germany. This explains why painstaking negotiations took place in the Council and why the related provisions had to be changed before eventually being approved by the Council and the EP (interview, Brussels, 28 March 2007). The Commission was reportedly more sympathetic to the market-making, liberal camp (the UK, the Nordic countries) until it realised that there was a blocking minority in the Council of Ministers and the EP, and a compromise between the two coalitions was therefore pursued (interview, Brussels, 14 June 2007).

The EP, especially the Committee on Economic and Monetary Affairs, reflected the views of industry (especially banks) as well as consumers. It favoured a higher level of regulation than was initially proposed by the Commission, with a view to improving consumer protection, but also embraced certain issues that were important to industry, such as limiting the scope of the directive (*European Voice*, 11 May 2006). In a report issued in 2004 (the rapporteur was Alexander Radwan), the EP:

> takes the view that prudential rules governing payment service providers should be made more uniform on a Europe-wide basis in order to ensure a level competitive playing field; takes the view that further fragmenting of prudential supervision provisions or a lowering of prudential supervision standards must be prevented; takes the view that, in the interest of all parties concerned (consumers, merchants, and banks), a new payment service provider status must not lead to a deterioration in the physical, prudential, financial, and economic security of the means of payment released onto the market.
>
> (EP 2004: 6)

This position, which was reiterated in the EP's report in 2006 (EP 2006) was quite sympathetic to the preferences expressed by banks. Moreover, the parliament also supported industry in limiting the application of the directive only to EU payments – the extension to non-EU payments would have been costly. Reportedly, German MEPs also successfully mobilized to extend the execution time, which posed major difficulties for the savings banks (interview, Brussels, 28 July 2007).

In its official opinion on the proposed Payment Services Directive, the ECB made clear that the scope of the directive, as originally drafted, was too broad, because payment institutions would receive deposits from their customers and could use this to provide credit. There was consequently an inconsistency between the permitted activities of payment institutions and the prudential and supervisory approach suggested, with credit institutions being placed at a regulatory disadvantage, as they would be subject to capital requirements and supervision on a consolidated basis. The ECB therefore suggested that capital requirements be introduced for payment institutions; that they should be prevented from carrying out credit functions; and that the ancillary services they could offer should be limited (ECB 2006a). This position was close to the preferences expressed by the banks.

The industry was divided into two main camps: the banks and the other payment institutions. As confirmed by interviews, the member states were also divided into two main camps: the market-making liberal countries (the UK, the Netherlands, Sweden and Finland), which wanted to widen the innovative use of payment cards and credit, and the market-shaping countries (France, Italy and Spain), which had a more traditional outlook on financial activities and insisted that non-bank payment companies should have strict capital requirements (*Financial Times*, 26 March 2007). Some of the new member states, in particular Poland and the Czech Republic, sided with the Northern group, because non-bank payment institutions already operate in these countries (interviews, Brussels, 9 April 2007). For example, it is possible to pay bills in supermarkets and through mobile phone companies.

Overall, the debate exposed a North–South divide in Europe (*Financial Times*, 26 March 2007), except that Germany and Belgium joined the Southern coalition (*Financial Times*, 28 February 2007). The Germans, who have a bank-based financial system and hence were concerned about the competitiveness of banks vis-à-vis payment institutions, were worried about the competitiveness of the public banks, which constitute approximately half of the banking system in the country (*Financial Times*, 28 February 2007). Germany's role was pivotal because it put forward a compromise during its presidency of the EU in the first semester of 2007, when the directive was eventually agreed.

TARGET2

The last initiative to be discussed with reference to payment services is TARGET2, which built on and replaced TARGET1. In October 2002, the governing council of the ECB decided to create TARGET2 in preparation for enlargement. It is based on a single shared platform for those central banks that decided to give up their own national platform and join it. The Banca d'Italia, the Banque de France and the Deutsche Bundesbank offered to build the technical platform, and in December 2002 users were invited to comment on its principles and structure. In December 2004 the governing council accepted the project plans prepared by the three national central banks and approved the building of the single settlement platform for TARGET2 operations. It became operative in 2007, and all Eurosystem central banks, together with the Danish central bank, participate, though the Swedish central bank and the Bank of England are not connected. The central banks of new member states participate as soon as they adopt the euro. Overall, the project was not controversial, unlike T2S examined below, because TARGET1 was already in place and TARGET2 was simply intended to supersede it. Moreover, at the national level, the central banks have traditionally been involved in the payment system.

The clearing and settlement of securities in the EU

The international, EU and national institutions involved in the regulation and supervision of securities markets have been analysed in Chapter 5. Here is it important to note that, as in the case of payment services, the clearing and settlement of securities can have systemic implications whenever important transfers are involved. For this reason, it is not uncommon for central banks to settle securities. For example, in the euro area, the National Bank of Belgium, the Banco de Portugal and the Bank of Greece provide such a service for government bonds, and the Banque de France, the Banco de España, the Banca d'Italia, and the Bank of England did so until recently.[4]

The Group of Thirty, which brings together leading bankers, central bankers and academics, performs the function of a think tank on international financial matters. In 2003 it formulated a series of twenty recommendations concerning best practice in clearing and settlement on a worldwide scale (Group of Thirty 2003). This document also stressed the concept of 'interoperability' in terms of both compatible technical requirements and compatible processes, business practices and fees. These recommendations were similar to the CPSS–IOSCO principles, but since the G30 represented the perspective of industry, its document prioritised issues such as efficiency and the removal of transcontinental barriers (Wymeersch 2006). The concept of interoperability subsequently became a core element of the code of conduct discussed below.

An overview of the main categories of actors involved in the clearing and settlement of securities should be provided before proceeding further. According to the glossary drawn up by the CPSS (2003; see also CEC 2005e), 'international central securities depositories' are depositories that clear and settle international securities or cross-border transactions in domestic securities. In Europe, there are two main such depositaries – Clearstream and Euroclear – which, unlike the central securities depositaries, also hold banking licenses. 'Central securities depositaries' are entities for holding securities, which enable securities transactions to be processed by book entry. A central securities depository may also incorporate clearing and settlement functions.

The 'intermediaries' are usually 'custodian banks', acting as 'agent banks' and/or 'global custodians'. Several banks have moved back and forth over time between these two categories (for example, Deutsch Banke is no longer a global custodian) and some banks, such as Citigroup and BNP Paribas, are active in both (Norman 2007). Agent banks are generally local banks with access to the national central securities depositaries and which hold securities for their customers; they may also provide various other services, such as clearance and settlement on their own books (CPSS 2003). Deutsche Bank is an agent bank in Germany, and Intesa-San Paolo is an agent bank in Italy. There are also multi-market agent banks, such as BNP Paribas and Citibank (Norman 2007). Global custodians are globally active banks, such as State

Street and the Bank of New York, which provide such services across borders. Central counterparties are institutions that typically act as intermediaries between the counterparties to trades.

In Europe, the main rivalry was traditionally between the two international central securities depositaries, Euroclear and Clearstream, and between the international central securities depositaries and the global custodians. However, the main competition is now between the agent banks (in particular Citibank and BNP Paribas) and Euroclear, because these companies compete for the settlement of equities and because their activities often overlap, especially after Euroclear's acquisition of national central securities depositaries (Norman 2007).

Regulating the clearing and settlement of securities in the EU

The background to the policy initiatives concerning clearing and settlement in the EU was the consolidation of trading and post-trading infrastructures that took place, first at the national level and subsequently at a pan-European level, through mergers and alliances (London Economics 2005). On the one hand, the international central securities depositaries based Europe operated as private monopolies in the settlement of securities. This also meant that there were potential systemic risks associated with securities settlement. The risk linked to the insolvency of a participant in such a system was partly dealt with by the Settlement Finality Directive adopted in May 1998. However, some concerns remained.

On the other hand, cross-border arrangements for the clearing and settlement of securities in the EU were complex and fragmented, generating costs and risks. At the beginning of the third stage of EMU, a member of the ECB executive board, Tommaso Padoa-Schioppa, noted that in the US there were two large payment systems, three securities settlement systems and three retail payment systems. In the euro area in 1999, when the final stage of EMU began, there were eighteen large value payment systems, twenty-three securities settlement systems and thirteen retail payment systems (Padoa-Schioppa 1999b). Defying expectations, no further consolidation took place after the establishment of EMU. As a result, the costs of cross-border clearing and settlement in Europe were much higher than in the United States. As in the case of payment services, the view of the ECB and the Commission was that this limited efficiency prevented the reaping of all the benefits of EMU (interview, Brussels, 13 June 2007).

The 'non-directive' on clearing and settlement of securities

The FSAP did not contain initiatives concerning clearing and settlement – this aspect was overlooked. In April 2001 the Commission launched a consultation, followed in November 2001 by the first report of the Giovannini Group (see Chapter 5) on cross-border clearing and settlement arrangements.

In May 2002 the Commission held a second consultation on the need for EU legislative measures, identifying two main objectives: the removal of barriers to individual cross-border transactions and the removal of competitive distortions (CEC 2002c). The responses suggested that some stakeholders regarded the removal of barriers as the primary role of the public authorities, while others maintained that harmonised rules were necessary for the creation of a level playing field. There was a majority in favour of a Lamfalussy-type framework directive (CEC 2002d), subject to a cost–benefit analysis.

The EP responded to the Commission's consultative document in December 2002 with the Andria Report (EP 2002c), first discussed in the Committee for Economic and Monetary Affairs and adopted in a plenary session in January 2003. The report expressed overall support for legislation on clearing and settlement as well as for the activities of the ESCB–CESR in transposing the CPSS–IOSCO recommendations into the level 3 measures mentioned below. Without going into too much technical detail, it also suggested changes that implied the unbundling of services provided by the international central securities depositaries and therefore the demise of their business model. Norman (2007) notes that these proposals were very similar to those articulated in a document produced by a group of custodian banks and in a consultation response by BNP Paribas. The Andria Report stirred up some opposition among MEPs, and a British and a Finnish MEP took charge of drafting subsequent reports on this matter. This episode also evidenced the overt politicisation of the regulation of clearing and settlement in Europe. Afterwards, lobbying from different parts of the industry intensified (ibid.).

The second report of the Giovannini Group on clearing and settlement arrangements was published in April 2003. In response to it, in April the following year, the Commission issued a communication proposing the preparation of a framework directive. This directive was intended to promote 'liberalisation and integration' by introducing rights of access for clearing and settlement providers to all EU markets and ensuring choice for investment firms, banks, central counterparties, central securities depositaries and markets. It would set up a 'common regulatory framework' concerning clearing and settlement, allowing the mutual recognition of systems across the EU, and introduce specific 'governance arrangements' – disclosure requirements, accounting separation and unbundling of specific services – for entities that play a crucial role in the clearing and settlement process (CEC 2004b, 2004d).

The Commission also envisaged establishing an advisory and monitoring group composed of high-level representatives of various private and public bodies, including the ESCB and the CESR. The Clearing and Settlement Advisory and Monitoring Expert group, created in July 2004, was followed in January 2005 by the Legal Certainty Group and the FISCO group to deal with legal and taxation matters concerning securities trading.

The majority of responses to the Commission's second communication were in favour of a directive, subject to two conditions, namely that it should be a framework, Lamfalussy-type directive, dealing only with high-level principles; and it should be subject to a cost–benefit analysis or regulatory impact assessment (CEC 2004c). In July 2005 the EP adopted a *Report on Clearing and Settlement in the European Union* (EP 2005a; rapporteur Piia-Noora Kauppi) to respond to the Commission's communication. This was rather lukewarm towards the prospect of legislating on clearing and settlement, urging an impact assessment by the Commission beforehand and expressing concern about potentially 'over burdensome legislation'. It also criticised the CESR–ESCB initiative on the regulation of clearing and settlement, as elaborated below (EP 2005a, 2005b).

In the meantime, the DG Competition had begun investigating anti-competitive practices in the clearing and settlement of securities. In 2004 it found Clearnet guilty of abuse of its dominant position in Germany. Subsequently the newly appointed commissioner, Neelie Kroes, commissioned a report from London Economics (2005), which criticised the 'vertical silos' structure of certain stock exchanges for restricting competition. In a vertically integrated model, the stock exchange incorporates both trading and post-trading services. This report was followed by a report from DG Competition (CEC 2006), which emphasised the concept of 'interoperability', already highlighted by the Group of Thirty, and which became a core part of the code of conduct. The report by the Commission was also negative about the vertical silos structure, and for this reason it was criticised by the German government, which made clear it would not support a clearing and settlement directive (Norman 2007). The position of the German authorities was that it was important to ensure a level playing field, whereas the measures proposed were seen as unduly penalising the German bourse model (interview, Berlin, 23 April 2008).

The Code of Conduct on Clearing and Settlement of Securities

In March 2006, the Competition and Internal Market commissioners issued a joint statement pointing out that they would act, proposing legislation, unless there was further movement by the industry before the summer. The following July, Commissioner Charles McCreevy made it clear that he favoured an industry-led approach to a more efficient and integrated post-trading market in the EU (McCreevy 2006). In November 2006 the three main industry associations – the Federation of European Stock Exchanges, the European Association of Central Counterparty Clearing Houses and the European Central Securities Depositories Association – prepared a code of conduct that was signed by all their members. The measures detailed in the code addressed three main issues: transparency of prices and services; access and interoperability; and the unbundling of services and accounting separation. The decision was taken not to involve the custodian banks in the drafting of the code, as this would have meant engaging another set of powerful players and making negotiations more difficult (Norman 2007). The concerns of the custodian banks are explained below.

Let us look in more detail at the main issues at stake and the preferences of the major policy-makers and stakeholders. The first issue was whether to issue legislation or to rely on market-led initiatives in order to promote the liberalisation and integration of securities clearing and settlement systems, eliminating the existing barriers. Some member states and stakeholders were against a directive, preferring to rely on market forces. As argued in the previous chapters, this is generally the approach preferred by the British authorities, and it was clear in the joint response to consultation issued by the UK Treasury, the Financial Services Authority and the Bank of England (see HM Treasury *et al.* 2004). This position was also shared by the British Bankers' Association (2004b), even though the London Stock Exchange (2004) supported a directive with limited scope. The German government preferred a code of conduct because a directive would challenge the 'vertically integrated model' of stock exchange (also referred to as 'silos model') used by the German bourse (which is the largest vertical silo in Europe) and the Spanish and Italian bourse (*Financial Times*, 11 July 2006). The new member states and the Nordic countries tended to be closer to the British approach (interview, Brussels, 14 June 2007).

French policy-makers were the main advocates of a directive on clearing and settlement. The French banking industry was in favour (Fédération Bancaire Française 2004), though it was concerned about the length of the negotiations and what the final outcome might be (interviews, Brussels, 28 March 2007; London, 2 July 2007; Frankfurt, 10 September 2007). BNP Paribas was reportedly very influential in shaping the position of the French authorities on this matter. Italy supported the idea of having a directive because its finance minister, Tommaso Padoa-Schioppa, who had been dealing with the dossier on payments and infrastructures while at the ECB, believed that the activity should be regulated (interviews, London, 2 July 2007; Brussels, 14 June 2007). Moreover, although the Italian bourse had a silos structure, it was along different lines to the German one, and hence would have been penalised less by a directive. Indeed, Monte Titoli, the settlement body of the Italian bourse, is one of the best performing in Europe in terms of transaction costs. Finally, the Italian banking industry also supported the proposal for a directive (Associazione Bancaria Italiana, 2004).

The second issue, inextricably linked to the first, was the content and the purpose of the legislation. The two main questions were governance arrangements and regulatory and supervisory arrangements. On the first, a transnational alliance of investment banks, financial groups and some (non-vertically integrated) stock exchanges was keen to use regulatory power to break up the vertical silos (*Financial Times*, 24 May 2006), arguing that they significantly raised the costs of cross-border trading, particularly when one of the counterparties lay outside the market of the silos stock exchange

(*Financial Times*, 20 February 2006). As mentioned above, DG Competition was also following this issue.

In 2004, the European Securities Forum, a lobby group, called for legislative action (*Financial Times*, 10 February 2004). In 2006, a statement issued by the group, which included some of the main banks, the London Investment Banking Association, the Italian Association of Financial Intermediaries and the French Association of Investment Firms, argued that silos created potential for 'severe competitive distortions' (*Financial Times*, 20 February 2006). Hence, they supported the 'imposition of the unbundling of the vertical silos' if private stakeholders did not begin the process on their own. However, bankers privately preferred a voluntary unbundling of exchange services rather than one imposed through an EU directive, which might take years to draft (*Financial Times*, 20 February 2006).

The 'silos' stock exchanges (but not the non-vertically integrated exchanges, such as the London Stock Exchange,[5] which supported the proposal for a directive) were wary of legislation as, together with the central counterparties and the central securities depositaries, they disagreed both with the principle of accounting separation and unbundling of services and with certain governance arrangements mentioned in the Commission's communication (Deutsche Börse Group 2004). The Spanish bourse argued that the investment banks most critical of the vertical silos were those hoping to compete directly with exchanges themselves (*Financial Times*, 11 July 2006). Governments were split on the issue, whereas a few securities regulators were in favour of binding rules.

The second main line of division on the content of the directive concerned the regulatory and supervisory arrangements and very much mirrored the debate that took place when the CESR–ESCB level 3 measures were discussed (CESR and ECB 2004a, 2004b). This issue pitted the custodian banks (especially the systemically important custodians) against the central securities depositaries (especially the international central securities depositaries), or, to put it another way, the 'intermediaries' against the 'infrastructure' (*Financial Times*, 4 August 2003). The specific points at the centre of the negotiations were the capital requirements and other prudential regulation to be applied to the custodians and the central securities depositaries; and the possibility of non-banks (i.e. central securities depositaries) undertaking credit activities without a banking licence.

Although these issues are elaborated further below, with reference to the first point it is important to mention that there are three possible approaches. The 'pure functional approach', preferred by the central securities depositaries and the central counterparties, was based on the principle 'same activity/function' equals 'same regulation', without taking risk considerations into account. The second approach, preferred by the banks, was that entities performing a similar function should not be regulated in exactly the same manner, and account should be taken of their risk profile. Third, the 'institutional approach' suggested that the central securities depositaries and the central counterparties should be subject to institutional regulation (CESR and ECB 2004a, 2004b).

Finally, the principles of 'home supervision' and 'mutual recognition' tended to pit the industry against the supervisory authorities and the central banks. Whereas industry – to be more precise, the most transnational part of it – was in favour of streamlining supervisory arrangements, hence favouring 'home country' competence, the supervisory authorities and the central banks, although aware of the need for greater cooperation, substantially disagreed. They preferred a flexible approach to cooperation on the ground of the systemic risk concerns of the host country, which should retain some supervisory power on entities operating within their national borders (CEC 2005d). This debate is similar to the one that unfolded when the role and powers of the home-host supervisors were discussed in the Capital Requirements Directive and the MiFID.

The Commission was internally divided on the directive: some members favoured legislation, others did not (interview, Brussels, 13 June 2007). The change in the College of the Commission and, especially, the appointment of a new Internal Market commissioner made a difference, because the Barroso Commission was in favour of 'better regulation' (i.e. less regulation and self-regulation) (Norman 2007). Commissioner Charles McCreevy seemed to be closer to an Anglo-Saxon approach than his predecessor, and it was no coincidence that the draft directive on clearing and settlement that had been initiated by Fritz Bolkenstein was eventually set aside by the new commissioner, as pointed out in several interviews with stakeholders. Moreover, research conducted by the Commission suggested that cross-border costs for clearing and settlement would be removed only following the harmonisation of tax laws (*Financial Times*, 10 February 2004). Last but not least, it was clear that there was not a critical mass of member states in favour of a directive (interview, Brussels, 13 June 2007).

In its response to the Commission's consultation on clearing and settlement, the ECB, which supported the main goals of the directive, was keen to point out that, given the fact that there was not a corresponding level 2 committee which could draft the level 2 implementing measures of the proposed directive, this task should be assigned to the CESR and the ESCB, which were already working together on this issue (ECB 2004c).

The CESR–ESCB standards/recommendations

Another regulative activity that highlights the interaction between international and EU rule-making concerns the transposition of the CPSS–IOSCO recommendations into EU standards. The work concerning the recommendations was carried out primarily by central banks and securities supervisors. Banking supervisors did not take part directly because banks are only marginally involved in clearing and settlement, albeit the situation varies across countries. Hence, custodian banks were not mentioned in the recommendations and banking supervisors did not participate in drafting the document (Wymeersch 2006). However, as explained below, the custodian banks were subsequently mentioned in the EU document. In their view, they were negatively affected by the draft CESR–ESCB standards, which were designed to transpose the international recommendations into EU level 3 measures, and they consequently engaged forcefully in the regulatory debate.

In October 2001, the governing council of the ECB and the CESR agreed to cooperate in the field of securities clearing and settlement, setting up a working group composed of representatives from the ECB, the national central banks and the CESR, with the Commission attending the meetings as an observer. The group began to work on the transposition of standards agreed at the international level by the CPSS–IOSCO into EU standards which can be enforced by the national authorities. When the ESCB and the CESR began to work on these level 3 measures, they had the support of the EP, as evidenced by the Andria Report in 2002 (EP 2002c).

In August 2003, the working group released two documents for public consultation: 'Standards for securities clearing and settlement systems in the European Union' and 'The scope of application of the ESCB–CESR in the field of safety, soundness and efficiency of securities clearing and settlement'. As regards the application of the standards, the views of market participants were split into two groups: the banks and their associations strongly opposed the proposal to include custodian banks in the scope of the standards (Association of Global Custodians 2005, 2004), whereas the (international) central securities depositaries and some stock exchanges and securities dealers' associations were in favour of extending the scope to cover all systemically important entities, including custodian banks (Euroclear 2004).

In response to the CESR–ECB consultation, the banking community argued that a distinction should be made between infrastructure and intermediaries. In particular, the (international) central securities depositaries were considered to be infrastructures, while the custodian banks were considered intermediaries (Association of Global Custodians 2004). The banks insisted that the (international) central securities depositaries de facto operated as a monopoly, while the custodian banks competed among themselves. Second, the systemic risks associated with the operations of the (international) central securities depositaries were seen as different from the types of risk associated with the activities of the custodian banks. Third, the custodian banks stressed that they were already subject to comprehensive banking regulations both at the national and the European level (CESR and ECB 2004a, 2004b)

The (international) central securities depositaries and the stock exchanges endorsed the extension of the standards to all entities operating systemically important systems, including custodian banks (ECSDA 2004). They argued that there was no difference between services being offered by the (international) central securities depositaries or by the custodian banks – the risks were the same. Third, they noticed that (international) central securities depositaries were subject to European banking regulation when they had banking status and provided credit services, but otherwise were subject to some form of (national) regulation (CESR and ECB 2004a, 2004b).

The basic concern was that any differences in the regulatory environment between the (international) central securities depositaries and the custodian banks would promote a shift of settlement activities from the former to the latter. At the same time, the custodian banks already subject to banking regulation did not want to be burdened by additional rules. With reference to the custodian banks, there was the issue of the definition or identification of the custodians to which the standards were to be applied, first and foremost the identification of 'systemically important banks' (the so-called significant custodians) that would lead to a two-tier custodian market (ECB and CESR 2004a, 2004b).

The ECB and the CESR attempted to straddle a middle way in the development of the standards, and thus the draft they produced in September 2004 took into account the fact that banks' risks were already dealt with by the Basel II Accord (CESR and ESCB 2004c). Yet, in the end, the new measures would increase the regulation of custodian banks, especially global custodians, potentially increasing their costs. The ECB governing council and the CESR endorsed the report in October 2004. However, at that stage, the German financial services authority, the BaFin, questioned the legal basis for the adoption of such standards in Germany. This was a rather unexpected turn of events, because the question had not been raised during previous discussions (Norman 2007). One explanation could be that, since Germany has a bank-based financial system, measures imposing additional costs on custodian banks attracted considerable opposition. In particular, some *Länder* banks perform a custodian function, and the proposed standards would have increased their operational costs (interview, Lisbon, 27 November 2008). This triggered political interference in the working of the CESR and the regulatory authorities gathered in this body.

Since the custodian banks were not happy with the drafted level 3 measures (Association of Global Custodians 2005, 2004), they decided to put their case to MEPs, some of whom proved sympathetic. The European Banking Federation also sided with the custodian banks and the Fair and Clear group (see European Banking Federation 2004, 2003). The so-called Kauppi Report was critical of the CESR–ESCB initiative on the ground that it could affect level 1 legislation being discussed at that time and that level 3 measures were being discussed before any level 1 legislation was adopted, despite the fact that the Commission was working in this direction (EP 2005a, 2005b; interview, Brussels, 30 March 2007). The EP considered that, in the light of existing banking regulation, the special rules proposed for 'significant custodians' were over-burdensome, and that just because some of the activities of local custodians are similar to or in competition with the central securities depositaries did not imply that they should be subject to the same regulation. The draft report called for a regulation that was 'risk-based', arguing that the risk profile of custodian banks was different from that of central securities depositaries, albeit there was some overlap between their functions (EP 2005a: 6).

On the one hand, this was surely an attempt by the EP to defend its role in EU policy-making as, prior to the reform of comitology in 2006, it co-decided level 1 legislation but had no formal power on the adoption of level 2 and 3 measures. On the other hand, the MEPs had been influenced by the fact that a section of the industry – the custodian banks – was unhappy with the content of the measures (interview, Paris, 25 April 2007). The ESCB–CESR standards were eventually put on hold, waiting for the Commission's position. The Commission eventually decided not to propose legislation on this mater, and opted instead for a code of conduct.

After three years of stalemate, on 3 June 2008 new political impetus was given to the ESCB–CESR measures by the ECOFIN Council, which, with respect to the 'safety and soundness of the post-trading infrastructure', decided the following:

The Council

- agrees that the work started with the former ESCB/CESR draft 'Standards for Securities Clearing and Settlement in the EU' should be completed, respecting the following principles:
- The adopted text should take the form of non-binding Recommendations solely addressed to public authorities;
- Its scope should include ICSDs [international central securities depositaries] and exclude custodians – whilst CEBS is invited to further review, in cooperation with CESR, the coverage of risks borne by custodians, taking into account that some CSDs [central securities depositaries]/ICSDs/CCPs [central counterparties] are also subject to the CRD [Capital Requirements Directive], so as to ensure a level playing field while avoiding inconsistencies in the treatment of custodians and double regulation by end 2008.

Hence, when the mandate of the ESCB–CESR group was renewed in June 2008, it was redefined so that the result should be a set of 'recommendations' addressed to public authorities only, rather than 'standards' addressed to industry. The scope of the work was limited to central securities depositories and central counterparties based on the assumption that the Capital Requirements Directive (discussed in Chapter 4) or other relevant banking regulation would address the relevant post-trading risks for custodian banks. The CEBS was invited, together with CESR, to conduct further work. This was the result of a political compromise in the Council to appease the Germans (interview, Lisbon, 27 November 2008).

The T2S

The last important development in the field of clearing and settlement of securities was the ECB's decision in 2007 to set up its own platform for the clearing and settlement of securities – the T2S – which would be attached to the TARGET2 platform. The objective of T2S was to provide efficient settlement services for securities transactions in central bank money, leading to the processing of both securities and cash settlements on a single platform through common procedures. The ECB made it clear that T2S would be a 'settlement platform', not a central securities depositary, hence it would not be dealing with activities such as dividend payments, redemptions, etc. (ECB 2007c). It would not open securities accounts for the users (i.e. the banks), an activity that would remain with the central securities depositaries, and joining T2S would be voluntary. This had reportedly not been the case initially, and the ECB's take on it changed only later (this issue was raised by Euroclear 2006; European Central Securities Depositaries Association 2007).

The consultation with industry carried out by the ECB suggested that banks were against financing the T2S platform on top of the existing platforms. Some central securities depositaries demanded that each securities transaction initiated by banks should first be sent to them, before being processed by the T2S platform. However, banks wanted to send their settlement orders directly to the settlement platform (Godeffroy 2006). A similar debate took place with reference to TARGET2, and it was ultimately decided that payment orders should be sent directly to the settlement platform without going through the national central banks. In TARGET2, the national central banks have access to the cash accounts of their banks, and it was suggested that a similar possibility could be offered to the central securities depositaries in T2S (ibid.).

In July 2006, the Eurosystem considered the opportunity of providing settlement services for securities transactions in central bank money, leading to the processing of both securities and cash settlements on a single platform through common procedures. The governing council of the ECB decided to consult central securities depositaries and other market participants concerning the setting up of a new service for securities settlement in the euro area. A questionnaire, 'TARGET2-Securities: initial assumptions and questions' (ECB 2006b), was distributed, and responses were received from the banking community, the central securities depositaries, the two international central securities depositaries, the European Savings Banks Group, the European Association of Public Banks and several stock exchanges. These responses basically rehearsed the views mentioned above. In October 2006, the governing council invited its Payments and Settlement Systems Committee to prepare a detailed feasibility study on the T2S project by February 2007.

Following this, several meetings took place between the ECB/Eurosystem, market participants and market infrastructures in December 2006 and

January 2007, when the ECB requested market participants to comment on a document entitled *Governance of Target 2 Securities: A Possibility* (ECB 2006c). In February 2007 the European Central Securities Depositories Association wrote to the ECB asking for a delay and calling for it to engage in more market consultation (ECSDA 2007).

According to the ECB, the rationale for the setting up of T2S was to improve the efficiency of the system for clearing and settlement (ECB 2007c). Its argument was that it had an interest in the proper functioning of securities clearing and settlement systems because any major malfunction could endanger the implementation of monetary policy, the functioning of payment systems, and the overall stability of the financial system in the euro area (*Financial Times*, 17 April 2007; ECB 2004c). Moreover, at the national level, the oversight of securities clearing and settlement systems was carried out by central banks, cooperating with other authorities such as securities regulators. Custodian banks were increasingly involved in operating securities settlement systems and the international central securities depositaries had bank status, hence cooperation with prudential supervisors was also important (ECB 2007b).

Before the start of EMU, some market participants called for the Eurosystem to undertake such a project. However, at that time the preference was for the market to deliver it (ECB 2004c). Given the fact that the market did not do so – Euroclear set up a settlement platform covering only part of central bank money settlement for euro-denominated securities (between one-fifth and one-third, depending on the criteria used) and catering for three national central securities depositaries in the euro area – the ECB decided to intervene directly to offer such a service (Godeffroy 2006). The ECB's argument was that T2S was designed to solve a market failure: the high cost of settlement resulting from the absence of a common platform created by the private sector.

Critics argued that this was an attempt by the ECB to expand its competence, that it could potentially be detrimental to the bank's primary task (conducting monetary policy with a view to maintaining price stability) and that it would lead to the creation of a public monopoly in this field (ECSDA 2007). Moreover, as Willem Buiter argued (*Financial Times*, 19 January 2007), whereas the strong degree of independence of the ECB could find some justification in the realm of monetary policy, this was not acceptable in performing the tasks envisaged as part of T2S, and which should be subject to public scrutiny. The consultation process of the ECB was initially criticized for being limited and not fully transparent (*Financial Times*, 17 April 2007; ECSDA 2007).

It is fair to say that the failure of the private sector to provide a common platform for settlement services was in part on account of the behaviour of the central banks in the euro area. Companies providing settlement services use central bank money to reduce the risk involved. Whereas some central banks, such as the Banque de France, allowed the operation of such accounts by the private sector, others, such as the Bundesbank, did not. Market operators wanted some harmonisation, so as to create a level playing field in the euroarea. Consequently, the ECB–Eurosystem faced two choices: either to outsource the use of central bank money or to insource the settlement of securities with T2S (*Financial Times*, 17 April 2007).

This was not a minor technical choice, and it stirred up a robust debate between national central banks in the Eurosystem and within the ECB governing council for over a year without reaching a compromise solution. There were two schools of thought in central banking (Norman 2007). On the one hand, there were the central banks, first and foremost the Bundesbank, Banca d'Italia and Banco de España, which considered the control of central bank money to be a core function of central banks, not to be trusted to the market because this could endanger financial stability. On the other hand, there were the central banks, such as the Banque de France, the National Bank of Belgium and the Dutch central bank, that supported outsourcing. The central banks were also keen to 'retain business in their territories that might otherwise be lost to providers through outsourcing' (ibid.: 253).

The T2S project was a way of ending the internal rift within the ECB–Eurosystem (Norman 2007). Reportedly, the national central banks that favoured outsourcing and had Euroclear-owned central securities depositaries operating on their territory decided not to oppose the project and actually became involved in setting it up. If the ECB had decided that T2S should be restricted to debt instruments as eligible collaterals, it would have been similar to the Fedwire system of the US Federal Reserve, but the ECB also extended it to equities (interview, London, 2 July 2007), an argument articulated by Clearstream (see ibid.).

While the members of the ECB's executive board tended to be in favour of T2S, it was relatively controversial both within the governing council of the ECB and in the ECOFIN Council. Some national central banks sitting in the governing council – for example, the central bank of Finland – were not supportive, as the project was seen to be beyond the remit of the ECB–Eurosystem (interviews, Brussels, 13 June 2007, 28 March 2007). In contrast, the national central banks of the three (subsequently four) large countries in charge of setting up TARGET2 backed up the idea of T2S.

After reviewing the project at a meeting in January 2007, the ECOFIN Council indicated that the ECB should delay its decision. At a second meeting, in February 2007, the finance ministers requested from the ECB a more elaborated business case, clear information on how T2S would comply with EU competition policy and the intended governance structure (*Financial Times*, 8 March 2007). The positioning in favour or against T2S taken in the Eurosystem was more or less reflected in the ECOFIN and the FSC, apart from the UK, which was lukewarm at best, even though it was clear that it could not prevent the project from moving ahead. Although they did not declare their position officially, neither the Belgian not the Dutch authorities were particularly in favour, on account of the importance of Euroclear's activities in their countries. The Finnish authorities also had some concerns about the project, because of the different way in which clearing and settlement operates in Finland and Greece – the so-called transparent holding system (interview, Brussels, 9 April 2007).

The Commission, for which making clearing and settlement of securities more efficient was a priority, supported the setting up of T2S, and DG Internal Market, in particular, worked very closely with the relevant units at the ECB (interviews, Frankfurt, 10 September 2007; Brussels, 13 June 2007). The main concern was whether the creation of what would be a public monopoly would infringe EU competition rules, and DG Competition pledged to look into the matter (*Financial Times*, 28 February 2007). The EP, traditionally wary of increasing the ECB's tasks, given its high degree of institutional independence, did not raise any substantial objections. This was reportedly because MEPs were concerned that the big US clearing and settlement groups might take over this function in the EU, which is also why some of them (especially those from the socialist group) were keen on a directive on clearing and settlement (interview, London, 2 July 2007).

Industry was divided on T2S. The main split was between banks and infrastructures (i.e. international central securities depositaries, central securities depositaries), as became evident in the responses by national financial markets to the ECB's initial questionnaire, as collected by the Banca d'Italia (2006), Banco de España (2006) and National Bank of Belgium (2006). In the euro area, the banking sector reacted positively, though it should be said that the European Banking Federation, which was internally divided on the issue, questioned the need for ECB intervention (*Financial Times*, 25 September 2006). This is because, even if in principle banks were to gain from T2S, in some countries they had expended a considerable amount to adapt to the existing system and it would be costly to change (interviews, London, 2 July 2007; Brussels, 2 April 2007). For example, the French Banking Federation was strongly in favour of T2S, making it the sole settlement platform for the eurozone securities settling in euro central bank money (Fédération Bancaire Française 2006), but Belgian banks were less enthusiastic (see the responses collected by the National Bank of Belgium 2006). Some entities outside the euro area (based in London, for example) expressed support for the project, which would facilitate their access to the euro area markets (Godeffroy 2006).

The central securities depositaries had mixed feelings, especially the large ones that were likely to lose part of their business. T2S will not embrace the services of custody, collateral management and securities lending provided by central securities depositaries. However, many depositaries that operate on thin margins, if they provide only those services, could be put under financial stress (*Financial Times*, 8 March 2007). On the other hand, some depositaries that already operated efficiently in the market had the potential to gain from T2S. Moreover, the banks, which are the clients of the central securities depositaries, were by and large supportive (Norman 2007). But Euroclear, the international central securities depositaries that already provided similar services, objected to the ECB's plans (Euroclear 2006), arguing that T2S would fragment the industry by splitting securities settlement from other services and settlements in different currencies (*Financial Times*, 29 September 2006).

An overview of the main regulatory measures concerning post-trading adopted by the EU over the last decade is provided in Table 6.2.

An overall assessment

The Commission was influential at the agenda-setting stage by proposing legislation or threatening to do so in order to spur the market into action. It consulted with national governments and industry on whether or not to legislate, as well as on the specific content of the various directives and their implementation. The case of the proposed directive on clearing and settlement also highlighted the importance of the policy preferences at the top level of the Commission for 'better regulation' – a synonym for less regulation and self-regulation. Obviously, the Commission and its proposals were more influential whenever they had the support of all or part of the industry and the main member states. For instance, the lack of sufficient support for a directive on clearing and settlement and the strong opposition from Germany (interview, Berlin, 23 April 2008) influenced the Commission's decision not to propose legislation.

The ECB is not a traditional regulatory body: it is first and foremost a central bank overseeing the functioning of the payment systems. It has minimal prudential supervisory functions and some regulatory powers in its areas of activity, where it cooperates with other Lamfalussy bodies, such as the CEBS and the CESR. In certain spheres, such as the Single Euro Payments Area, the ECB, like the Commission, with the support of public authorities, was keen for market-led activities to take place. On one occasion – T2S – the ECB's view was that direct public (ECB) intervention was needed. The benign view was that the bank genuinely aimed to correct market failures by intervening (*Financial Times*, 17 April 2007), even if this resulted in a de facto public monopoly, which was nevertheless preferable to de facto private monopolies. The less benign view is that the ECB behaved as a traditional bureaucracy by trying to expand its areas of competence, as predicted by bureaucratic politics theories (for a review, see Peters 2004), rather than necessarily acting in the public interest (a benevolent welfare maximiser), as generally assumed by mainstream theories concerning monetary policy and central bank independence (for a review, see Cukierman 1992). Moreover, as Norman (2007) argues, proposing the T2S project was a way of ending an internal drift within the governing council of the ECB and the Eurosystem.

The EP was a powerful player at the decision-making stage, as demonstrated by the fact that the Payment Services Directive was substantially redrafted incorporating its amendments; however, these amendments were also supported (indeed, many were advocated) by industry (interview, Berlin,

Table 6.2 The main regulatory measures on payments and clearing and settlement over the last decade (international rules in shaded boxes)

Regulation	Date of adoption	Institutions/bodies	Scope/objectives
Core Principles for Systemically Important Payment Systems	2001	CPSS	To set international standards for systemically important payment systems
Recommendations for securities settlement systems	2001	CPSS–IOSCO	To set international standards for securities settlement systems
Recommendations for central counterparties	2004		To set international standards for central counterparties
Single Euro Payment Area (SEPA)	2008	European Payments Council	To create an integrated market for payment services To develop common standards with a view to removing technical, legal and commercial barriers between the current national payment markets To enhance competition and improve payment services
TARGET2	2007	ECB, Eurosystem	To provide real-time processing, settlement in central bank money and immediate finality To settle central bank operations, large-value euro interbank transfers and other euro payments
TARGET2 securities	2008 (agreed)	ECB, Eurosystem	To provide a single, borderless pool of pan-European securities, as well as a core, neutral, state-of-the-art settlement process
Code of Conduct for Clearing and Settlement	2006	Industry associations dealing with clearing and settlement	To deal with issues related to transparency of prices and services; access and interoperability; the unbundling of services and accounting separation in clearing and settlement
CESR–ESCB guidelines	Adoption pending	CESR and ESCB	To increase the safety, soundness and efficiency of securities clearing and settlement systems and central counterparties

23 April 2008). The parliament was also keen to safeguard its competence at level 1, as evidenced by its reaction to the CESR and the ECB drafting of the level 3 measures on clearing and settlement. Hence, it was sometimes a powerful player pursuing its own institutional prerogatives, whereas most of the time it was a target for lobbying by industry – though it also actively sought the latter's input, as suggested in several interviews. Overall, the EP was sympathetic, providing a channel through which industry could articulate its policy preferences.

Sometimes, these policy preferences played out in the EP, triggering internal debates. The MEPs formed competing coalitions, depending on their nationality and political orientation. For example, the socialists were in favour of a directive on clearing and settlement, whereas the liberals and conservatives were against it (interview, Brussels, 25 June 2007). Sometimes, such as in the making of the Payment Services Directive, the member states in the Council teamed up with their MEPs to pursue their national priorities. For example, the German and British MEPs were involved in the negotiations of the Payment Services Directive. Overall, the EP proved to be a good ally of industry. It was sympathetic to business concerns, but also to consumer protection, depending on the political group and nationality of the MEPs: socialist MEPs from Southern European countries tended to give more prominence to consumer protection, whereas conservative and liberal MEPs from Northern Europe privileged financial innovation, competition and market efficiency. The different policy preferences played out even more strongly in the Council, where the member states generally tried to promote their national interests. However, it was a matter not only of different national interests but of the dissimilar public policy priorities.

The main industry divide in the regulation of the clearing and settlement of securities was between the (international) central securities depositaries and the custodian banks, especially the global custodians. This is interesting because most of the literature on international political economy tends to assume similar preferences among transnational companies and global players (Bieling 2003, 2006; Apeldoorn 2002). In this case, the main divide was among international market players, namely, infrastructures versus custodians. The two main international central securities depositaries in Europe, Euroclear and Clearstream, which had been rivals in the past (see Norman 2007), presented a relatively united front in the 'battle' against the agent banks. Agent banks from ten European countries formed the group 'Fair and Clear', led by Citibank and BNP Paribas, to coordinate their response to consultations and their 'fight' against the international central securities depositaries, especially Euroclear.

The picture of industry's preferences was, however, more complicated. French banks were in principle in favour of a directive, albeit in practice they were worried about the length of the legislative process and its unpredictable outcomes. They also strongly supported T2S. The British Bankers' Association and London Investment Banking Association were neutral, but in principle against new legislation. The European Banking Federation tended to favour a directive, though it was concerned about the end result after time-consuming negotiations. It was divided on T2S, because some of its members had invested heavily in the existing system (*Financial Times*, 25 September 2006; interview, London, 5 July 2007). There was no uniform view even within the large banks, because, for example, in Germany some banks are also shareholders of the Deutsche Börse, which would have been affected negatively by the directive (interview, Berlin, 23 April 2008). As far as T2S is concerned, the German banks reportedly first supported it, then subsequently took issue with the governance structure (interview, London, 2 July 2007; Frankfurt, 10 September 2007). The European Banking Federation also expressed concerns about the governance framework of T2S (European Banking Federation 2007). In the Payment Services Directive, the main divide was between banks (credit institutions) and payment institutions.

As the European Savings Banks Group (2006: 2) argued in its response to the consultation on T2S – though this observation could be extended to almost all post-trading activities – there are different constituencies within many national markets. Such constituencies consist of central banks, central securities depositaries, savings banks, cooperative banks and commercial banks. 'Indeed, the views of some of these constituencies may differ within a single national market but be very similar to another constituency in a different national market.' Hence, it was not a 'battle of the systems' along national lines (Story and Walter 1997): national systems and industry were both divided on this issue. Industry spent time and resources in lobbying, using multiple channels of access and fighting their battles in various arenas. For example, when the custodians lost their case in the drafting of the CESR–ECB standards, they made their case to the EP, in particular the Committee on Economic and Monetary Affairs.

Conclusions

Payment services and the clearing and settlement of securities seem to be among the most 'technical' areas of financial services. However, the analysis conducted in this Chapter suggests that politics matter a great deal in the governance of these activities. Indeed, as one interviewee remarked, these technical issues have become so political that they are now discussed at a high level in the ECOFIN and the EFC (interview, Berlin, 23 April 2008). The agenda-setting role of the Commission and of the ECB were highlighted, even though the influence of the member states at this early stage of the process was stressed, at least when there is not a critical mass of support. The EP was a channel through which industry articulated its preferences, but the parliament also had its own institutional preferences.

National governments were aware of their national interests, which were largely based on domestic political economy considerations – that is, derived from the configuration of national financial structures. These interests were taken into consideration when defining the national positions to be articulated in the EU policy process, principally in the Council. However, in several instances, national industry and transnational operators were divided on the issues. Furthermore, the national authorities were informed by specific policy paradigms in their decisions. Of course, these policy paradigms or regulatory approaches were not independent of the structural context in which policymakers operated, which is why this research does not juxtapose, but rather combines, interests and ideas. This point is elaborated further in the following chapter.

In the governance of payment services there was, on the one hand, the Northern market-making approach, which favoured competition, financial innovation and consumer choice, opening up the market for the provision of payment services. On the other hand, the Southern market-shaping approach, which on this occasion was also fully espoused by Germany, wanted to restrict the activities of payments institutions as well as impose some capital requirements on those institutions. This was presented as prioritising consumer protection and financial stability. In the clearing and settlement of securities, whereas France and the Southern group (with some distinctions) tended to prefer public intervention through a directive and through the ECB's T2S, the Northern group preferred soft rules and private sector governance.

As far as the clearing and settlements of securities is concerned, the T2S project was partly originated by the need to reconcile two central banking schools of thought (Norman 2007). It is also noteworthy that, in the governance of securities post-trading activities in the EU in the early 2000s, two main projects were put forward, underpinned by different regulatory paradigms. The code of conduct was industry-led, based on soft law, and fully embraced private sector governance; it exemplified the Northern market-making approach and, indeed, was driven by Commissioner McCreevy. The T2S project was led by the ECB and the main Eurosystem central banks, and was based on a direct intervention by the public authorities in the market by setting up a settlement system. The project represented an extreme case of the market-shaping approach.

Across the financial services examined in this volume, this is the policy sector where the direct participation of industry in the policy process is strongest. Because this area is very technical and complex even for experts, the public authorities really need stakeholders and experts from the marketplace to make informed decisions, to chart policy and to implement it. The following chapter will discuss the main similarities and differences in the governance of the various financial services considered in this book, feeding into the broader theoretical debate on European financial integration.

7 An overall cross-sectoral assessment

This chapter compares the main findings of the previous chapters. It begins by highlighting the main similarities and differences across the governance of the financial services examined in this book, all of which are to a different extent interconnected. The second section presents an overall cross-sectoral assessment of the analytical leverage of the various theoretical approaches discussed in Chapter 2, identifying which policy-makers and/or stakeholders are most influential, how and why. This is followed by a concise discussion of the formation of policy-makers' and stakeholders' preferences and coalitions, dwelling on specific regulatory paradigms that play out in the policy-making processes under consideration. The final section touches upon the issue of democracy in financial services governance in the EU.

A cross-sectoral comparison of financial services governance in the EU

Taking a cross-sectoral comparative perspective, there are both similarities and differences concerning the governance of the financial services examined in this book – banking, securities, and post-trading activities. The main differences are a dissimilar degree of financial market integration and regulation; a different use of 'hard' and 'soft' rules; and dissimilar styles and formats of supervision, including the power of the supervisory authorities. The main similarities are the blurring of roles and boundaries between the public authorities and industry; the intensification of lobbying in the EU; and the interconnection and the interactions between levels of governance (national, EU, international). All these issues are examined in turn in this section.

There has traditionally been a dissimilar degree of market integration and regulation across financial services. As noted in Chapter 3, until the late 1990s, financial market integration, regulation and supervision was more advanced in the banking sector than in securities trading and post-trading activities. However, during the last decade, the most intense areas of regulatory activity have been securities trading and, most recently, post-trading services, mainly because a catching-up process was very much overdue.

It should, however, be noted that integration has taken place mainly in the wholesale market and to a much more limited extent in the retail market, where distinctive consumer preferences and the market power of 'national brands' are paramount. Domestic players, some of which oppose further financial integration, are more active in the retail than in the wholesale sector, and hence are less willing to open the sector up to foreign competition. In specific segments of retail financial services, such as consumer credit and mortgages, industry has been lukewarm about further market integration, even though different firms have different views on this issue.

For example, Germany is lukewarm towards new EU rules to promote integration in the retail sector because this is opposed by the domestically powerful savings banks, even though the big German private banks are keen to expand their customer base (interviews, Paris, 18 July 2007; Frankfurt, 12 September 2007; Brussels, October 2007). British-based banks are also reportedly hesitant about further integration in the retail market, partly because they fear excessive EU re-regulation as a result, partly because there are only a few providers in domestic retail banking in the UK. This status quo was criticised by the British competition commission (see Cruickshank 2000) with reference to the banking services offered to consumers, and specifically the provision of funding to SMEs.

There are also institutional factors that explain the limited policy-making activity concerning the integration of retail markets across Europe. An institutional weakness of the Lamfalussy sectoral committees is that horizontal matters, such as retail finance, are not the specific competence of any one committee (Lannoo 2005). Moreover, these issues are part of consumer protection policies, which are dealt with not by DG Internal Market but by DG Health and Consumer Protection.

Across financial services, there has been a different use of 'hard' and 'soft' rules. Banking governance in the EU relies mainly on legislation, whereas 'soft rules' and other non-legislative measures are used relatively more often in regulating securities markets and post-trading activities. Moreover, cross-border regulation and cooperation have always been more advanced in banking than in any other financial sector, both in the EU and internationally. The importance of international rules is highlighted by the fact that the most important directive passed in the banking sector has been based on the incorporation of the rules set by an international agreement, the Basel II Accord.

Besides differences concerning the types of rules, there are important differences concerning the style and format of supervision. The issue of different styles of supervision across the three main financial sectors came to the fore when the Financial Conglomerates Directive (see also Joint Forum 1999) was negotiated, and banking, insurance and securities supervisors were wary of any attempt to impose one sectoral mode or style of supervision on the other sectors.

Supervision in the banking sector focuses on institutions (i.e. banks and entities performing banking activities) and has greater implications for the stability of the financial system. It is generally assumed that less sophisticated (i.e. knowledgeable) consumers are present in the banking sector (Joint Forum 2001). Supervision in securities markets focuses on transactions, an activity that is intrinsically less risky for financial stability (unless a very large transfer of securities is involved), whereas micro-supervisory issues such as rules of conduct and transparency are actually more important, given the fact that they affect investor decisions (ibid.). It is interesting to note that the supervisors of securities markets are generally referred to as regulators (for example, the CESR is the Committee of European Securities *Regulators*, whereas the equivalent committee in the banking sector is the Committee of European Banking *Supervisors*). Moreover, unlike in the banking sector, the powers of supervisors (or regulators) in the securities sector varies greatly across countries, as pointed out by the members of the CESR in the so-called Himalaya Report (CESR 2004), which called for greater convergence of supervisory powers among the CESR members (see also CESR 2007). This issue is also raised by the Francq Report (FSC 2006).

There are three crucial similarities concerning the governance of various financial services in the EU. First, there is an increasing interaction and blurring of roles between the public authorities and industry, which also has implications for lobbying activities. On the one hand, there is greater involvement of the private sector in rule-making and implementation. In the making of hard law, industry is consulted intensively at the drafting stage, and it remains active through lobbying at the decision-making stage. As far as soft law is concerned, industry is often asked to draft, agree and implement voluntary codes of conduct, such as that on clearing and settlement. Moreover, the private sector contributes to monitoring the implementation of hard law, providing feedback to the public bodies, notably the Commission and the Lamfalussy committees. Another example is the activity of the Clearing and Settlement Advisory and Monitoring Expert Group for the removal of market barriers, mentioned in Chapter 5.

On the other hand, the public authorities may decide to intervene directly in the market, for example providing services competing with or replacing those provided by parts of industry – the most notable example being T2S. Or they can threaten the adoption of legislative measures in the event of inaction, as in the case of the Single Euro Payments Area and the code of conduct on clearing and settlement. Industry participation, at least in a consultative form, is encouraged by the public authorities, in particular the Commission, the EP, and the national governments and supervisors.

Regulation and supervision generate economic costs and benefits for market players, which therefore have an incentive to attempt to influence the policy-making process by engaging in lobbying activities (Mügge 2006). Because of the resources at their disposal, private actors can be influential lobbyists in various policy arenas and organize their activities at the national, EU and international levels (Knill 2001; Knill and Lehmkuhl 2002). Indeed, the increased involvement of industry in financial governance is a worldwide trend (see Hall and Biersteker 2002; Porter 2005). This also applies to the making of international agreements (Underhill and Zhang 2008), where intense consultation is conducted by both national authorities and international bodies. In these instances, the main industry participants tend to be from the US, the UK and, to a more limited extent, Germany, France and Italy.

As far as lobbying in the EU is concerned, EU associations, especially the banking associations, have become more important in the policy process over time, though it depends on the issue negotiated (on lobbying in the EU, see the special issue of the *Journal of European Public Policy* 14, 3). There is also some evidence that, in general, the Commission and the EP prefer to deal with EU associations, which are regarded as EU-wide representatives, rather than with national associations or private firms (Bouwen 2002, 2004), which are regarded as more 'parochial'. Sometimes, further aggregation is sought at the EU level. For example, the Commission strongly encouraged the six main EU banking associations to form a common platform, the European Banking Industry Committee, in order to present a coherent position. The catalyser of this initiative was the negotiation and implementation of the Capital Requirements Directive (interviews, Brussels, 28, 30 March 2007).

Many national associations have increased their external lobbying activities vis-à-vis EU bodies and other international bodies, such as the BCBS. For example, all national associations are generally members of EU associations and some national associations have offices in Brussels. Depending on the circumstances and issues being discussed, national associations can be more important than EU associations, especially when the latter are internally divided. On the MiFID, the European Banking Federation was internally divided between the French and Italian banks on one side and the British banks on the other (interview, Brussels, 27 June 2007). Similarly, on the T2S, the European Banking Federation took a cautious position, because some banks had invested heavily to adapt to the system of clearing and settlement system already in place.

In the securities sector, the Federation of European Stock Exchanges and the European Fund and Asset Management Association experience the same problems as EU banking associations: their national member associations might have different policy preferences, or priorities, which need to be reconciled in the positions taken by the respective European associations. Hoewver, it should be noted that, while this activity is more common for the big banks than for the small ones, most banking associations are involved in securities regulation, as many of their members trade in securities.

The third main similarity across the financial services examined in this book is that governance is inherently multi-level. In the banking sector, the most important piece of legislation, the Capital Requirements Directive, transposed with some amendments the Basel II Accord. In securities markets and payment services, the soft rules agreed by international bodies such as the IOSCO–CPSS were transposed into soft EU rules (level 3 measures).

The national level remains important because most EU legislation (i.e. all directives) needs to be transposed into the individual legislation of the member states, which can use national discretion. This often means additional national rules (gold-plating), a complaint often vented by industry representatives during interviews. Existing national legislation, institutions and supervisory arrangements also shape the preferences articulated by the various national authorities and/or by interest groups in EU fora (CEBS 2007b). Moreover, the financial industry tends to lobby national authorities in the first instance (Grossman 2004) – this is particularly the case with the most domestic and less internationalised interest groups (Greenwood 2003).

The presence of multiple levels of rule-making and the variety of actors involved at each level and across levels means that a multiplicity of policy locations and channels of access are available to industry (Knill 2001; Eising 2004). Battles lost in one policy arena or at a certain stage of the policy process – the agenda-setting phase, when the Commission drafts the directive, the decision-making stage, such as a vote in the Council or a vote in the EP, or the implementation stage, such as the measures adopted by level 3 committees – can be reopened at negotiations in other policy locations. For example, when the banks failed to have their policy preferences incorporated into the level 3 measures drafted by the ESCB and the CESR, they resorted to the EP, which managed to block the measures (interviews, Brussels, 13 June 2007; Paris, 25 April 2007).

These multiple channels are available not only to industry but also to the national governments and the national supervisors. In a few instances, when an issue was too complex for agreement to be reached at level 1, it was deliberately passed down to level 2 (interviews, Brussels, 13 June 2007; Berlin, 23 April 2008). This was the case with certain provisions concerning the supervision of branches in the MiFID and the approval of the prospectus in the Prospectus Directive. At other times this was done less deliberately, but the result was the same – the political issues were reopened at the technical level.

National supervisors occasionally engaged in 'venue shopping'. For example, whenever the Commission chose not to follow the advice given by the level 3 committees in adopting level 2 legislation, the CESR resorted to the level 2 committee (the European Securities Committee) and the EP to make its case (interview, Brussels, 28 March 2007). Similarly, when supervisors lost a battle in discussions taking place in the level 3 committee, they made their case either to their national representatives sitting on the level 2 committees or to MEPs.

A theoretically-informed cross-sectoral assessment

Let us now look in more detail as to whether liberal intergovernmentalism or supranational governance/neo-functionalism has better analytical leverage, or if they can be combined in order to elucidate financial services governance in the EU. As noted in Chapter 2, European integration theories largely overlap with competing understandings of political economy of financial market regulation. This is done through the sequencing of various theories, according to the main stages of the policy process. This section first discusses the role and preferences of the EU supranational authorities – the Commission, the ECB and the EP. It then examines the preferences and the influence of the member states (the national governments and the supervisory authorities) in regulating financial services. The final part dwells on the policy preferences and channels of influence of the private sector – the market.

The Commission is an influential supranational actor (Posner 2005; Jabko 2006) at the agenda-setting stage, in that it drafts and officially proposes legislation, and at the implementation stage, in that it adopts the level 2 implementation measures with the assistance of the level 2 committees and advice from the level 3 committees. It also monitors national implementation. The clearest example of the influence of the Commission at the agenda-setting stage was the FSAP, which basically offered the blueprint for the relaunch of financial market integration in Europe. However, the FSAP was also endorsed by several member states and had both the backing of the British presidency of the EU and the support of transnational industry (Mügge 2006). Hence, as in the case of the EP, it is not easy to distinguish the preference and influence of the Commission from those of the national authorities and industry, especially those that have most to gain from financial market integration.

The Commission had less agenda-setting power in the regulation of the banking sector because the content of the main piece of legislation, the Capital Requirements Directive, was agreed in the BCBS, where the Commission sat as observer. Similarly, the Financial Conglomerates Directive largely incorporated the principles agreed by the Joint Forum in Basel. However, the interviews conducted suggest that the member states negotiating in these fora liaised quite closely with the Commission, as they were aware that these international norms would be transposed into EU legislation. The Commission was therefore indirectly an influential player in the Basel process.

Moreover, given the fact that the Commission and the ECB sat as observers in the BCBS and had no formal decision-making power, they were not formally bound by the decisions taken there (interview, Brussels, 27 June 2007). Consequently, the Commission had some agenda-setting power in proposing amendments to the Basel II Accord while drafting the Capital Requirements Directive. However, in practice, it had to take into account the preferences and policy positions expressed by the member states (especially the largest ones), the EP and industry. All these players were consulted by or interacted with the Commission at the drafting stage, as confirmed by several interviews (Christopoulos and Quaglia 2009).

The Commission formally had full agenda-setting power in the making of the Lamfalussy directives concerning securities trading. A notable example in which such power was used was the belated insertion of the transparency provisions into its official draft of the MiFID. However, in practice, the Commission consulted quite intensively with the member states and industry – for some directives more than for others (reportedly, limited consultation took place before the drafting of the Prospectus Directive and the Market Abuse Directive). Its decision as to whether or not to propose legislation depended on the support (or lack of it) of a critical mass of member states and the EP – as the decision not to propose a directive on the clearing and settlement of securities made clear.

The content of legislation was also influenced at the drafting stage by the policy preferences of the (main) member states and, to some extent, the EP and industry. For example, the Northern coalition felt that the first draft of both the MIFID and the Prospectus Directive was close to the approach preferred by the Southern coalition. Several member states lamented that a liberal approach was chosen by the Commission in drafting the proposal for the Payment Services Directive, despite the fact that is was clear that those with traditionalist views on payment services had problems with it (interview, Brussels, 28 March 2007). These policy episodes also highlighted the fact that the change of the guard at the Commission in 2004 made a difference in shaping its policy orientation, moving it closer to the coalition embracing the market-making paradigm.

In the adoption of market-led measures, the Commission actually had more influence than the EP and the Council, which are not involved in the adoption of soft law. This, together with the change at the top level of the Commission in 2004, contributes to explaining its preference for soft law, given that, as discussed above, it also engaged in some institutional turf wars vis-à-vis the EP, the Council and the Lamfalussy committees.

Unlike the EP and the Commission, the third supranational institution, the ECB, was eager to keep industry at arm's length (interview, Frankfurt, 17 January 2006). The main exceptions were its consultation with the CESR before the drafting of some level 3 measures and, most importantly, the project T2S. Like the Commission and the EP, the ECB had its own (bureaucratic) policy agenda (Quaglia 2009a), a point generally overlooked by supranational governance approaches. For example, it tried, rather unsuccessfully, to expand its role in the Lamfalussy negotiation process. The T2S project was criticised by some observers for creating a public monopoly (see Willem Buiter's letter in the *Financial Times*, 19 January 2007).

Interestingly, the preferences of the member states played out not only in the Council of Ministers but also to some extent in the EP, at least for the two most controversial Lamfalussy directives and the Payment Services Directive. This lends some support to the liberal intergovernmentalist explanation because, in these instances, the MEPs can be seen as acting as national rather than supranational representatives. Hence, divisions in the EP ran along national lines in addition to party lines. By contrast, in the negotiations concerning the prospect of a directive on clearing and settlement, the split in the EP was mainly between the socialists on the one side and the conservative and liberal groups on the other (interview, Brussels, 13 June 2007). At the same time, the EP was engaged in a power game with other EU institutions and was eager to safeguard its institutional prerogatives, an issue overlooked by supranationalist approaches. The clearest example of this was the controversy over the renewal of the comitology procedure, which led to the comitology decision in 2006.

The EP's general dislike of soft legislation in its quest for 'institutional balance' and its interest in safeguarding its influence in the policy-making process is explained partly by the fact that it is excluded from this process. For this reason, it opposed the proposed CESR–ESCB standards on clearing and settlement, even though MEPs had been lobbied strongly by industry, principally the banks (interviews, Brussels, 13 June 2007; Paris, 25 April 2007). Indeed, the EP is a prime target for lobbyists in the financial sectors. On the other hand, it is keen to seek interaction with industry, from which MEPs elicit information and expertise on the issues under consideration.

Overall, the EP is an important actor, in line with the supranational governance approach, with one important caveat. It is true that, in the negotiations of some of the Lamfalussy directives concerning securities trading, there were clear instances in which the Commission's draft had to be substantially changed as a result of the amendments proposed by the EP. However, the proposed changes were often endorsed by the Council (or by some of the member states therein) and by parts of the industry, which makes it difficult to separate out the particular influence of the EP. The EP also managed to block the adoption of some level 3 measures and contributed to sinking the proposal for a directive on clearing and settlement, although there was no critical mass in favour of it in the Council (interviews Brussels, 13–14 June 2003; London, 2 July 2007).

The member states remain crucial actors in financial services governance (Grossman 2004), their influence being paramount at the decision-making stage. Yet, paraphrasing Story and Walter (1997), 'the battle of the systems', which runs along national lines and the parameters of which are determined by the configuration of national financial systems, has been compounded by cross-cutting and varying lines of attrition. The process of national preference formation (or the aggregation of domestic preferences) is much more complex than that postulated by liberal intergovernmentalism (Mügge 2006). Sometimes policy preferences cut across national borders. National preferences are diversified because different domestic groups and transnational companies based in the member states have different interests or priorities.

The member states were not unitary actors, and did not behave as such, even in negotiations for legislation that exhibited the greatest degree of political conflict among them, such as the Capital Requirements Directive, the MiFID, the Prospectus Directive, and the Payment Services Directive. In order to form a national negotiating position, governments had to reconcile different and, at times, conflicting preferences among the various parts of the domestic industry and the multinational and transnational financial groups based in their territory (Macartney forthcoming).

Nonetheless, several instances and features of 'the battle of the systems' remain. In the negotiations of the Basel II Accord and the Capital Requirements Directive, the main divide in Europe was between those countries that have a bank-based financial system and an extensive part of their economy derived from SMEs, such as Germany, Italy and France, and those countries, principally the UK, which have a securities-based financial system and several non-bank investment firms. The former group was worried about the potentially negative effects of the new capital requirements on the cost of lending to SMEs (interviews, Frankfurt, 17 January 2006; Rome, 23 June 2006) and also opposed exclusive reliance on external rating, as their firms, in particular SMEs, had no rating tradition (Wood 2005). By contrast, for the UK, the cost of lending to SMEs was a not an important issue, given the structure of the British economy; the UK prioritised instead the trading book in securities (interview, London, 19 June 2006). In the securities sector, especially in the MiFID and the Prospectus Directive, the two main competing factions were the Northern market-making coalition and the Southern market-shaping coalition, with Germany switching between the two, depending on its domestic political circumstances.

However, in the governance of payments services, Germany was firmly in the market-shaping Southern or continental camp, and was actually more financially 'conservative' than either Italy or France (interviews, Brussels, 14 June 2007, 9 April 2008). In this instance, as in the case of the regulation of securities markets, the main line of division was between financially 'conservative' (or 'traditionalist') countries, such as Germany, France, Belgium, Italy and the other Mediterranean countries, and the 'liberal' Anglo-Saxon and Nordic countries, along with Poland and the Czech Republic (interview, Brussels, 28 June 2007). Finally, there was an unusual configuration of coalitions as regards the governance of post-trading activities, specifically on the possibility of issuing a directive on clearing and settlement, whereby France was strongly in favour and Germany and the UK were against, though for very different reasons (interviews, Frankfurt, 10 September 2007; Brussels, 13–14 June 2007; London, 2 July 2007).

Liberal intergovernmentalism assumes that interest groups lobby their national governments in order to pursue their objectives and articulate their preferences in EU negotiations. However, the empirical record of the making of the main directives on financial services reveals that they also lobbied the EP and the Commission and other member states in the Council of Ministers – especially when their preferences were not duly taken into account by their own government and/or other national governments had similar preferences – as well as EU associations. The latter, in turn, lobbied EU bodies, whenever they were not ridden by internal divisions, as their members (national associations) had different preferences on certain issues (interviews, Brussels, 30 March 2007, 27 June 2007).

In some circumstances, national authorities did not completely follow the policy preferences expressed by their domestic industry, especially when this affected their institutional prerogatives. In these instances, the process was closer to 'traditional' intergovernmentalism. For example, some large British, German and French transnational banks and financial groups would have either preferred the establishment of a 'lead supervisor' in the Capital Requirements Directive and the Financial Conglomerates Directive (European Banking Federation 2003a; British Bankers' Association 2003) or supported the creation of a European system of national supervisors, analogous to the ESCB (EUROFI 2002b; Deutsche Bank 2000). However, national governments and supervisors, particularly in the main member states, strongly opposed this solution (interview, Berlin, 23 April 2008), as they were eager to preserve national supervisory arrangements and policy competence.

The national governments, principally the permanent representations in Brussels, liaised with national and EU associations in order to lobby MEPs (though sometimes they did so directly). An example is when the UK Treasury wished to make the case for the solo model in the Capital Requirements Directive and to amend the transparency requirements in the MiFID (interviews, London, 20 April 2006, 2 April 2007). It is a circular process of lobbying, where 'everyone lobbies everybody else' (interview, Brussels, 27 June 2007). This aspect is overlooked by intergovernmentalist accounts, which, by definition, focus on negotiations among national governments.

Not surprisingly, national preferences played out, or at least surfaced, not only in the ECOFIN Council but also in the working of the level 2 committees, especially the European Securities Committee, when level 2 measures were voted on for adoption – an example being the 'politically liquid shares' mentioned in Chapter 5. Interestingly, national preferences (or the preferences of national industry) sometimes played out in the level 3 committees, which are supposed to be 'technical' committees of supervisors, as in the case of the CESR–ESCB standards (recommendations). The level 3 committees and supervisors also tried to preserve their policy competence vis-à-vis other EU bodies, primarily the Commission. The national supervisors were reluctant to abandon their own rules and practices despite the need to foster convergence. This occasionally caused problems in the adoption of level 2 and level 3 measures, which were then the result of the papering over and/or adding together of national rules and practices. In some cases, it was minimum rather than maximum harmonisation. Another sensitive issue among supervisors was the division of powers between the home and host authorities.

As postulated by liberal intergovernmentalism, the outcome of the negotiations was within the Pareto frontier (or win set) of the main member states. However, the negotiations were more complex than what generally takes place purely between governments, especially when the EP and the level 2 and 3 committees were involved, as 'national interests', 'institutional prerogatives', 'bureaucratic politics' and 'political party preferences' in the EP compounded the difficulties in the policy-making process and the search for a compromise. Consequently, the regulatory outcome was a compromise not always based on the most rational solution. Examples are the definition of liquid share and the establishment of the threshold that would not trigger pre-trade transparency in the MiFID; the possibility of national waiver in the Financial Conglomerates Directive; the threshold for bond issuers in the Prospectus Directive; national discretion in the choice of the model for the calculation of capital requirements in the Payment Services Directive; and the initial number of national discretions in the Capital Requirements Directive, which approached one hundred. Indeed, whenever clauses concerning 'waivers', 'national discretions', and the substitution of 'will/shall' (legally biding) with 'may/could' (optional) appear in legal documents, it means that at least one member state had a problem with that specific provision and a compromise was necessary.

Let us now look at the preferences and the influence of industry, where there were national lines of division with some homogeneity of preferences. As argued above, this seems to be the case in the negotiations of several financial services directives, which pitted the Northern coalition against the Southern coalition, similar to the case in the negotiations of key directives in financial services in the later 1980s and early 1990s (see Story and Walter 1997; Underhill 1997). However, a fine-grained analysis reveals that national positions were diversified (see Macartney forthcoming).

The German private banks were pitted against the public banks on the issue of intra-group exposure in the Capital Requirements Directive, but they shared the concern of making sure that the new rules would not penalise the SMEs, the backbone of the German economy (interview, Frankfurt, 17 January 2006). With reference to the Payment Services Directive, all banks wanted some capital requirements to be imposed on non-bank payment institutions, but they did not want additional burdens placed on banks and opposed a 'one-leg' system. German private banks were rather relaxed about the strict execution time foreseen in the initial draft by the Commission, whereas this was a problem for the savings banks.

In the regulation of securities markets, some big French investment banks reportedly revealed Anglo-Saxon policy preferences on the MiFID, and some big Italian banks were actually very happy with the MiFID when it was implemented (interview, Brussels, 27 March 2007). By contrast, it was mainly a burden for small banks. In the negotiations of measures concerning clearing and settlement, the main conflict was between *international* central securities depositories (often referred to as market infrastructure, e.g. Euroclear) and *global* custodians (big banks, e.g. Deutsche bank, Goldman Sachs, BNP Paribas), which were all international market players. In the negotiations of the Payment Services Directive, the line of attrition was between banks and other payments institutions (i.e. non-banks, operators without a banking license – diffuse in the UK, for example). Furthermore, the silos stock exchanges had different preferences from the non-vertically integrated exchanges in regulating (or not) clearing and settlement activities.

A domestic political economy perspective would emphasise the presence of competing interest groups, whose domestic battle for power played out at the EU level. EU regulation can provide (or deny) comparative advantages to specific market players in the member states – several examples, particularly from Germany, have been mentioned. Moreover, EU regulation can entail considerable adjustment costs for certain parts of the industry, but not for others, and the benefits of market integration can also be unevenly spread (Egan 2001). Finally, the extent to which the financial market has been opened up to competition and the effects of market integration vary within countries.

The process of market integration and regulatory and supervisory convergence in the EU is deemed to benefit transborder operators, MNCs and big financial firms by strengthening their comparative advantages and/or reducing their operating costs across various jurisdictions, as well as facilitating access to previously protected domestic markets (Mügge 2006). By contrast, this process is likely to be detrimental to small domestic financial companies, through imposing adjustment costs resulting from the change of the national regulatory and supervisory framework, exposing them to direct competition from the main transnational financial companies.

However, contrary to what is claimed by most political economy literature (Mügge 2006; Bieling 2006, 2003), the main lines of attrition in the regulation of financial services in the EU were not necessarily between the large financial groups representing transnational capital, on one hand, and the small domestic financial firms, operating mainly in national markets, on the other. On only a couple of issues did this division come to the fore. A notable example was the call for the creation of a European system of national supervisors, which was a priority for cross-border operators but not for domestic ones, which preferred to continue dealing with their national supervisory authorities, using their usual procedures.

On the one hand, it is true that, as in other policy areas (see Eising 2007), the main market players – big banks and their associations, large financial conglomerates, big securities dealers and their associations – tend to have better access to policy-makers because they have the financial and human resources to engage in a variety of consultations and lobbying activities. Moreover, they can bring technical knowledge to bear in articulating their points. On the other hand, as elaborated in the following section, at least in principle, the consultation process is open, and arguably successful lobbying requires targeted strategic action rather than vast resources (though, of course, these help). Several interviewees from industry as well as qualified observers argued that, if a stakeholder had a valid point to make in the policy discussion, this contribution was taken into consideration by the Commission, regardless of the size of the business represented.

In the banking sector at least, regulators are aware of the bias in the consultation process (and, more generally, in the policy process) in favour of large companies and transnational operators. They are also aware that small banks constitute a large part of the banking sector in the EU (CEBS 2007b; Nouy 2007), though the proportion is larger in some countries (among the big four, Germany, France and Italy) than in others (the UK). In a hearing before the EP, the chairwoman of the CEBS also highlighted the fact that 'small and local banks raise different supervisory concerns from large and sophisticated global firms'. 'Proportionality is the key concept' on which to rely (Nouy 2007: 4), which suggests that big market players should be subject to stricter supervisory provisions.

Taking a step back (or going a step further): explaining preference formation

This research proceeded in an inductive way in order to identify the preferences of policy-makers and stakeholders in the regulatory game by analysing the empirical record. An examination of the responses to consultations and other policy papers was conducted, and corroborated by a systematic review of relevant press coverage and more than eighty interviews. In the previous chapters, the preferences of the main policy-makers and stakeholders were concisely explained by examining the economic costs and benefits ensuing from the EU regulatory activity for the actors concerned, which in turn depended on the specific characteristics of national financial systems and the degree of transnationalisation and competitiveness of the financial firms operating therein. Given the very large numbers of actors involved, this assessment was carried out in general terms; it was not possible to explore the specific position of each participant.

However, while conducting fieldwork, it became clear that the conventional interest-based explanation would not provide a full picture of the preferences of policy-makers and stakeholders and hence the formation of policy coalitions. This was especially the case for the preferences of the regulators: the importance of regulatory paradigms – ideas about the main objectives of and instruments for financial regulation – was alluded to in many of the interviews conducted (not only those with regulators). This feeds into the conventional debate in political science that juxtaposes interests with ideas (Checkel 1997; Pollack 2001; Jupille *et al.* 2003). Let us examine how these two approaches score against the empirical record in order to explain the preferences of policy-makers and stakeholders and the formation of coalitions.

A 'traditional' (interest-based) political economy approach would stress 'the battle of the systems' (Story and Walter 1997), triggered by competing national interests. As mentioned above, regulation and supervision can provide (or deny) comparative advantages to financial systems and/or stakeholders based in the member states. EU regulation can result in considerable costs of adjustment in the member states and can advantage (or disadvantage) financial operators based therein. Both national governments and technical authorities are sensitive to this. It was clear to all the participants in the making of the Basel II Accord and the Capital Requirements Directive that this was 'financial diplomacy' (interview, Frankfurt, 17 January 2006). A similar reasoning applies to the most 'political' of the Lamfalussy directives – the Prospectus Directive and the MiFID – which pitted the financial system, industry preferences, and regulatory and supervisory arrangements in Northern Europe against those in Southern Europe, albeit with all the caveats mentioned above about the absence of 'monolithic' national positions and the fragmentation and fluidity of the policy coalitions.

A senior French policy-maker explained that 'an internal market in financial services cannot be based solely on deregulation and the free market, because if, for example, an undercapitalized insurance company goes bust in Ireland, this could affect millions of French consumers who have bought insurance contracts from that company' (interview, Paris, 24 April 2007). An Italian policy-maker stated:

> We are more concerned than British policy-makers about consumer protection and in particular the protection of small savers, as they are mostly located in Southern Europe. The City of London mainly hosts wholesale markets, and professional market operators do not need detailed rules for investor protection. The level of financial literacy is also higher in Northern Europe than in Southern Europe, which is why the latter needs prescriptive rules for consumer protection.
>
> (Interview, Brussels, June 2007)

The point about the low level of financial literacy and the need for both investor protection and the prevention of financial crime was also made by financial negotiators of the new member states (interviews, Brussels, 9 April 2007).

A British policy-maker pointed out that 'financial industry in Southern Europe is much less competitive than British industry. The argument of consumer protection is actually an attempt to protect the national industry, limiting competition' (interview, London, 17 May 2007). A continental policy-maker reversed this argument on its head, arguing that

> British policy makers are keen to set in place EU regulation that would advantage London as a financial centre. Hence, they prefer light-touch principle-based regulation, which leaves more room for manoeuvre to national regulators in the application of rules. This is a clear attempt to play the 'regulatory game' to British advantage, attracting business to the City of London.

British financial policy-makers, in turn, are eager to point out that the City is a European asset, not purely a British one.

Nonetheless, it was a matter not just of different and competing national interests but of the two different ideas about the completion and regulation of the Single Market in financial services. The market-making and market-shaping paradigms were identified on the basis the interviews conducted with policy-makers and stakeholders involved in financial services across Europe and are presented in a rather stylised form, mostly repeating terms and expressions that were used by the interviewees themselves. The ontological starting points are normative beliefs about the market, which can be summarised as 'market trust' for the Northern coalition and 'market distrust' for the Southern one. Light-touch principle-based regulation is endorsed by the market-making group, which prefers to rely on instruments of soft law and private sector governance, based on the involvement of industry through consultation and the implementation of soft law. Detailed and prescriptive rules are favoured by the market-shaping group, which prefers instruments of hard law under the steering action of the public authorities. These regulatory instruments are also embedded in different legal systems: common law and Roman law, respectively.

These different regulatory approaches came to the fore when interviewing senior national policy-makers involved in the negotiations. The Anglo-Saxon camp would see the continental approach as being over-regulated and over-prescriptive, de facto limiting competition and consumer choice. Moreover, according to the British view, the light touch regulatory approach adopted in the UK has not been proved less effective, and there has not been a larger number of policy failures in the UK than in continental Europe. The continental camp would argue that the public authorities have the responsibility to ensure sound regulation, and that, despite the operation of the Single Market, national governments have a responsibility towards national consumers if something goes wrong. They would also point out that there were some serious policy failures in the UK in the 1990s, and as further evidence would refer to how the global financial crisis played out in the UK, where four of the ten largest banks had to be rescued in various ways (some-what selectively forgetting that the French and German banking systems were also substantially affected, see Hardie and Howarth 2009).

The competing regulatory paradigms came to the fore primarily in the regulation of securities markets (especially the Prospectus Directive and the MiFID) and some post-trading activities. They were less evident in the regulation of banking because, as explained previously, banking regulation in the EU and internationally is well developed: it dates back to the 1970s, and the gap between different regulatory paradigms has by now been reduced, at least concerning the key tenets of banking governance. Moreover, the fact that central bankers form a well-established and well-integrated 'epistemic community' (Verdun 1999) has contributed over time to reconciling different approaches to banking regulation. Yet this does not mean that all the main regulatory differences have been sorted out, as suggested by more than 100 national discretions initially left in the Capital Requirements Directive. Nor does it mean that central bankers and banking regulators are immune from bureaucratic politics, as suggested by the discussions of the home–host country allocation of responsibilities.

The existence of different national regulatory and supervisory paradigms across the EU is recognised by policy-makers themselves and, indeed, was evident in several of the interviews conducted: regulators usually prefer the expression 'regulatory and supervisory philosophies'. The specific contents of the various paradigms are difficult to pin down, since they move beyond the general features pointed out above and because they differ from country to country, from financial service to financial service, from issue to issue, and even within the two main coalitions identified.

In the explanation of the preferences of the main actors and policy coalitions, two sets of factors – interest-market structures and ideas-regulatory paradigms – are very much intertwined and mutually reinforcing. The regulation and supervision of financial services is intended to secure the public goods of financial stability, consumer protection and market efficiency. However, national policy-makers attach different priorities to these objectives, and prefer to rely on certain regulatory instruments and supervisory strategies rather than others, partly because they are embedded in a specific domestic structural context (primarily a given configuration of the national financial system), and partly because they subscribe to distinctive regulatory paradigms.

Democracy and financial services governance

It was quite deliberate that this research did not engage in an explicit evaluation of democracy in financial services governance in the EU, because such an exercise would have required a different research design and a normative theoretical underpinning. The main scope of this book has been to explain how the policy process works, why, and with what effects on the outcome: financial regulation. By providing a reliable and empirically accurate account of the policy-making process of all the main EU measures adopted in the last decade concerning the regulation of banking, securities markets, and post-trading activities, the reader is left free to make up their own mind about democracy in financial services governance.

However, there are three main points that can guide readers in their assessment. Some of these remarks apply only to financial services regulation in the EU, whereas others apply to financial services governance *tout court*. They are drawn from the literature on democracy in the EU, in particular the work of Fritz Scharpf (1999), which distinguishes between input-oriented legitimacy and output-oriented legitimacy, rather than being informed by the specific literature on the accountability and independence of financial regulators (see Masciandaro and Quintyn 2007). This section dwells on the democratic input into the process, whereas it is too early and beyond the purpose of this volume to evaluate the output-oriented dimension, which focuses on the effectiveness of policies and the results delivered, as many rules are still in the process of being implemented in the member states. This would also require a different top-down research design, used in implementation studies.

The democratic input into the policy-making process is generally equated with the influence of parliaments at the national level and, even more, at the EU level. The formal role of the EP in financial services regulation has increased over time. On the one hand, all level 1 legislation is subject to co-decision between the EP and the Council, and the 2006 revision of the comitology procedure has given the EP the power to block level 2 implementing measures adopted by the Commission and the Lamfalussy committees. The preceding analysis of the main level 1 legislative measures showed that the EP exerted real influence in the policy-making process and was able to affect the outcomes substantially. The interaction between MEPs and the private sector was also highlighted, including cases in which MEPs gave in to lobbying by industry – which is, however, part and parcel of the democratic process.

On the other hand, the EP is not formally involved in the making of soft law, such as codes of conduct, which explains its growing reluctance to endorse such regulatory instruments. Moreover, it does not have a formal say in the projects that are the exclusive competence of the ECB, such as TARGET2 and the more controversial T2S, and level 3 measures remain the competence of national supervisory authorities. However, in at least one instance – the CESR–ESCB standards – the EP was able to block the measures agreed at level 3, even though it should be said that a large section of the industry (principally the custodian banks) was also unhappy with those measures.

Although the situation varies from country to country, national parliaments are generally excluded from the making of EU legislation and are formally involved only in passing legislative measures transposing EU directives into national law (Maurer and Wessels 2001; Katz and Wessels 1999; O'Brennan and Raunio 2007). This is the case even more in financial services regulation, given the highly complex and technical nature of the subject matter, where finance ministries and national supervisors are the prime movers in the implementation of EU rules.

The second important point about democracy in financial services governance in the EU (as elsewhere) concerns the limited involvement of consumer organisations and, more generally, non-financial organisations (IIMG 2007a, 2007b; Moloney 2006). On the one hand, although formal consultation and participation are not the same as real influence, there has been an attempt to open up the policy process, at least at the consultative stage, to these groups (see, for example, the consultation with the FINUSE group).[1] On the other hand, even formal participation is limited by the scarce resources (in terms of finance, personnel, expertise) available to these organisations, which are also affected by the 'logic of collective action' (Olson

1971). Whereas consumers of financial services would collectively and individually benefit from certain provisions concerning financial regulation, their incentive to lobby and to invest resources to do so is limited by the fact that benefits would be diffuse. By contrast, financial associations and their members have a direct interest in opposing certain rules that would be costly for service providers to implement. These market players have considerable resources to engage in lobbying activity.

The third point about democracy and financial services concerns the role of experts and non-majoritarian institutions (financial regulatory agencies and central banks) (on this debate, see Majone 1996). Given the technical and complex nature of the issues surrounding financial services regulation and supervision, technocracies and 'experts' (civil servants with a specific economic and/or legal background) tend to be heavily involved. Indeed, this was the main rationale underpinning the creation of the Lamfalussy framework. However, a number of technical issues have considerable political implications and hence involve political as well as technical choices. On the one hand, the direct (or indirect) intervention of the political authorities in technical discussions (for example, at levels 2 or 3) is sometimes unhelpful and is resisted by the technical bodies. On the other hand, the technical bodies sometimes have to deal with political issues that were passed on to them because they could not be settled through political negotiations at level 1 (CEBS 2007a).

A related issue is the 'double-hatted' role of the national supervisory authorities sitting on the level 3 committees. The members of these committees are technical authorities that are expected by EU institutions and transnational industry to promote the convergence of supervisory practices. At the same time, they are national representatives with a national mandate and subject to national accountability systems (interviews, Paris, 18 July 2007; Frankfurt, 12 September 2007; see also Bini Smaghi 2007). Within the current setting, 'CESR members may have no alternative but to respect legitimate national discretions' (CESR 2007: 2).

To overcome this dilemma, the Francq Report (FSC 2006) proposed to give a European mandate to all the members of the level 3 committees. Subsequently, the idea was floated of either conferring legal personality on these committees or transforming them into EU agencies (CEC 2007; IIMG 2007a). This proposal was explicitly put forward by the Italian treasury minister, Tommaso Padoa-Schioppa, reflecting on the lessons to be learned from the financial turmoil of the summer 2007, in a letter to the ECOFIN ministers in November of that year.

At the following ECOFIN Council meeting in December 2007, the British and German authorities, backed by other countries such as Spain, Belgium, Finland and Austria, did not support the proposal (*Financial Times*, 4 December 2007), arguing that the existing supervisory framework was adequate and its potential had to be fully exploited (see HM Treasury and FSA 2007). Reportedly the proposal attracted some encouragement from France and the

Netherlands (*Financial Times*, 4 December 2007). The worsening of the financial crisis in 2008 reopened this debate, as mentioned in Chapter 8, which discusses the proposal put forward in early 2009 by the de Larosière Group and subsequently endorsed by the ECOFIN Council.

Conclusion

In an overall cross-sectoral assessment it is argued that financial services in the EU are characterised by the presence of two variable and internally fragmented coalitions of public and private actors, articulating diversified interests and exposing different regulatory paradigms. These coalitions compete for influence in the regulatory process for the completion of the Single Market in financial services.

The Northern European market-making coalition, which coalesces around the UK, includes Ireland, the Netherlands, Luxembourg and the Scandinavian countries, while the Southern European market-shaping one, which coalesces around France and Italy, includes Belgium and the Mediterranean countries. The new member states, which were involed only belatedly in the negotiations of several policy measures discussed in this book, joined one group or the other, depending on the circumstances, as did Germany, which was also ridden with domestic political economy conflicts. These coalitions espouse two competing regulatory paradigms, which affected the perceptions of interests of their members and vice versa, in that the structural context influenced the prevailing national regulatory approach.

Before the eruption of the global financial crisis, the market-making paradigm was gaining acceptance in the EU, as suggested by the very objective of the FSAP and the content of most of the regulatory measures adopted for the completion of the Single Market in financial services. Nonetheless, as elaborated in the following chapter, the financial turmoil challenged the attractiveness of the Anglo-Saxon model and provided new ammunition to the supporters of the market-shaping regulatory paradigm.

8 The EU response to the global financial turmoil in 2007–9

The bulk of the empirical research in this book has examined the regulatory activity that took place in the EU from the issuing of the FSAP in 1999 to its near completion after 2004. However, just as the new regulatory framework for financial services came into force in the EU, Europe was hit by global financial turmoil.

It is beyond the scope of this chapter and this book to conduct an in-depth analysis of the causes and consequences of and the responses to this global financial turmoil. There are three objectives to this chapter: the first is to provide an overall picture of the institutional arrangements for financial stability in the EU, parts of which have been mentioned in the previous chapters; the second section sketches out the EU response to the global financial crisis, as of June 2009; the third section teases out (but does not attempt to address) some of the key issues that were raised by the financial crisis, contextualising them in the ongoing debates in the literature and policy-making circles; and the last section feeds into the theoretical debate outlined in Chapter 2.

The institutional arrangements for financial stability in the EU

'Financial stability' involves crisis prevention and crisis management. 'Crisis prevention' comprises financial regulation, financial supervision (these terms were defined in Chapter 2) and cooperation between supervisors, which is paramount in crisis management (ECB 2007a).

Whereas in Europe financial regulation is in general set at the EU level and then implemented in the member states, financial supervision is largely carried out at the national level. Hence, in the multi-level governance of financial services, there is a 'disjunction' between EU regulation and national supervision. This statement, however, needs to be qualified. To begin with, the EU directives regulating banking (see, for example, the Capital Requirements Directive; Chapter 4), securities (the four 'Lamfalussy directives'; see Chapter 5) and financial conglomerates (the Financial Conglomerates Directive; see Chapter 4) were often based on a minimum common denominator, resulting from convoluted compromises and trade-offs during the negotiation process. Moreover, in the rule-making process, regulators often had to cave in to pressure from different parts of the industry, in the EU as elsewhere, such as in the negotiations of the Basel II Accord (discussed in Chapter 4).

Furthermore, in some cases, such as the Capital Requirements Directive, ample use of national discretion in the transposition and implementation of EU rules remained. In a letter sent to the ECOFIN Council in the wake of the financial chaos, the Italian treasury minister, Tommaso Padoa-Schioppa, noted the lack of a unified 'rule book' in the EU (Padoa-Schioppa 2007). This 'regulatory patchwork' (Héritier 1996) makes uniform supervision across countries more difficult. Moreover, some of the key directives regulating financial services in the EU incorporated rules agreed in international regulatory fora. A clear example was the Capital Requirements Directive, which incorporated into EU legislation the Basel II Accord. However, before the global financial crisis there were financial activities that were subject to only minimal regulation at the EU level, internationally and nationally. Notable examples, some of which were at the centre of the financial upheaval, were derivatives, credit rating agencies and hedge funds. Partly as a response to the financial crisis, the EU has undertaken sustained regulatory activity concerning some of these financial services (Quaglia 2009c).

Financial supervision is carried out mainly at the national level, by the central bank (whenever it is responsible for banking supervision) or the banking supervisory authority (if separated from the central bank) and the supervisors of other financial activities (e.g. securities trading). However, there are EU committees of national supervisors in which the activity of national supervisors is (or should be) coordinated. These are the Lamfalussy committees and the Banking Supervision Committee of the ESCB (which were examined in Chapters 4 and 5).

'Crisis management' concerns the cooperation between financial supervisors, central banks and national governments (treasuries) at the national level and across borders, on the basis of bilateral and multilateral memoranda of understanding and supervisory coordination and exchange of information in relevant fora (ECB 2007a). 'Crisis resolution', which might require private sector solutions or public sector intervention, ultimately bailing out insolvent institutions, can be seen as the last stage of crisis management, though it is sometimes treated separately (see EFC 2007). Four main types of crisis management and/or resolution measures can be identified and were deployed during the height of the financial crisis: provision of liquidity to the system and to specific institutions; injections of capital into banks (the state's acquisition of capital shares in banks and the purchase of 'toxic assets'); mergers; and state guarantees of both new debt issued by banks and banks' deposits.

In the euro area, the provision of emergency liquidity assistance to markets that are drying up is performed by the ECB – for example, the interventions that took place at the outset of the crisis in August 2007. The provision of emergency liquidity to specific institutions that pledge eligible collaterals (the function of lender of last resort *strictu sensu*; see Deutsche Bank 2008) is performed by the national central banks in the Eurosystem, as in the case of the Bundesbank's and BaFin's intervention in two German banks in late 2007. Both episodes are discussed briefly in the following section. Outside the euro area, this function is carried out by national central banks. Capital injections – for example, buying ordinary or preferences shares or purchasing toxic assets from banks – are the responsibility of national treasuries, which might also help to orchestrate mergers, subject to competition law. State guarantee of banks' deposits and of new debt issued by banks is also the responsibility of national treasuries, the former subject to the minimum threshold set by the EU deposit guarantee scheme.

The institutional arrangements for crisis management in the EU are set out in Table 8.1.

There are a variety of memoranda of understanding in the EU designed to promote supervisory cooperation in crisis management. These memoranda of understanding, unlike the legislation examined in the previous chapters, are not legally binding and concern only the parties that sign them. They set out areas of interest and common lines of action. To begin with, following the recommendations of the Economic and Financial Committee in 2001 (EFC 2001), a memorandum of understanding on high-level principles of cooperation between the banking supervisors and central banks in crisis management situations was adopted in March 2003, under the auspices of the Banking Supervision Committee of the ESCB. In September 2003, a simulation exercise involving central banks and banking supervisors was carried out in order to test the provisions of the memo adopted (ECB 2007a). In addition, in January 2001, a memorandum of understanding on the cooperation between banking supervisors and central banks in their capacity as payment systems

Table 8.1 The institutional framework for crisis management in the EU

Actions	Institution/body responsible
Liquidity provision	
– to the markets	ECB in euro area; national central banks outside
– to specific institutions	National central banks within and outside the euro area
Recapitalisation of financial institutions	National treasuries Subject to EU competition law
Mergers	Private sector, intervention of national treasuries Subject to EU competition law
State guarantees	
– deposits	National treasuries, minimum threshold set by EU directive
– new debt issued by banks and interbank lending	National treasuries

overseers was signed. Although this agreement does not specifically focus on crisis management, it contains provisions dealing with the exchange of information in the event of liquidity or solvency problems (ibid.).

Second, as a follow-up to the priorities set by the EFC in 2004, a memorandum of understanding on cooperation between the banking supervisors, the central banks and the finance ministries in financial crisis situations was signed in May 2005 (*Financial Times*, 15 May 2005). This also included arrangements for the development of contingency plans for the management of crisis situations, along with stress testing and simulation exercises. A simulation exercise was carried out in April 2006, involving the ECB, national central banks, national banking supervisors and finance ministries, in order to assess whether they could effectively work together to contain a financial crisis (*Financial Times*, 9 April 2006).

Nonetheless, before the financial turmoil erupted in 2007, there were no specific EU rules for crisis management and the sharing of the financial costs of public intervention in a crisis situation. As a response to the financial disorder, in September 2007 the EFC produced a report that outlined 'common principles for cross-border crisis management' and 'burden sharing' (EFC 2007: 10). These (rather vague) principles were subsequently endorsed by the ECOFIN Council in October 2007 and in the spring of 2008 were incorporated in the existing memoranda of understanding signed in 2005.

Third, there are regional and national memoranda of understanding – for example, the memorandum of understanding between the central banks of the Nordic region and that between the Dutch and Belgian authorities. The supervisory authorities in these countries were proactive in signing these memos both on account of the long-standing cooperation between them and because they supervise some very large cross-border financial groups (the Nordea group in the Nordic countries and the Fortis group in the Benelux). These memoranda were severely tested during the financial crisis, as in the case of the acrimonious winding-up of the Fortis group by the Benelux authorities (see Quaglia *et al.* 2009).

At the national level, a memorandum of understanding in the UK established a framework for cooperation concerning financial stability between the Treasury, the Bank of England and the Financial Services Authority. This arrangement was severely tested in the autumn of 2007, when the central bank had to provide emergency liquidity to the Northern Rock bank (for an in-depth discussion of this episode, see Treasury Committee 2008a). The memorandum was subsequently revised, and a special resolution regime was introduced under the Banking Bill (see Bank of England, HM Treasury and FSA 2008). Similarly, following the liquidity and solvency problems experienced by a couple of banks, and the way in which the issue was dealt with by the Bundesbank and the BaFin, the arrangements for supervisory cooperation came under scrutiny in Germany (*Financial Times*, 28 August 2007).

Despite these arrangements for financial stability, before the outbreak of the global financial crisis the IMF (2007, 2006) and other commentators and policy-makers (Padoa-Schioppa 2007) noted the need to adjust the largely nationally based EU supervisory framework to cope with increasing financial integration. The shortcomings of the existing arrangements were underscored by the delayed and piecemeal EU policy response to the global financial upheaval (see also Pauly 2008).

The EU policy response to the financial turmoil in 2007–9

The financial turmoil was caused by several interrelated factors (for a review of the main causes, see FSF 2008; see also Treasury Committee 2008a, 2008b). It took place in an international context of macro-economic imbalances, with an increasing surplus in the balance of payments of many Asian economies and a persistent deficit in the US balance of payments, compensated by capital inflow into the US from surplus economies (Pauly 2009). The crisis started off as an 'old fashioned bubble', whereby banks and financial institutions borrowed to invest in assets the value of which it was believed could only rise. This led to excessive levels of debt that were not backed up by enough capital.

In the US, where the problem originated, there was a credit boom in 'subprime' mortgages, the practice of 'predatory loans', and the widespread use of securitised mortgages that were then divided and repackaged into complex structured financial instruments and passed on to other investors. These activities were hardly regulated at either the federal or the state level (Committee on Oversight and Government Reforms 2008a). The 'originate to distribute' model meant that the financial instruments created in this way were not kept on the books of the financial companies that originated them; they were instead sold on, ending the relationship between banking and securitised mortgages. Moreover, they were incorrectly rated by credit rating agencies, partly because of the intrinsic difficulty of performing this task on complex financial products, partly because of the conflict of interest to which the credit rating agencies were subject, for they were also involved in advising the issuers on how to place these products on the market (Committee on Oversight and Government Reforms 2008b).

Once massive delinquency in the US sub-prime mortgages became apparent, a contagion spread among financial institutions, which stopped lending to each other because it was unclear which institutions held financial products based on badly performing loans. Furthermore, on account of the high level of uncertainty, financial institutions began to hoard cash. This crisis of confidence resulted in the seizing up of the interbank market, which is the wholesale market through which banks lend to each other. Since several financial institutions, among them the Northern Rock, relied on short-term loans in the wholesale market to fund their long-term investments, such institutions faced a liquidity shortage (Treasury Committee 2008a, 2008b). All this led to the so-called credit crunch.

In some cases the liquidity crisis became a solvency crisis, causing failures and the winding down of financial institutions, mergers and acquisitions, and direct interventions by the public authorities. When the investment bank Lehman Brothers filed for bankruptcy in the US in September 2008, the crisis gained full force: panic spread in the market, as it became clear that large financial institutions would be allowed to go under, contradicting the widely held view of being 'too big to fail'. The last stage unfolded when the crisis of confidence spread to the real economy, with direct negative effects on economic growth and employment. Many countries, including the euro area and the UK, entered into economic recession in late 2008.

During the first outbreak of chaos in the summer of 2007, the ECB intervened repeatedly in the market in a timely manner, injecting emergency liquidity into the financial system of the euro area (*Financial Times*, 15 August 2007; IMF 2008). At the national level, liquidity interventions also took place in 2007 under the aegis of the national central banks. For example, German public banks were among the most exposed to the credit squeeze and liquidity crunch in Europe (see Hardie and Howarth 2009), and the Bundesbank, together with the German financial supervisory authority, rescued the operations of two banks (*Financial Times*, 22, 28 August 2007).

Unlike the ECB, the Bank of England intervened belatedly, having previously indirectly criticised the ECB's interventions (*Financial Times*, 12 September 2007). The argument put forward by the governor of the Bank of England was that 'the provision of liquidity support undermines the efficient pricing of risk by providing ex post insurance for risky behaviour. That encourages excessive risk taking and sows the seeds of a future financial crisis' (King 2007: 7). Only after the Northern Rock crisis erupted in September 2007 did the Bank of England change its stance. The different response of the two banks suggests that there are different regulatory philosophies in the EU and different approaches to maintaining financial stability, as elaborated below.

International cooperation also took place in an attempt to deal with the problem. In December 2007, the ECB, the Federal Reserve, the Bank of England, the Bank of Canada and the Swiss central bank undertook concerted action to provide liquidity with a view to easing pressure on the money market and tackling the credit squeeze (*Financial Times*, 13–14 December 2007). When the global financial crisis gained full force in autumn the following year, on 8 October the US Federal Reserve, the Bank of England, the Bank of Canada, the Swiss central bank and Sveriges Riksbank carried out a coordinated cut in the interest rate of half a percentage point.

Following the failure of Lehman Brothers in the US in September 2008, the unsecured interbank money market froze worldwide. In the euro area, banks became increasingly dependent on ECB liquidity operations and overnight borrowing. This triggered the height of the credit crunch, and the ECB decided to ease the procedures for the provision of liquidity for as long as this was deemed necessary (ECB 2008). On 7 October, the ECOFIN discussed a coordinated response, relating in particular to support for systemic financial institutions and the definition of common principles for action. The member states committed themselves 'to take all necessary measures' (European Council 2008: 6) to protect the stability of the banking system and the deposits of individual savers. Yet more specific measures were not adopted. It should be noted that the possibility of creating a European stabilisation fund, mainly for bank recapitalisation, had briefly been considered by the French presidency but quickly dismissed due to strong German opposition. The new member states were also lukewarm towards the scheme, which would have benefited primarily banks headquartered in the old member states (interview, Paris, 7 May 2009), even though such banks had subsidiaries and branches in the new member states. The Netherlands was reportedly the main proponent of the scheme, which was also supported by Italy and France, though the latter was more ambivalent (*Financial Times*, 7 October 2008).

On 12 October, the heads of state in the euro group, acting in agreement with the European Commission and the ECB, approved a concerted action plan and urged the other EU countries to adopt its principles. By and large, this plan followed the template set by the plan announced by the British government a few days before the euro group meeting (Quaglia 2009b). It provided for individual national governments to take coordinated measures to facilitate bank funding (government guarantees for new medium-term debt issuance) and recapitalisation (government subscription of preference shares or other instruments) (Eurogroup 2008). This framework was fully endorsed by the European Council on 15 and 16 October. Afterwards, the national governments adopted their specific national plans, broadly following the guidelines outlined in the concerted action plan, though subject to some national variations.

On 15 October, the ECB expanded its list of assets eligible for use as collateral in its credit operations and increased the provision of longer-term liquidity by fully meeting banks' demand for liquidity at maturities of three and six months (ECB 2008). The list was subsequently tightened up, allegedly because some banks were 'gaming the system' (*Financial Times*, 5 September 2008), providing low quality collateral in credit operation with the ECB.[1] On 6 November, the ECB cut interest rates by half a point.

Several meetings of the three or four largest member states (France, Germany, the UK and sometimes Italy) took place, but lip service was paid to the elaboration of a joint response to the crisis and they resulted mainly in somewhat vague joint statements. This was clearly revealed by the Summit of European G8 members on 4 October (Summit of European G8 Members 2008) in that, shortly after the end of one of the meetings, the German government unexpectedly and unilaterally issued a statement concerning the state guarantee on bank deposits in Germany, apparently without previously informing the other member states, including those participating to the restricted meeting (*Financial Times*, 25 November 2008). Ireland had previously extended a state guarantee of all bank debt.

On 2 December, the ECOFIN Council approved a European recovery plan prepared by the Commission (CEC 2008), which was endorsed by the European Council on 11–12 December. In particular, the Council supported an economic stimulus amounting to 1.5 per cent of EU GDP (€200 billion), made up of budgetary expansion by the member states of €170 billion (around 1.2 per cent of EU GDP) and EU funding in support of immediate action of €30 billion (approximately 0.3 per cent of EU GDP) (ibid.: 6). The plan stated that the member states must coordinate their activities and choose the most appropriate measures concerning expenditures and revenues, prioritising those with a short-term impact. The Council stressed the need to establish national schemes to support the banking sector, comprising guarantees and recapitalisation plans.

The regulatory response to the financial crisis has been coordinated mainly in international fora, principally the FSF, and is still evolving. The FSF comprises representatives from central banks, supervisory authorities and treasury ministries, plus senior officials from international financial institutions (IMF, BIS, OECD, World Bank) and international regulatory bodies (BCBS, IOSCO, IAIS, IASB), as well as the CPPS and the ECB. In 2008 it included representatives from G7 countries plus Hong Kong, Singapore, Australia and the Netherlands. In 2009 it was transformed into the Financial Stability Board, with an enlarged membership and a more robust institutional structure.

Angeloni (2008) notes that the FSF was at the forefront in the elaboration of the response to the crisis. By contrast, EU fora took something of a back seat for two reasons. First, some member states, rather than strengthening the EU framework for financial stability outlined in the previous section, preferred less binding international solutions. For example, the possibility of increasing the power and status of the so-called Lamfalussy committees was resisted by the UK (ibid.; HM Treasury and FSA 2007). Second, arguably, given the international origins and implications of the financial crisis, it made sense to elaborate a regulatory response in international financial fora (which included the US, where the problem originated) rather than in the EU. Third, British policy-makers have constantly been (and are still) worried about the negative effects that could ensue from EU regulation on the City of London, which is one of the main international financial centres to compete with European and non-EU jurisdictions for business.

The FSF was asked by the G7 ministers and central bank governors to evaluate the causes of the crisis and to put forward recommendations to address the existing weaknesses, and in April 2008 it produced a report in collaboration with the other main international supervisory fora dealing with financial services. The report suggested 'strengthening capital, liquidity and risk management', 'enhancing transparency and valuation' and reviewing the role of credit rating agencies. The G7, which met in the spring of 2008, endorsed the report, highlighting the priorities for action in the short and medium term (Group of Seven 2008). The ECOFIN Council by and large reiterated the policy prescriptions put forward by the FSF.

The following list of measures is by no means exhaustive, but it is designed to give the flavour of the hectic regulatory activity that took place in the EU in 2008–9, often following or preceding international regulatory activity or regulatory changes in other non-EU jurisdictions, primarily the US. First, the Deposit Guarantee Scheme Directive, which dated back to 1994, was revised, raising the minimum deposit guarantee from €20,000 to €50,000, with a view to bringing the minimum threshold to €100,000 in the future. This directive had not been revised as part of the FSAP. The Capital Requirements Directive is also being revised, in parallel with international discussions concerning the revision of the Basel II Accord by the BCBS. In both instances, the policy debate has focused on the revision of risk weighting for securitised products, the trading book review and new rules about liquidity risk management, all of which had been bones of contention when the rules were negotiated in the early 2000s. At that time, industry, supported by some member states, had successfully lobbied for provisions that would basically lower capital requirements. After the crisis, the need to enhance international capital standards to address tendencies towards procyclicality was recognised (Group of Thirty 2009).

In April 2009, the EU issued a regulation on credit rating agencies, which were regarded as some of the main culprits of the crisis. As explained in Chapter 4, the use of external rating had been contentious in the making of the Basel II Accord and was hardwired into legislation when the accord was signed. The EU regulation contained several elements of the revised code of fundamentals for credit rating agencies, initially issued by the IOSCO in 2006 and revised in 2008 (Quaglia 2009c). Also in April 2009, the Commission proposed a directive on hedge-fund managers (to be precise, alternative investment fund managers, which take in private equities funds), currently under negotiation. The Commission has liaised with industry with a view to creating a (private) European counterparty for derivatives trading, and there have been ongoing discussions concerning the strengthening of the colleges of supervisors for cross-border groups in the EU – these colleges had been created in the banking sector by the Capital Requirements Directive. The Financial Stability Forum has put forward proposals for the creation of international colleges of supervisors for cross-border groups.

Last but not least, proposals for the reform of financial supervision in the EU have been put forward. In February 2009, the de Larosière Group, chaired by the former governor of the Banque de France, produced a report that recommended two main institutional changes related, respectively, to macro-prudential and micro-prudential supervision. The report proposed the creation, first, of the European Systemic Risk Council, comprising the ECB/

ESCB General Council, plus the chairpersons of CEBS, CEIOPS, CESR and the Commission, and second, of a European System of Financial Supervision in two stages, 2009–10 and 2010–12, with a review after stage 2. This involved the transformation of the Lamfalussy level 3 committees into European sectoral authorities – the European banking authority, the European securities authority and the European insurance authority.

The new European authorities would have the same functions as the existing Lamfalussy level 3 committees. In addition, they would have a legally binding mediation role vis-à-vis cross-border institutions, be in charge of licensing and supervising cross-border financial institutions such as credit rating agencies, and adopt binding standards. The boards of the authorities would comprise the chairs of the national supervisory authorities. The chairperson and the secretary general would be full-time independent professionals, and the appointment of the chairperson for a period of eight years would be subject to confirmation by the Commission, the EP and the Council. The European authorities would be endowed with autonomous budgets. This blueprint has been endorsed by the ECOFIN Council, and in June 2009 the Commission presented some proposals towards its implementation.

On the whole, the EU response to the financial turmoil in 2007–8 was somewhat delayed and uncoordinated, even though some aspects – such as the provision of liquidity by the ECB–Eurosystem – functioned better than others (see the positive assessment of the IMF 2008) – such as the coordination of national recapitalisation plans or the rules on depositors' protection schemes (for a more in-depth assessment of the EU coordination – or the lack of it – during the crisis, see Quaglia *et al.* 2009; for an analysis of the European responses to the global financial crisis, see Hodson and Quaglia 2009b). After the high point of the crisis had passed, the response consisted of a series of proposals for the regulation of activities previously not regulated by the EU, such as credit rating agencies and alternative investment funds, and the revision of existing legislation that was found wanting, such as the Capital Requirements Directive.

Open issues highlighted by the EU response to the financial turmoil

The EU response to the financial turmoil has highlighted some open issues concerning the arrangements for financial stability in Europe (see Hodson and Quaglia 2009a). More generally, such arrangements are under review worldwide, following the work of the FSF (2008). Hence, some of the issues discussed in this section concern primarily the EU, whereas others are of more general relevance. The purpose of this section is mainly to raise these issues for reflection, rather than attempting to answer them in a limited amount of space.

First, the responsibility for financial supervision remains largely with the national authorities, whereas financial markets are increasingly integrated, and, following the FSAP and the wave of regulatory measures examined in this book, cross-border activities of banks and other providers of financial services are widespread, especially in the EU. This begs the long-standing question of whether financial supervision should be transferred to the EU level and, if so, which institutions should be responsible for it (Goodhart 2000; Buiter 1999; Andenas and Avgerinos 2003; Begg *et al.* 1997, 1998). For instance, should a European financial supervisor be established, or should this function be transferred to the ECB (a debate that was hinted at in Chapter 3)?

The second issue, which is linked to the previous one, is whether central banking functions should be separated from supervisory functions, and whether supervisory functions should be divided among different authorities (Goodhart and Schoenmaker 1995; Masciandaro and Quintyn 2007; Mayes *et al.* 2001; Padoa-Schioppa 2003, 2004b; Group of Thirty 2009; Department of the Treasury 2008). As explained in the previous chapters, different institutional arrangements are in place in the member states (Masciandaro 2005), and there is no widely recognised 'best model' for financial supervision – unlike, for example, the model in monetary policy of an independent central bank (Busch 2004). The issue concerning the best model for financial supervision was brought to the fore by the events that took place in 2007 in the UK and Germany, where the coordination between the national authorities proved to be unsatisfactory. Yet countries where the central bank was responsible for banking supervision, such as the Netherlands, were also severely affected by the financial crisis.

Third, there is the issue of the interaction between EU and international arrangements for financial stability and financial regulation. Financial services are inherently subject to multi-level governance, being regulated in different ways in a variety of jurisdictions and policy locations (Cerny 1993, 1995; Cohen 1996; Helleiner 1994; Porter 2005, 2003). Sometimes, they escape regulation altogether. On the one hand, regardless of the rules set in place in one jurisdiction, it would be very difficult for such a jurisdiction to isolate or to protect itself from what happens elsewhere, partly as a consequence of the rules – absent or inadequate – set in place in other jurisdictions. Financial services are truly a globalised activity, and the financial crisis in 2007–9 originated outside the EU. On the other hand, a more robust regulatory framework in the EU would have lessened its impact on European financial markets and would have improved the response of the public authorities.

The Basel II Accord set minimum (not maximum) international standards for capital requirements. In principle, in the Capital Requirement Directive, the EU could have set stricter standards (i.e. higher capital requirements), which would have provided a better capital base to withstand the global financial chaos. Yet stricter standards would have been criticised for being detrimental to the competitiveness of the financial industry in Europe and for creating problems for banks operating across borders within and outside the EU. Higher capital requirements would have met opposition from industry and some member states, in particular those with strong financial transatlantic links and hosting large financial centres.

For example, in 2000 Spain adopted 'dynamic provisioning', whereby the banks were forced to build up reserves against future hypothetical losses. At the time Spanish banks resisted the regulation, fearing they would lose ground against competitors. Yet these rules gave Spanish financial institutions the capital cushions to use during the economic downturn. Arguably, this regulatory approach helped them to weather the financial storm, despite the collapse of the country's housing bubble. In 2008 the Bank of England pushed for the Spanish example to be discussed at an international level, and the Financial Stability Forum began to study the Spanish case (*Wall Street Journal*, 10 November 2008).

Fourth, there is the need to minimise moral hazard. As pointed out by the governor of the Bank of England (King 2007), there is the need, on the one hand, to safeguard financial stability and, on the other, to penalise (and hence discourage) risky behaviour by financial operators. The difficulty is to strike a balance between the two, bearing in mind that this might vary depending on the regulatory approach adopted, as evidenced by the different policy response of the ECB–Eurosystem and the Bank of England to the financial crisis.

If public funding is needed, the challenge is to decide how to share the costs, which in turn affects the incentive (or disincentive) for cooperation between the home and the host country authorities, creating potential conflicts of interest between the member states. The rules for burden sharing in the event of a financial crisis are still rather fuzzy (indeed, they are 'principles'), as explained in the previous section. This is largely because, as in other episodes of financial regulation analysed in this book, the member states and the EU institutions involved were unable to reach an agreement, and the compromise solution put forward, based on the minimum common denominator, proved to be inadequate to the task in hand, at least in some respects. Moreover, this issue tends to be politically sensitive because taxpayers' money is involved.

Fifth, in some instances the content of financial regulation was not fit for purpose. This was owing to a variety of reasons. To begin with, industry had lobbied in favour of 'light rules' – or, at any rate, rules that favoured competition and minimised the adjustment costs of financial operators. Furthermore, and related to this, different sections of the industry sometimes disagreed on the content of the rules, as did the public authorities. This was the result not only of different market configurations across countries but also of different regulatory paradigms. Consequently, the search for a compromise meant that often the rules agreed did not form a coherent whole and were not the most effective for sound regulation.

Finally, it is important to bear in mind that there is no full common understanding concerning the basic tenets of financial stability, as evidenced by the debates on rules versus principles; on how to deal with failing banks, hedge funds/complex financial instruments and moral hazard; and the allocation of power between home and host supervisors (Fonteyne and van der Vossen 2007). Also, in this case, different regulatory paradigms play a role.

A concise theoretically-informed assessment

Feeding into the theoretical debate developed in the previous chapters, it is possible to conclude that the EU response to the global financial turmoil in 2007–8 was largely intergovernmental. Under the French presidency in the second semester of 2008, the member states gathered first in the euro group and later in the Council were the key decision-makers, but disagreements among the member states and weak institutional arrangements for financial stability were the main causes of the delayed and piecemeal EU response. The concerted rescue plan adopted in October 2008 followed the lines set by the British national rescue plan, outlined by Prime Minister Gordon Brown at the euro group meeting in Paris. The fiscal stimulus plan package adopted in December 2008 left the member states with considerable room for manoeuvre in national implementation.

The role of the Commission was limited to the relaxation of the rules on state aid and mergers with reference to the application of national rescue plans and the drafting of the fiscal stimulus plan, subsequently adopted by the Council. However, supported by certain national governments, it has taken the lead in proposing new legislative measures, such as the regulation of credit rating agencies, and revising existing rules, first and foremost the Capital Requirements Directive and the deposit guarantee scheme. The EP was almost absent in elaborating the EU response in 2007–8, but was very active during the regulatory debate that ensued in the aftermath of the crisis. The ECB–Eurosystem successfully managed liquidity provision in the euro area and cut interest rates on several occasions, often in concerted action with other central banks both inside and outside the EU. However, the function of lender of last resort vis-à-vis specific financial institutions was performed at the national level by the national central banks of the Eurosystem.

In the debate on states and markets, the national rescue plans that contained provisions for the injection of public capital into financial companies, the *de jure* or de facto nationalisation of banks, the state guarantees of new debt issued by banks, the stepping up of national protection schemes for depositors, the end of the self-regulatory regime for credit rating agencies, and the attempt to regulate hedge-fund managers sanctioned the retreat of the market in the EU as elsewhere, first and foremost the US. For example the US has also tightened up its national regulatory regime for credit rating agencies and is considering doing the same for hedge funds.

The market-friendly regulatory approach that was particularly influential in shaping EU financial regulation over the previous decade has suffered a setback, at least in the short and medium term. For example, the so-called Turner review (FSA 2009), named after the chairman of the British authority that produced it, engaged in the revision of fundamental theoretical issues concerning (financial) market regulation, acknowledging that efficient markets can be irrational and that there had been 'misplaced reliance on sophisticated maths' and a 'failure of market discipline' in the build-up to the crisis. An interesting political consequence has been to strengthen the hand of the market-shaping coalition in the EU, as well as the negotiating position of the Union in international regulatory fora such as the G20 meetings. An example of this was the G20 meeting in London in April 2009, where the EU called for tougher international rules, such as the regulation of hedge funds and clamping down on tax heavens (Group of Twenty 2009). The regulatory response that ensued in 2009, after the most dramatic period of the crisis had passed, seems to have been informed by a market-making regulatory paradigm and a shifting balance of power (at least temporarily) between the main coalitions at play in the regulation of financial services in the EU.

Conclusion

The delayed and piecemeal EU response to the financial turmoil can be explained by the relatively 'thin' and somewhat fragmented arrangements for financial stability. On the one hand, over the last decade, the EU has developed a rather detailed and encompassing regulatory framework with a view to completing the Single Market in financial services. More or less harmonised rules have been set in place with the objective of market-making and, to some extent, market-shaping, as explained in the previous chapters. On the other hand, less attention has been paid to the development of sound arrangements for financial stability.

Although the two issues are intertwined, the rules for financial market integration have overall enjoyed broad support, even though their content has at times been subject to heated political discussion and painstaking negotiation, as highlighted in several instances in this book. By contrast, the arrangements for financial stability, in particular crisis management and resolution, are more politically sensitive, as they may involve the use of taxpayers' money for rescue operations. This feature strikes at the heart of national sovereignty, and the incomplete framework for financial stability can largely be ascribed to the fact that the EU lacks some state-like features and is still a polity in the making (Caporaso 1996; Wallace 1983).

Conclusions

The overarching question that informed this research was where the power lies in the governance of banking, securities and post-trading activities in the EU – basically, as Dahl (1961) put it, 'who governs' financial services in the EU. This question is all the more topical following the intense regulatory activity that has taken place in the EU over the last decade and the global financial turmoil that hit the Single Market in financial services in 2007–9. The answer is that power is dispersed across various national, European and international policy locations. Within these locations, the large member states and the most internationalised and competitive parts of the financial industry are very influential.

However, the large member states as well as the financial operators located in their territories often have different policy preferences that are articulated in the negotiation of EU rules, leading to the formation of fluid and fragmented coalitions (Grossman 2004). Hence, the final outcomes of the negotiations – EU financial regulation, including 'hard' and 'soft' rules – are the result of a series of compromises, brokered by the Commission, taking into account also the preferences of the EP. Besides the largest member states, some of the old member states, particularly the Benelux countries and the Nordic member states, are also active participants in the policy-making process because they have relatively large financial sectors.

By contrast, the new member states tend to be marginal participants for several reasons. First, they joined the EU only in 2004, when many of the new rules concerning financial services had already been agreed upon. Furthermore, in the first few years of membership, they had to grapple with more pressing matters concerning the post-accession phase (interview, Brussels, 9 April 2008). Second, and related to the previous point, their resources for dealing with the dossiers on financial regulation are rather stretched, especially in the permanent representations, even though the situation varies from country to country. Third, the new member states have small and largely foreign-owned financial sectors. That said, the new member states are gradually becoming more engaged in financial services regulation, and they take an active part in debates if they have a strong direct interest in the issues being negotiated. For example, given the fact that they play host to many foreign financial groups, they tend to defend the prerogatives of the host supervisors.

In almost all the directives concerning banking and securities markets, as well as in the Payment Services Directive, the main line of division has been between the North and the South, on account of both the different configuration of national financial systems and their competitiveness (hence 'interests') and the different policy paradigms (hence 'ideas') about financial services regulation, its priorities and instruments. This is the market-making regulatory paradigm, rooted in the ontological principle of market trust and privileging the objectives of competition and market efficiency, versus the market-shaping paradigm, rooted in the ontological position of market distrust and prioritising financial stability, consumer protection, and the protection of national markets. The first approach relies on the policy instruments of light-touch, principle-based regulation, rooted in the common law system, soft law and intense engagement with the private sector, while the second is rule-based, rooted in the Roman law system, and entails a limited interaction between the public authorities and the private sector. Direct intervention of the public authorities in the market is also envisaged under specific circumstances – T2S being the main example.

Large financial operators, which are generally transnational, have very good access to both national and EU policy-makers, and hence the push for further market integration has come from this section of the industry, which has most to gain from it (Mügge 2006; Bieling 2003, 2006; Macartney forthcoming). Anecdotal evidence suggests that the big banks and investment firms, many of which are US owned, have very good access to MEPs, or at least some of them. However, contrary to what is suggested by some international political economy literature, the preferences of the financial industry, even the most transnational part of it, as to the specific content of EU regulation are not identical across countries and sectors. Sometimes, indeed, they are very different, as evidenced by the policy discussions on the governance of the clearing and settlement of securities or payment services. Moreover, small and/or domestically oriented companies can also enjoy good access to policy-makers at the national level (e.g. the Länder in Germany) and in the EP (primarily the MEPs from their country or region).

The interviews conducted also suggest that MEPs seek contact with consumer organisations and are well disposed towards consumer protection, – not so much for idealistic reasons, but because 'consumers vote at the European elections' (interview, Brussels, 13 June 2007). Many MEPs are eager not to be seen as too sympathetic to the 'interest of big capital', and some actually lean in the opposite direction, though this depends on their nationality, party affiliation and constituency. Obviously, Southern European socialist MEPs are less likely to be sympathetic to the financial industry than Northern European conservative and liberal MEPs.

Partly on account of diversified policy preferences, there is no evidence of the Commission's regulatory capture by interest groups. Moreover, as one of the interviewees put it, given the fact the Commission consults or has contact with more than 100 financial associations and firms, all of which may have different priorities and policy preferences, this is quite unlikely. Overall, the Commission is willing to listen to industry, not least because the market-making, principle-based views articulated by the most internationalised section are in line with the its goals. This was even more the case after the change of the College of the Commission in 2004, when the Commission and its 'better regulation' agenda moved closer to the market-making approach. In the making of a Single Market in financial service, the Commission often elicited or relied upon the support of the big market players (Posner 2005; Jabko 2006).

An important caveat to be pointed out in this concluding chapter is that this research, which has examined the intense regulatory activity following the adoption of the FSAP and the setting in place of key rules for the governance of banking, securities and post-trading activities, has paid particular attention to issues that were contentious. This is because such controversies formed the main hindrances to the completion of the Single Market in financial services and because the question of 'who governs' comes to the fore in situations of conflict. As one policy-maker remarked, for several measures examined in this volume, there was by and large consensus among policy-makers and stakeholders on 80 per cent of the content. Yet the remaining 20 per cent, which was crucial in shaping the fundamentals for the regulation of financial services in the EU, was controversial and politically contested (interview, Brussels, 9 April 2008). Similarly, some controversial issues emerged in the EU response to the global financial turmoil in 2007–9, stressing that arrangements for financial stability are incomplete. This is mainly because these matters go to the very heart of national sovereignty and the various member states all have different views.

It was not the purpose of this research to evaluate the costs and benefits of the EU rules adopted in the financial sector during the last decade, or to prescribe what their content should have been, how they should be implemented and amended, and what future rules should look like. These issues are usually of interest to practitioners, and an economist and/or a lawyer would have been better suited than a political scientist to conducting such a regulatory impact assessment.

However, what this research suggests is that, regardless of the best economic model for financial services governance and the most effective regulation to be adopted in the EU, there is the unavoidable issue of the 'political' acceptability of such rules and regulatory models by the national governments, industry, and EU institutions themselves. In other words, the core question is not simply what is the best model and the best set of rules for financial services governance in the EU (i.e. the most cost-efficient and effective regulation) but also what is politically feasible in in the present circumstances. In a way, the answer to the first question is irrelevant for policy if such rules cannot be adopted in practice and cannot be implemented in the member states on account of political opposition. Moreover, the 'best rules' depend on the underlying structural conditions (the configuration of the financial system and market structure) as well as the main priorities selected for a specific policy (regulatory objectives). And these factors vary across the EU. Paraphrasing Héritier (1996), this has resulted in a 'regulatory patchwork' which was not 'robust' or 'coherent' enough to withstand the impact of the global financial crisis.

What does this research tell us about theories of EU policy-making and competing understandings of the political economy of financial market regulation in the EU? The findings do not support a purely intergovernmentalist explanation, albeit, as shown, the large member states remain crucial players – perhaps more than in other EU policy areas – or a purely supranational one, not least because, even though they tend to support financial market integration, there are some turf wars between the Commission, the EP and the ECB. There are several instances of 'bureaucratic politics' at play in the interaction of these bodies and their participation to the policy process. Moreover, the Lamfalussy committees are themselves a hybrid between intergovernmental fora, supranational bodies and technical committees of experts. Different policy-makers are particularly influential at different stages of the policy process, which is why it is useful to combine traditional theories of European integration with a public policy approach based on the different phases of the 'policy cycle'.

Market forces tend to interact closely with the public authorities in regulatory activity at both national and EU levels, promoting their diversified preferences, but also providing information, technical expertise and even human resources (seconded personnel). The private sector is also important in the implementation of EU rules, an issue that was not discussed in this book. Furthermore, many directives agreed as part of the FSAP are still in the process of being implemented and their effects have to be evaluated in the member states. The heavy involvement of industry in shaping the content of financial regulation in a variety of ways (not only pushing for further integration; see Haas 1968) is somewhat overlooked by the traditional theories of European integration. Another consequence of the increasing influence of industry in the regulatory process in the EU and elsewhere (e.g. in the US or in international regulatory fora) is that many of the rules set in place have tended to be 'market-friendly', though not the most suitable to safeguard financial stability.

What does this research tell us about financial market integration in the EU and the EU response to the global financial turmoil? Following the 'regulatory wave' of the early 2000s with a view to implementing the FSAP for the completion of the Single Market, financial market integration is proceeding at a steady pace, though it will be slowed down by the crisis and the economic recession that followed it. Moreover, some domestic constraints discussed in the previous chapters are likely to remain in place for the foreseeable future, delaying the integration of retail banking and mortgage services.

Some important institutional issues remain unresolved, as evidenced by the delayed and piecemeal EU response to the financial upheaval. Among these, some concrete proposals are currently being discussed concerning the creation of a European System of Financial Supervision and the transformation of the Lamfalussy committees into European authorities, as envisaged by the report of the de Larosière Group (2009). More generally, there is the topical issue of the regulatory reforms needed following the financial crisis and how to safeguard financial stability in the EU and worldwide. These reforms are being discussed not only in the EU, but also in other countries such as the US (see Department of the Treasury 2008) and in international regulatory fora (see Group of Thirty 2009; Brunnermeier *et al.* 2009), as mentioned in chapter 8. In 2009 the EU undertook a series of regulatory activities that seemed to be informed more by the market-shaping paradigm – or, according to some (mainly British) policy-makers and industry representatives, the tendency to 'over-regulate' – than by the market-making approach that had previously carried more weight in EU policy-making.

Regulatory cooperation and financial services trade negotiations with the US will become more important in the future, as the latter made clear that, for this to happen, further market integration and regulatory convergence was needed in the EU. An example considered in this volume was the EU directive on financial conglomerates, which led to the discussion on the 'equivalence' of supervisory arrangements concerning conglomerates in the EU and the US (Posner 2009). Moreover, the worldwide financial instability in 2007–9 highlighted the interconnection among global financial systems, their inherent fragility, and the need to set in place a suitable regulatory and supervisory framework. This requires not only such a coherent and effective framework in the EU, but also intense transatlantic and more generally international cooperation in governing financial services. Indeed, the crisis originated in the US, and partly for this reason the regulatory response to it was led by international regulatory fora. The multi-level governance of financial services is set to become more and more intertwined.

Interviews

The interviewees are listed in alphabetical order, indicating their primary institutional affiliation at the time they were interviewed, though there are some exceptions, and some interviewees had several 'hats'. All the interviews were conducted on a non-attributable basis. They were triangulated, and the information gathered was cross-checked against available primary documents and a systematic survey of press coverage.

1 Susana Andrepova, secretariat of the Committee on Economic and Monetary Affairs, Brussels
2 Alan Bruce Beverly, secretary of the European Insurance and Occupational Pension Committee, European Commission, Brussels
3 Françoise Buisson, Autorité des marchés financiers, Paris
4 Adelaide Morais Cavaleiro, Banco do Portugal and CEBS, Lisbon
5 Giacomo Caviglia, ECB, Frankfurt
6 Daniele Ciani, Italian Permanent Representation, Brussels
7 Ben Cohen, FSF, Basel
8 Alberto Corinti, CEIOPS, Frankfurt
9 Manuel Ribeiro da Costa, Portuguese Securities Market Commission and CESR, Lisbon
10 Rob Curtis, FSA, London
11 Howard Davies, formerly chairman of the FSA, London
12 Fabrice Demarigny, CESR, Paris
13 Catherine Dias, Autorité des marchés financiers, Paris
14 Gerald Dillinburg, Bundesbank and CEBS, Frankfurt
15 Carmine Dinoia, Associazione fra le società italiane per azione, Brussels
16 Johannes Engels, BaFin, Frankfurt
17 Andrea Enria, CEBS, London
18 Simon Fish, HSBC, formerly UK Treasury, London
19 Stephen Fisher, European Banking Federation, Brussels
20 Florence Fontan, BNP Paribas, Paris
21 Giuseppe Forese, Italian Treasury Ministry, EBC and Financial Conglomerates Committee, Rome
22 Edward Foreshaw, FSA, alternate in the CESR, London

23   Noémie Francheterre, European Banking Federation, Brussels
24   Thierry Francq, French Treasury and FSC, Paris
25   Udo Franke, German Ministry of Finance and FSC, Berlin
26   Judith Hart, Federation of European Stock Exchanges
27   Annette Hauff, Deutsche Bank, Brussels
28   Simon Hills, British Bankers' Association, London
29   Chris Huhne, MP, formerly MEP, London
30   Patricia Jackson, Ernst and Young, formerly Bank of England, London
31   Stéphane Janin, Association française de la gestion financière, Paris
32   Nicolas Jeanmart, European Savings Banks Group, Brussels
33   Piia Nora Kauppi, MEP, Committee on Economic and Monetary
     Affairs, Brussels
34   Dr Werner Kerklo, German Finance Ministry, European Securities
     Committee, European Insurance and Occupational Pension Committee,
     Berlin
35   Doris Kolassa, European Commission, secretary of Clearing and
     Settlement Advisory and Monitoring Expert Group, Brussels
36   Christian König, European Building Societies Federation, Brussels
37   Sebastiano Laviola, Bank of Italy and CEBS, Rome
38   Olivier Lefebvre, formerly executive director of Euronext, Brussels
39   Tomas Mackie, European Commission and EBC, Brussels
40   Stefan Mai, Duetsche Börse, Frankfurt
41   Tuomas Majuri, Permanent Representation of Finland, Brussels
42   David Manning, FSA and CESR, London
43   Daniela Marilungo, Italian Banking Association, Brussels
44   Antonio Mas Sirvent, Spanish Securities Market Commission and
     CESR, Madrid
45   Marcus Mecklenburg, Bundesverband Investment und Asset
     Management eV, Frankfurt
46   Walburga Memetsberger, European Association of Public Banks,
     Brussels
47   Stefano Micossi, Associazione fra le società italiane per azione, Rome
48   Alois Müller, Bundesbank, Frankfurt
49   Xavier Musca, French Treasury, Paris
50   Mario Nava, European Commission, Brussels
51   Nikolaus Nordhorfer, Deutsche Bank, Frankfurt
52   Achim Oelgarth, Association of German Banks, Brussels
53   Carsten Ostermann, German Ministry of Finance, BaFin and European
     Securities Committee, Berlin
54   Francesca Palisi, Italian Banking Association, Rome
55   Alberto Parenti, European Commission, secretary of the European
     Securities Committee, Brussels
56   Mark Paskins, UK Treasury, London
57   Elisabeth Pauly, Banque de France/Commission bancaire and CEBS,
     Paris

58 Patrick Pearson, European Commission and Financial Conglomerates Committee, Brussels
59 Alessandra Perrazzelli, Bancaintesa, Brussels
60 John Purvis, MEP, Committee on Economic and Monetary Affairs, Brussels
61 Andreas Reinhardt, German Ministry of Finance and Bundesbank, EBC, Berlin
62 Finn Rieder, Association of German Banks, Berlin
63 Alessandro Rivera, Italian Treasury, European Securities Committee and FSC, Rome
64 Gary Roberts, UK Permanent Representation, Brussels
65 Serge Segre, National Bank of Belgium, Brussels
66 Giuseppe Siani, European Commission, Brussels
67 Peter Skinner, MEP, Committee on Economic and Monetary Affairs, Brussels
68 Lars Sorsen, secretariat of the Committee on Economic and Monetary Affairs, Brussels
69 Bernard Speyer, Deutsche Bank, Frankfurt
70 Patrick Starkman, EP adviser, Committee on Economic and Monetary Affairs, Brussels
71 Philipp Sudeck, BaFin and CESR, Frankfurt
72 Paul Symons, Euroclear, London
73 Greg Tanzer, IOSCO, Madrid
74 Mick Thom, European Commission, Brussels
75 John Tiner, formerly FSA, London
76 Daniel Trinder, Goldman Sachs, formerly UK Treasury
77 Tomas Trnka, Permanent Representation of the Czech Republic, Brussels
78 Vincent van Dessel, executive director, Euronext, Brussels
79 Alejandro Vargas, Banco de España and CEBS, Madrid
80 Philippe Vigneron, Belgian Permanent Representation and National Bank of Belgium, ESC, Brussels
81 Tobias Volk, Bundesbank, Frankfurt
82 Reinhold Vollbricht, Bundesbank, Frankfurt
83 Uta Wassmuth, European Banking Federation, Brussels
84 Clare Waysand, French Treasury and EFC, Paris
85 Sonia Wollny, secretariat of the Committee of Economic and Monetary Affairs, Brussels

Notes

2 The research design

1 A traditional intergovernmentalist approach has de facto been applied to several studies of how EMU came about (McNamara 1998; Dyson and Featherstone 1999), which show that the private sector was not an influential player. It was actually hardly consulted in the decision-making stage, even though the account is different if one takes into account the implementation stage, which involved industry.
2 The literature on ideas in political economy is vast, even excluding neo-Gramscian interpretations. See Blyth 2002; Campbell 1998; Hall 1989, 1993; Garrett and Weingast 1993; Goldstein 1993; McNamara 1998; Marcussen 2000; Parsons 2000, 2002; Woods 1995; Yee 1996.

3 The making of the Single Market in financial services

1 This part draws heavily from Quaglia (2007).
2 The members of the committee were Bengt Ryden, chief executive of the Stockholm Stock Exchange; Cornelius Herkströter, a director of Billiton plc and professor of international management at Amsterdam University; Luigi Spaventa, president of the Italian Bourse authority; Nigel Wicks, former permanent secretary of the UK Treasury; and Norbert Walter, chief economist at the Deutsche Bank Group. The rapporteur was David Wright, director financial markets, Directorate General for Internal Markets, European Commission, and the secretary was Pierre Delsaux.
3 'Comitology' refers to the delegation of implementing powers by the Council to the Commission for the execution of EU legislation. Representatives of the member states, acting through 'comitology committees', assist the Commission.
4 The Committee of Wise Men was also indirectly involved in this tug-of-war, as in the final version of the report it rejected the EP's request for a call-back clause.

4 Governing banking in the EU

1 www.bis.org/bcbs/ (accessed 10 January 2007).
2 www.bis.org/bcbs/jointforum.htm (accessed 10 January 2007).
3 The papers included were the following: 'Capital Adequacy Principles'; 'Supplement to the Capital Adequacy'; 'Fit and Proper Principles'; 'Framework for Supervisory Information Sharing'; 'Principles for Supervisory Information Sharing'; 'Coordinator Paper'; 'Supervisory Questionnaire'.
4 www.c-ebs.org/CEBScharter.htm (accessed 20 January 2007).

5   In March 2002, the European Council asked the Commission to prepare a report on the consequences of the Basel II Accord for all sectors of the European economy, with particular attention to SMEs in light of the fact that the accord's content was to be transposed into EU legislation (PricewaterhouseCoopers 2004). The report estimated a beneficial outcome for SMEs.

6   For a social network analysis of the Capital Requirements Directive, see also Christopoulos and Quaglia (2009).

7   For an overview, see http://europa.eu.int/rapid/pressReleasesAction.do?reference = MEMO/04/178&language = en&guiLanguage = en (accessed 20 May 2006).

8   The Bunsdesbank received more than 200 letters and policy documents from the public, including, among other bodies, churches. This is because Basel II has implication for the financial treatment of church taxation in Germany.

9   http://ec.europa.eu/internal_market/finances/docs/general/20050914_fsc_eu_us_paper_en.pdf.

5   Governing securities markets in the EU

1   http://ec.europa.eu/internal_market/securities/esc/index_en.htm   (accessed   27 February 2007).

2   To be precise, before 1997 in the UK there were several self-regulatory organisations dealing with supervisory issues.

3   http://ec.europa.eu/internal_market/securities/abuse/2004–01-contributions_en.htm (accessed 15 March 2007).

4   See also www.eupolitix.com/EN/News/200403/2780cf05-f17a-404d-b8d7-d15 f8376f93e.htm.

5   Euronext, following its alliance with the New York Stock Exchange (NYSE), has been renamed NYSE-Euronext.

6   For example, the president of the French Banking Federation is from BNP Paribas. The president of the Italian Banking Association is from a savings bank.

6   Governing post-trading in the EU

1   The National Bank of Belgium, Bank of Canada, Bank of France, Deutsche Bundesbank, Hong Kong Monetary Authority, Bank of Italy, Bank of Japan, Netherlands Bank, Monetary Authority of Singapore, Sveriges Riksbank, Swiss National Bank, Bank of England, Board of Governors of the Federal Reserve System and Federal Reserve Bank of New York.

2   www.bis.org/cpss/cpssinfo01.htm (accessed 17 August 2007).

3   www.ecb.eu/paym/target/html/index.en.html (accessed 1 August 2007).

4   For a more complete description of the clearing and settlement process – as well as specific cross-border features – see *Cross-Border Securities Settlements*, a report prepared by the CPSS of the central banks of the G10 (March 1995), and *Recommendations for Securities Settlement Systems*, the report of the CPSS–IOSCO Joint Task Force on Securities Settlement Systems (January 2001).

5   In 2007, the London Stock Exchange acquired the Italian Bourse. This might change the position of the London Stock Exchange on this issue (interview, Berlin, 23 April 2008).

7   An overall cross-sectoral assessment

1   The FINUSE group, selected by the European Commission, consists of consumer protection and small business experts, academic researchers and staff from major consumer and small business organisations. The group monitors and

References

Albert, M. (1993) *Capitalism versus Capitalism*, New York: Three Windows, Four Walls Press.

Allen, F., and Gale, D. (2000) *Comparing Financial Systems*, Cambridge, MA: MIT Press.

Andenas, M., and Avgerinos, Y. (eds) (2003) *Financial Markets in Europe: Towards a Single Regulator?*, The Hague: Kluwer Law International.

Angeloni, I. (2008) *Testing Times for Global Financial Governance*, Brussels: Bruegel.

Apeldoorn, B. van (2002) *Transnational Capitalism and the Struggle over European integration*, London: Routledge.

Armstrong, K., and Bulmer, S. (1998) *The Governance of the Single European Market*, Manchester: Manchester University Press.

Association of Global Custodians (2004) *Revised ESCB/CESR Standards for Securities Clearing and Settlement Systems*, 25 May.

—— (2005) *Public Statement: Follow-up Work by the ESCB/CESR*, 13 September.

Association of Private Client Investment Managers and Stockbrokers (2001) *Response to EU Commission proposal for a directive of the European Parliament and of the Council on the prospectus to be published when securities are offered to the public or admitted to trading*, 22 August.

—— (2003) *Review of Capital Requirements for Banks and Investment Firms: Response to the Consultative Paper 3*, London, 1 July.

Association of Private Client Investment Managers and Stockbrokers *et al.* (2002) *A European Capital Market for the 21st Century*, position paper prepared by the Association of Private Client Investment Managers and Stockbrokers, the European Association of Securities Dealers, the Futures and Options Association, the International Primary Market Association, the International Securities Market Association, the International Swaps and Derivatives Association, the London Investment Banking Association and the Bond Market Association, May.

Associazione Bancaria Italiana (2003) *Position Paper of the Italian Banking System on the European Commission Consultative Document: CAD 3*, Rome, October 2003.

—— (2004) *Communication from the Commission about Clearing & Settlement in the European Union: The Way Forward*, 2 August.

Bache, I., and Flinders, M. (eds) (2004) *Multi-Level Governance*, Oxford: Oxford University Press.

Baker, A. (2006) *The Group of Seven: Finance Ministries, Central Banks and Global Financial Governance*, London: Routledge.

Banca d'Italia (2006) *Target2 – Securities: Initial Assumptions and Questions, Reply of the Italian Market Participants, CSD, CCP and Stock Exchanges*, 11 September.

Banco de España (2006), *Target2 – Securities: Initial Assumptions and Questions, Spain Answer*, 8 September.

Bank of England, HM Treasury and FSA (Financial Services Authority) (2008) *Financial Stability and Depositor Protection: Strengthening the Framework*, London, January.

BCBS (Basel Committee on Banking Supervision) (2001) *Basel II: The New Basel Capital Accord – Second Consultative Paper*, Basel, January.

—— (2005a) *Basel II: International Convergence of Capital Measurement and Capital Standards: A Revised Framework*, Basel.

—— (2005b) *Amendment to the Capital Accord to Incorporate Market Risks*, Basel, November.

—— (2005c) *QIS 4: National Impact Studies and Field Tests in 2004 or 2005*, Basel.

Begg, D., De Grauwe, P., Giavazzi, F., Uhlig, H. and Wyplosz, C. (1998) *The ECB: Safe at Any Speed?*, Monitoring the European Central Bank 1, London: CEPR.

Begg, D., Giavazzi, F., Von Hagen, J., and Wyplosz, C. (1997) *EMU: Getting the End-Game Right*, Monitoring European Integration 7, London: CEPR.

Beyers, J. (2002) 'Gaining and seeking access: the European adaptation of domestic interest associations', *European Journal of Political Research*, 41: 585–612.

—— (2005) 'Multiple embeddedness and socialization in Europe: the case of Council officials', *International Organization*, 59: 899–936.

Bieling, H.-J. (2003) 'Social forces in the making of the new European economy: the case of financial market integration', *New Political Economy*, 8, 2: 203–23.

—— (2006) 'EMU, financial integration and global economic governance', *Review of International Political Economy*, 13, 3: 420–48.

Bini Smaghi, L. (2007) 'The fear of freedom: politicians and the independence and accountability of financial supervisors in practice', in D. Masciandaro and M. Quintyn (eds), *Designing Financial Supervision Institutions*, Cheltenham: Edward Elgar, pp. 41–62.

Blyth, M. (1997) 'Any more bright ideas?', *Comparative Politics*, 29: 229–40.

—— (2002) *Great Transformations: Economic Ideas and Institutional Change in the Twentieth Century*, Cambridge: Cambridge University Press.

Borio, C. (2003) 'Towards a macroprudential framework for financial supervision and regulation?', *CESifo Economics Studies*, 49, 2: 181–215.

Bouwen, P. (2002) 'Corporate lobbying in the European Union: the logic of access', *Journal of European Public Policy*, 9, 3: 365–90.

—— (2004) 'Exchanging access goods for access: a comparative study of business lobbying in the European Union institutions', *European Journal of Political Research*, 43: 337–69.

Branch, A., and Ohrgaard, J. (1999) 'Trapped in the supranational–intergovernmental dichotomy: a response to Stone Sweet and Sandholtz', *Journal of European Public Policy* 6, 1: 123–43.

British Bankers' Association (2003) *Comments on the Commission Services Working Document on the Review of Capital Requirements for Banks and Investment Firms*, London, 22 October.

—— (2004a) *Letter to the Rapporteur of the EP concerning the Capital Requirements Directive*, London.

—— (2004b) *Response to the European Commission's Communication on Clearing and Settlement*, 29 July.

British Bankers' Association and London Investment Banking Association (2003) *Response to the Consultative Paper 3 on the Basel II Accord*, London.

Brown, P. (1997) 'The politics of the EU single market for investment services: negotiating the Investment Services and Capital Adequacy directives', in G. Underhill, (ed.), *The New World Order in International Finance*, London: Macmillan, pp. 124–43.

Brunnermeier, M., Crockett, A., Goodhart, C., Persaud, A. D., and Shin, H. (2009) *The Fundamental Principles of Financial Regulation*, Geneva Reports on the World Economy 11, Geneva: International Center for Monetary and Banking Studies.

Buiter, W. (1999) 'Alice in Euroland', *Journal of Common Market Studies*, 37, 2: 181–209.

—— (2007) 'High degree of ECB independence in securities sector is undesirable', letter to the *Financial Times*, 19 January.

Bundesverband deutscher Banken (2003) *Response to the Consultative Paper 3 on the Basel II Accord*, Berlin.

Busch, A. (2004) 'National Filters: Europeanisation, institutions, and discourse in the case of banking regulation', *West European Politics*, 27, 2: 310–33.

Campbell, J. (1998) 'Institutional analysis and the role of ideas in political economy', *Theory and Society*, 27: 377–409.

Caporaso, J. A. (1996) 'The European Union and forms of state: Westphalian, regulatory or post-modern?', *Journal of Common Market Studies*, 34, 1: 29–52.

—— (1999) 'Toward a normal science of regional integration', *Journal of European Public Policy*, 6, 1: 160–64.

CEBS (Committee of European Banking Supervisors) (2005) *Report of Activities*, London.

—— (2007a) *CEBS Contribution to the Lamfalussy Review*, London, 12 November.

—— (2007b) *Assessing CEBS's Progress So Far*, London, 9 May.

CEC (Commission of the European Communities) (1998) *Financial Services: Building a Framework for Action*, Communication of the Commission to the Council and European Parliament, 28 October.

—— (1999) *Financial Services: Implementing the Framework for Financial Markets: Action Plan*, Communication from the Commission to the Council and European Parliament, Brussels, 11 May.

—— (2000a) *Towards an EU Directive on the Prudential Supervision of Financial Conglomerates*, Consultation Document, Brussels.

—— (2000b) *Upgrading the Investment Services Directive (93/22/EEC)*, 16 November.

—— (2001a) *ISD Feedback: Synthesis of Responses to COM (2000) 729*, July.

—— (2001b) *Overview of Proposed Adjustments: Detailed Presentation*, 24 July.

—— (2002a) *Commission Document on a Possible Legal Framework for the Single Payment Area in the Internal Market – Summary of Responses*, Brussels, 17 October.

—— (2002b) *The Follow up of the Second Mapping Exercise on EU Financial Conglomerates – A Summary of the Findings by the Mixed Technical Group*, Brussels.

—— (2002c) *Consultation Document: Clearing and Settlement in the European Union: Main Policy Issues and Future Challenges*, 28 May.

—— (2002d) *Commission Communication on Clearing and Settlement – Summary of Responses*, 18 December.

—— (2003) *A New Legal Framework for Payments in the Internal Market*, Communication from the Commission to the Council and the European Parliament, 2 December.

—— (2004a) *Financial Services: Turning the Corner, Preparing the Challenge of the Next Phase of European Capital Market Integration*, tenth progress report.

—— (2004b) *Clearing and Settlement in the European Union – The Way Forward*, Communication from the Commission to the Council and the European Parliament, 28 April.

—— (2004c) *Commission Communication on Clearing and Settlement – Summary of Responses*, 18 December.

—— (2004d) *Clearing and Settlement in the European Union: Main Policy Issues and Future Challenges*, Communication from the Commission to the Council and the European Parliament, *Official Journal of the European Union*, C 38 E, 12.2.2004.

—— (2005a) *The Green Paper on Financial Services Policy (2005–2010)*, Brussels.

—— (2005b) *The White Paper on Financial Services Policy (2005–2010)*, Brussels.

—— (2005c) *Proposal for a Directive of the European Parliament and of the Council on Payment Services in the Internal Market and Amending Directives 97/7/EC, 2000/12/EC and 2002/65/EC*, Brussels.

—— (2005d) *Communication on Clearing and Settlement in the European Union – The Way Forward, Summary of the Responses*, 21 March.

—— (2005e) *Working Document on Definitions of Post-Trading Activities*, Working document/MARKT/SLG/G2(2005)D15283.

—— (2006) *Competition in EU Securities Trading and Post Trading*, 24 May.

—— (2007) *Review of the Lamfalussy Process, Strengthening Supervisory Convergence*, Communication from the Commission.

—— (2008) *A European Recovery Plan*, Communication from the Commission to the European Council, Brussels, 26 November.

CEC (Commission of the European Communities) and ECB (European Central Bank) (2006) *Single Euro Payments Area*, Joint statement, 4 May.

Cecchini, P., with Catinat, M., and Jacquemin, A. (1988) *The European Challenge 1992: The Benefits of a Single Market*, Aldershot: Wildwood House [Cecchini Report].

Cecchini, P., Heinemann, F., and Jopp, M. (eds) (2003) *The Incomplete European Market for Financial Services*, Bonn: Springer Verlag.

Cerny, P. (ed.) (1993) *Finance and World Politics*, Aldershot: Edward Elgar.

—— (1995) 'Globalization and the changing logic of collective action', *International Organization*, 49, 4: 595–625.

CESR (Committee of European Securities Regulators) (2004) *Which Supervisory Tools for the EU Securities Markets? Preliminary Progress Report*, Paris [Himalaya Report].

—— (2007) *A Proposed Evolution of EU Securities Supervision Beyond 2007*, Paris.

CESR (Committee of European Securities Regulators) and ECB (European Central Bank) (2004a) *Summary of Responses to the Consultation on the Report on Standards for Securities Clearing and Settlement Systems in the European Union*, 23 September.

—— (2004b) *Summary of Responses to the Joint Consultation on Standards for Securities Clearing and Settlement Systems in the European Union*, 12 January.

—— (2004c) *Standards for Securities Clearing and Settlement in the European Union*, September.

CESR (Committee of European Securities Regulators), CEBS (Committee of European Banking Supervisors), and CEIPOS (Committee of European Insurance and Occupational Pensions Supervisors) (2006) 'Cross border consolidation', letter to Mr McCreevy, 29 September.

Checkel, J. (1997) 'International norms and domestic politics: bridging the rationalist–constructivist divide', *European Journal of International Relations*, 3, 4: 473–95.

Christiansen, T., and Larsson, T. (eds) (2007) *The Role of Committees in the Policy-Process of the European Union: Legislation, Implementation, Deliberation*, Cheltenham: Edward Elgar.

Christiansen, T., and Piattoni, S. (eds) (2004) *Informal Governance in the European Union*, Northampton, MA: Edward Elgar.

Christiansen, T., and Vaccari, B. (2006) 'The 2006 reform of comitology', *EIPAscope*, 3: 9–17.

Christopoulos, D., and Quaglia, L. (2009) 'Influence and brokerage: network constraints in EU banking regulation', *Journal of Public Policy*, 29, 2: 1–22.

Ciani, D. (2006) 'La Direttiva 2004/39/ce: un resoconto dall'interno dei difficili lavori preparatori', in M. Lamandini and C. Motti (eds), *Scambi su merci e derivati su commodities: quali prospettive?*, Milan: Giuffrè, pp. 35–48.

Cini, M. (2007) *From Integration to Integrity: Administrative Ethics and Reform in the European Commission*, Manchester: Manchester University Press.

Citi, M., and Rhodes, M. (2006) 'New modes of governance in the European Union: a critical survey and analysis', in K. Jorgensen, M. Pollack and B. Rosamond (eds), *Handbook of European Union Politics*, London: Sage, pp. 463–82.

Claessens, S., Underhill, G. R. D., and Zhang, X. (2008) 'The political economy of Basle II: the costs for poor countries', *World Economy*, 31, 3: 313–43.

Coen, D., and Thatcher, M. (2005) 'The new governance of markets and the non-majoritarian regulators', *Governance*, 18, 3: 329–46.

—— (2008) 'Network governance and multi-level delegation: European networks of regulatory agencies', *Journal of Public Policy*, 28, 1: 49–71.

Cohen, B. J. (1996) 'Phoenix risen: the resurrection of global finance', *World Politics*, 48, 2: 268–96.

Coleman, W. (1994) 'Policy convergence in banking: a comparative study', *Political Studies*, 42: 274–92.

—— (1996) Financial Services, Globalisation and Domestic Policy Change, London: Macmillan.

Coleman, W., and Underhill, G. (1998) 'Globalism, regionalism, and the emergence of international securities markets: the case of IOSCO and EU financial integration', in W. Coleman and G. Underhill (eds), *Regionalism and Global Economic Integration: Europe, Asia, and the Americas*, London: Routledge, pp. 223–48.

Committee of Wise Men (2000) *Initial Report of the Committee of Wise Men on the Regulation of Securities Markets*, Brussels.

—— (2001) *Final Report of the Committee of Wise Men on the Regulation of Securities Markets*, Brussels.

Committee on Oversight and Government Reforms (2008a) *Hearing on the Role of Federal Regulators in the Financial Crisis*, Washington, DC, 23 October.

—— (2008b) *Hearing on the Credit Rating Agencies and the Financial Crisis*, Washington, DC, 22 October.

Council of the EU and EP (2002) Directive on the Supplementary Supervision of Credit Institutions, Insurance Undertakings and Investment Firms in a Financial Conglomerate, 2002/87/EC.

—— (2006) 'Directive 2006/49/EC of the European Parliament and of the Council of 14 June 2006 on the capital adequacy of investment firms and credit institutions (recast)', *Official Journal of the European Union* L 177/201, 30 June.

Cowles, M. G. (1995) 'Setting the agenda for a new Europe: The ERT and EC 1992', *Journal of Common Market Studies*, 33, 4: 501–26.

CPSS (Committee on Payment and Settlement Systems) (2003) *A Glossary of Terms Used in Payments and Settlement Systems*, March, www.bis.org/publ/cpss00b.pdf.

Cruickshank, D. (2000) *Competition and Regulation in Financial Services: Striking the Right Balance*, London: HM Treasury [Cruickshank Report].

Cukierman, A. (1992) *Central Bank Strategy, Credibility, and Independence: Theory and Evidence*, Cambridge, MA: MIT Press.

Dahl, R. A. (1961) *Who Governs? Democracy and Power in an American City*, New Haven, CT: Yale University Press.

Davies, R., Dufour, A., and Scott-Quinn, B. (2006) 'The MiFID: competition in a new European equity market regulatory structure', in G. Ferrarini and E. Wymeersch (eds), *Investor Protection in Europe*, Oxford: Oxford University Press, pp. 163–97.

Deeg, R. (1999) *Finance Capitalism Unveiled: Banks and the German Political Economy*, Ann Arbor: University of Michigan Press.

—— (2005) 'The comeback of Modell Deutschland? The new German political economy in the EU', *German Politics*, 14, 3: 332–53.

Deeg, R., and Lütz, S. (2000) 'Internationalization and financial federalism: the United States and Germany at the crossroads?', *Comparative Political Studies*, 33, 3: 374–405.

de Larosière Group (2009) *The High Level Group on Financial Supervision in the EU*, Brussels, 25 February.

DeLeon, P. (1999) 'The stages approach to the policy process: What has it done? Where is it going?', in P. A. Sabatier (ed.), *Theories of the Policy Process*, Oxford: Westview Press.

De Nicoló, G., Bartholomew, P. F., Zaman, J., and Zephirin, M. G. (2003), *Bank Consolidation, Internationalization and Conglomeration: Trends and Implications for Financial Risk*, IMF working paper 03/158, Washington, DC: IMF.

Department of the Treasury (2008) *Blueprint for a Modernized Financial Regulatory Structure*, Washington, DC, March.

Deutsche Bank (2000) 'Regulation and banking supervision: caught between the nation state and global financial markets', *EMU Watch*, no. 86, 29 June.

—— (2002) 'EU prospectus on the home straight', *EU Financial Market Special*, 16 December.

—— (2003) 'The new ISD – better regulation for EU investment services?', *EU Financial Market Special*, 25 June.

—— (2004a) 'Bank performance in Europe: great progress through consolidation – except in Germany', *EU Monitor Financial Market Special*, no. 13, 28 June.

—— (2004b) 'Italy's savings banks: first reforms create big universal banks with untapped potential', *EU Monitor Financial Market Special*, no. 17, 25 November.

—— (2004c) 'Spain's cajas: deregulated but not depoliticised', *EU Monitor Financial Market Special*, no. 20, 13 December.

—— (2005a) 'Payments in Europe: getting it right,' *EU Monitor Financial Market Special*, no. 27, 29 August.

—— (2005b) 'Savings banks reform in France: plus ça change, plus ça reste – presque – le même', *EU Monitor Financial Market Special*, no. 22, 3 May.

—— (2008) 'Price stability vs. lender of last resort', *EU Monitor*, no. 52, 26 March.

Deutsche Börse Group (2004) *Response to the Communication from the Commission about Clearing and Settlement in the European Union – The Way Forward*, Frankfurt, July.

De Visscher, C., Maiscocq, O., and Varone, F. (2008) 'The Lamfalussy reform in EU securities markets: fiduciary relationships, policy effectiveness and balance of power', *Journal of Public Policy*, 28, 1: 19–47.

Di Giorgio, G., and Di Noia, C. (2007) 'Financial supervisors: alternative models', in D. Masciandaro and M. Quintyn (eds), *Designing Financial Supervision Institutions: Independence, Accountability and Governance*, Cheltenham: Edward Elgar.

Dimitrakopoulos, D. (ed.) (2004) *The Changing European Commission*, Manchester: Manchester University Press.

Drezner, D. W. (2007) *All Politics is Global: Explaining International Regulatory Regimes*, Princeton, NJ: Princeton University Press.

Duisenberg, W. (2002) *Testimony before the Committee on Economic and Monetary Affairs of the European Parliament*, 8 October and 3 December; www.ecb.int/press/key/date/2002/html/index.en.html.

Dür, A. (2008) 'Fortress Europe or liberal Europe? The external impact of the EU's single market programme', paper presented at the UACES conference, Edinburgh.

Dyson, K. (1994) *Elusive Union*, London: Longman.

—— (2000) *The Politics of the Eurozone*, Oxford: Oxford University Press.

Dyson, K., and Featherstone, K. (1999) *The Road to Maastricht*, Oxford: Oxford University Press.

Dyson, K., and Marcussen, M. (eds) (2009) *The Changing World of Central Banking*, Oxford: Oxford University Press.

Eberlein, B., and Kerwer, D. (2004) 'New governance in the European Union: a theoretical perspective', *Journal of Common Market Studies*, 42, 1: 121–42.

ECB (European Central Bank) (2001a) *The Role of National Central Banks in Prudential Supervision*, Frankfurt.

—— (2001b) *Opinion of the ECB at the Request of the German Ministry of Finance on a Draft Law Establishing an Integrated Financial Services Supervision*, 8 November, CONV/2001/35.

—— (2003a) *Comments of the European Central Bank (ECB) on the Third Consultative Document of the European Commission on Regulatory Capital Review*, Frankfurt, November.

—— (2003b) *Developments in National Supervisory Structures*, Frankfurt.

—— (2003c) *The Transformation of the European Financial System*, Frankfurt.

—— (2004a) *Report on European Banking Structure*, Frankfurt, November.

—— (2004b) *Towards a Single Euro Payments Area – Third Progress Report*, Frankfurt, 2 December.

—— (2004c) *Communication on Clearing and Settlement in the European Union: The Eurosystem's Response*, Frankfurt, 22 July.

—— (2006a) 'Opinion of the European Central Bank (ECB) of 26 April 2006 on a proposal for a directive on payments services in the internal market', *Official Journal of the European Union* C109/10.

—— (2006b) *Target 2 Securities: Initial Assumptions and Questions*, Frankfurt, 10 August.

—— (2006c) *Governance of Target 2 Securities: A Possibility*, Frankfurt, December.

—— (2007a) 'The EU arrangements for financial crisis management', *Monthly Bulletin*, Frankfurt, February.

—— (2007b) *Reply to Letter from ECSDA to ECB on Target 2 Securities*, Frankfurt, February.

—— (2007c) *Target 2 Securities: The Blueprint*, Frankfurt, 8 March.

—— (2008) *Financial Stability Review*, Frankfurt, December.

ECSDA (European Central Securities Depositaries Association) (2004) *Response to the ESCB/CESR Standards for Securities Clearing and Settlement Systems in the European Union*, May.

—— (2007) *Letter from ECSDA to the ECB on Target 2 Securities*, www.ecb.int/ paym/market/secmar/integr/pdf/T2SECSDAletter.pdf.

EFC (Economic and Financial Committee) (2000) *Report on Financial Stability*, Economic Paper of the European Commission 143, Brussels, May [first Brouwer Report].

—— (2001) *Report on Financial Crisis Management*, Brussels, April [second Brouwer Report].

—— (2002) *Report on Financial Regulation, Supervision and Stability*, revised to reflect the discussion at the 8 October meeting of the ECOFIN Council, Brussels, 9 October.

—— (2007) *Developing EU Financial Stability Arrangements*, Brussels, 5 September.

Egan, M. (2001) *Constructing a European Market: Standards, Regulation, and Governance*, Oxford: Oxford University Press.

Egeberg, M. (1999) 'Transcending inter-governmentalism? Identity and role perceptions of national officials in EU decision-making', *Journal of European Public Policy*, 6, 3: 456–74.

Eising, R. (2004) 'Multilevel governance and business interests in the European Union', *Governance*, 17, 2: 211–45.

—— (2007) 'The access of business interests to EU institutions: towards elite pluralism?', *Journal of European Public Policy*, 14, 3: 384–403.

Engelen, K. (2002) 'Central bank losers: the inside story of how the ECB and the Bundesbank are being pushed aside as financial regulators', *International Economy* summer.

EP (European Parliament) (2001) *Report on the Commission Communication on Upgrading the Investment Services Directive 93/22/EEC Final*, Committee on Economic and Monetary Affairs, Brussels, 23 March.

—— (2002a) *Report on a Proposal for a Directive on the Supplementary Supervision of Credit Institutions, Insurance Undertakings and Investment Firms in a Financial Conglomerate*, Committee on Economic and Monetary Affairs, Brussels, 27 February.

—— (2002b) *Recommendation for a Second Reading on the Council Common Position with a View to the Adoption of a Directive on the Supplementary Supervision of*

Credit Institutions, Insurance Undertakings and Investment Firms in a Financial Conglomerate, Committee on Economic and Monetary Affairs, Brussels, 5 November.

—— (2002c) *Report on the Communication from the Commission entitled Clearing and Settlement in the European Union*, Committee on Economic and Monetary Affairs, Brussels, 4 December [Andria Report].

—— (2004) *Report on a Legal Framework for a Single Payment Area*, Committee on Economic and Monetary Affairs, Brussels, 18 March.

—— (2005a) *Report on Clearing and Settlement in the European Union*, Committee on Economic and Monetary Affairs, Brussels, 6 June.

—— (2005b) 'Resolution on clearing and settlement in the European Union', *Official Journal of the European Union* C 157 E/485.

—— (2006) *Report on the Proposal for a Directive on Payment Services in the Internal Market*, Committee on Economic and Monetary Affairs, Brussels, 20 September.

Euroclear (2004) *Response to the European Commission's Communication on Clearing and Settlement*, July.

—— (2006) *Target 2 Securities: Euroclear Group's Response to the ECB's Questionnaire*, 8 September.

EUROFI (2002a) *Banking and Financial European Integration: Proposals for Regulation on Securities Markets*.

—— (2002b) *An integrated European Financial Market*, Preliminary report, 26 November.

Eurogroup (2008) *Summit of the Euro Area Countries: Declaration on a Concerted European Action Plan of the Euro Area Countries*, 12 October.

Euronext (2002) *Internalisation*, January.

European Banking Federation (2002) *Statement on the Revised Investment Services Document*, 14 June.

—— (2003) *Response to the ESCB/CESR Consultation on Clearing & Settlement*, 1 November.

—— (2004) *FBE's Final Response to the Second Consultation on the CESR–ESCB Standards for Clearing and Settlement*, 21 June.

—— (2007) *Governance of Target 2 Securities: A Possibility*, 31 January.

European Banking Federation, European Savings Banks Group, European Association of Cooperative Banks, European Mortgage Federation, European Federation of Building Societies, European Association of Public Banks, Comité Européen des Assurances, and Federation of European Stock Exchanges (2002) *Prospectus Directive Modified Proposal*, 31 July.

European Banking Federation, Institute of International Finance, International Swaps and Derivatives Association, London Investment Banking Association, and Bond Market Association (2004) 'Trading book review', joint letter to the Basel Committee on Banking Supervision, 9 December.

European Council (2008) *Presidency Conclusions*, Brussels, 11–12 December.

European Savings Banks Group (2003) *Response to the Consultative Paper 3 on the Basel II Accord*, Brussels.

—— (2006) *Position of the European Savings Banks Group on the Target – Securities Project*, Brussels, 21 September.

European Securities Markets Expert Group (2007) *Report on Directive 2003/71/EC of the European Parliament and of the Council on the Prospectus to be Published when Securities are Offered to the Public or Admitted to Trading*, Brussels, 5 September.

Expert Group on Banking (2004) *Financial Services Action Plan: Progress and Prospects*, Brussels, May.

Expert Group on Securities (2004) *Financial Services Action Plan: Progress and Prospects*, Brussels, May.

Fédération Bancaire Française (2004) *Comments and Observations concerning Communication from the Commission to the Council and the European Parliament 'Clearing and Settlement in the European Union: The Way Forward'*, Paris, 5 August.

—— (2006) *Target 2 – Securities: Initial Assumptions and Questions, Fédération Bancaire Française Answers*, Paris, 4 September.

Federation of European Stock Exchanges (2003) *Position Paper by the FESE in Response to the Commission Proposal on the Revision of the Investment Services Directive*, Brussels, 28 February.

Ferran, E. (2004) *Building an EU Securities Market*, Cambridge: Cambridge University Press.

Ferran, E., and Goodhart, C. (eds) (2001) *Regulating Financial Services and Markets in the Twenty First Century*, Oxford: Hart.

Ferrarini, G., and Recine, F. (2006) 'The MiFID and internalisation', in G. Ferrarini and E. Wymeersch (eds), *Investor Protection in Europe*, Oxford: Oxford University Press, pp. 235–70.

Ferrarini, G., and Wymeersch, E. (eds) (2006) *Investor Protection in Europe: Corporate Law Making, the MiFID and Beyond*, Oxford: Oxford University Press.

Finnemore, M., and Sikkink, K. (2001) 'Taking stock: the constructivist research program in international relations and comparative politics', *Annual Review of Political Science*, 4: 391–416.

Fioretos, K.-O. (1997) 'The anatomy of autonomy: interdependence, domestic balances of power and European integration', *Review of International Studies*, 23, 3: 293–320.

Fonteyne, W., and van der Vossen, J.-W. (2007) 'Financial integration and stability', in J. Decressin, H. Faruqee, and W. Fonteyne (eds), *Integrating Europe's Financial Markets*, Washinghton, DC: IMF, pp. 199–237.

Fratianni, M., and Pattison, J. (2001) 'The Bank for International Settlements: an assessment of its role in international monetary and financial policy coordination', *Open Economies Review*, 12, 2: 197–222.

FSA (Financial Services Authority) (2009) *The Turner Review: A Regulatory Response to the Global Banking Crisis*, London, March.

FSC (Financial Services Committee) (2006) *Report on Financial Supervision*, Brussels, February [Francq Report II].

FSF (Financial Stability Forum) (2008) *Report of the Financial Stability Forum on Enhancing Market and Institutional Resilience*, Basel, 7 April.

Garrett, G., and Weingast, B. R. (1993) 'Ideas, interests, and institutions: constructing the European Community's internal market', in J. Goldstein and R. Keohane (eds), *Ideas and Foreign Policy: Beliefs, Institutions, and Political Change*, Ithaca, NY: Cornell University Press, pp. 173–206.

George, S. (1998) *An Awkward Partner: Britain in the European Community*, Oxford: Oxford University Press.

Giovannini Group (2001) *Cross-Border Clearing and Settlement Arrangements in the European Union*, Brussels, November.

—— (2003) *Second Report on EU Clearing and Settlement Arrangements*, Brussels, April.

Godeffroy, J. (2006) *Speech by Jean-Michel Godeffroy, Director General/Payment Systems and Market Infrastructure, ECB, to the British Bankers' Association*, London, 20 September.

Goldstein, J. (1993) *Ideas, Interests, and American Trade Policy*, Ithaca, NY: Cornell University Press.

Goodhart, C. (ed.) (2000) *Which Lender of Last Resort for Europe?*, London: Central Banking.

Goodhart, C., and Schoenmaker, D. (1995) 'Should the functions of monetary policy and banking supervision be separated?', *Oxford Economic Papers*, 47: 539–60.

Gowland, D. (1990) *The Regulation of Financial Markets in the 1990s*, Aldershot: Edward Elgar.

Greenwood, J. (2003) *Interest Representation in the European Union*, Basingstoke: Palgrave.

Griffith-Jones, S. (2003) letter, *Financial Times*, 12 May.

Grossman, E. (2004) 'Bringing politics back in: rethinking the role of economic interest groups in European integration', *Journal of European Public Policy*, 11, 4: 637–54.

—— (2005) 'European banking policy: between multi-level governance and Europeanization', in A. Baker, D. Hudson and R. Woodward (eds), *Governing Financial Globalisation*, London: Routledge, pp. 130–46.

—— (2006) 'Europeanization as an interactive process: German public banks meet EU state aid policy', *Journal of Common Market Studies*, 44, 2: 325–48.

Group of Seven (2008) *Statement of G-7 Finance Ministers and Central Bank Governors*, 11 April.

Group of Ten (2001) *Consolidation in the Financial Sector*, Basel.

Group of Thirty (2003) *Global Clearing and Settlement: A Plan of Action*, Washington, DC.

—— (2009) *Financial Reform: A Framework for Financial Stability*, Washington, DC.

Group of Twenty (2009) *A Global Plan for Recovery and Reform*, London, April.

Haas, E. (1968) *The Uniting of Europe: Political Social and Economic Forces 1950–57*, Stanford, CA: Stanford University Press.

Hall, P. (1989) (ed.) *The Political Power of Economic Ideas*, Princeton, NJ: Princeton University Press.

—— (1993) 'Policy paradigm, social learning and the state: the case of economic policy making in Britain', *Comparative Politics*, 25: 275–96.

Hall, P., and Soskice, D. (eds) (2001) *Varieties of Capitalism: The Institutional Foundations of Comparative Advantage*, Oxford: Oxford University Press.

Hall, R. B., and Biersteker, T. (eds) (2002) *The Emergence of Private Authority in Global Governance*, Cambridge: Cambridge University Press.

Hancher, L., and Moran, M. (eds) (1989) *Capitalism, Culture, and Economic Regulation*, Oxford: Clarendon Press.

Hardie, I., and Howarth, D. (2009) 'The financialisation of French and German banking systems and the credit crunch', *Journal of Common Market Studies*, 47, 4.

Hayes-Renshaw, F., and Wallace, H. (2006) *The Council of Ministers*, New York: St Martin's Press.

Heinemann, F., and Jopp, M. (eds) (2002) *The Benefits of a Working European Retail Market for Financial Services*, Report to the European Financial Services Round Table, available at: ftp://ftp.zew.de/pub/zew-docs/div/erffinal.pdf.

Helleiner, E. (1994) *States and the Reemergence of Global Finance: From Bretton Woods to the 1990s*, Ithaca, NY: Cornell University Press.

Héritier, A. (1996) 'The accommodation of diversity in European policy-making: regulatory policy as patchwork', *Journal of European Public Policy*, 3, 3: 149–67.

—— (ed.) (2002) *Common Goods: Reinventing European and International Governance*, Lanham, MD: Rowman & Littlefield.

Hix, S. (1998) 'The study of the European Union II: the "new governance" agenda and its rival', *Journal of European Public Policy*, 5, 1: 38–65.

Hix, S., Noury, A. G., and Roland, G. (2007) *Democratic Politics in the European Parliament*, Cambridge: Cambridge University Press.

HM Treasury (2003a) *The New Capital Adequacy Directive, CAD 3: The Transposition of the New Basel Accord into EU Legislation*, consultation document, London.

—— (2003b) *Consultation on CAD3: Summary of Responses*, London.

HM Treasury and FSA (Financial Services Authority)(2007) *Strengthening the EU Regulatory and Supervisory Framework: A Practical Approach*, November.

HM Treasury, Financial Services Authority and Bank of England (2004) *Joint Response to the Commission's Communication on Clearing and Settlement*, London, 27 July.

Hodson, D., and Quaglia, L. (2009a) 'European perspectives on the global financial crisis: introduction', *Journal of Common Market Studies*, 47, 5: 939–53.

—— (2009b) 'European perspectives on the global financial crisis', *Journal of Common Market Studies*, 47, 5 [special issue].

Hoffman, S. (1966) 'Obstinate or obsolete? The fate of the nation state and the case of Western Europe', *Daedalus*, 95, 3: 862–915.

Hooghe, L. (2001) *The European Commission and the Integration of Europe: Images of Governance*, Cambridge: Cambridge University Press.

Hooghe, L., and Marks, G. (2001) *Multi-Level Governance and European Integration*, Lanham, MD: Rowman & Littlefield.

—— (2003) 'Unraveling the central state, but how? Types of multi-level governance', *American Political Science Review*, 97: 233–43.

House Committee on Financial Services (2003a) *The New Basel Accord – Sound Regulation or Crushing Complexity?*, 27 February.

—— (2003b) *The New Basel Accord – In Search of a Unified US Position*, 19 June.

Howarth, D., and Loedel, P. (2005) *The European Central Bank*, 2nd ed., Basingstoke: Palgrave.

Huhne, C. (2002) letter, *Financial Times*, 5 November.

IIMG (Inter Institutional Monitoring Group) (2007a) *Final Report Monitoring the Lamfalussy Process*, Brussels, 15 October.

—— (2007b) *Second Interim Report Monitoring the Lamfalussy Process*, Brussels, 26 January.

IMF (International Monetary Fund) (2006) *Euro Area Policies: Selected Issues*, Country Report no. 06/288, August.

—— (2007) *Euro Area Policies: 2007 Article IV Consultation – Staff Report; Staff Supplement; Public Information Notice on the Executive Board Discussion; and Statement by the Executive Director for Member Countries*, Country Report no. 07/260, July.

—— (2008) *Euro Area Policies: Article IV Consultation*, Country Report no. 08/262, August.

International Swaps and Derivatives Association (2001) *International Swaps and Derivatives Association's Comments on the Proposal for a Directive on Insider Dealing and Market Manipulation (Market Abuse)*.

Jabko, N. (2006) *Playing the Market: A Political Strategy for Uniting Europe, 1985–2005*, Ithaca, NY: Cornell University Press.

Jachtenfuchs, M. (2001) 'The governance approach of European integration', *Journal of Common Market Studies*, 39, 2: 245–64.

Jacobs, F., Corbett, R., and Shackleton, M. (2007) *The European Parliament*, London: John Harper.

Jacobsen, J. K. (1995) 'Much ado about ideas: the cognitive factor in economic policy', *World Politics*, 47, 1: 283–310.

Joint Forum (1999) *Supervision of Financial Conglomerates*, Basel, February.

—— (2001) *Core Principles: Cross-Sectoral Comparison*, Basel, November.

Josselin, D. (1997) *Money Politics in the New Europe: Britain, France and the Single Financial Market*, Basingstoke: Macmillan.

Judge, D., and Earnshaw, D. (2003) *The European Parliament*, New York: Palgrave Macmillan.

Jupille, J., Caporaso, J., and Checkel, J. (2003) 'Integrating institutions: rationalism, constructivism, and the study of the European Union', *Comparative Political Studies*, 36, 1–2: 7–40.

Kaltenthaler, K. (2006) *Policy-Making in the European Central Bank: The Masters of Europe's Money*, Lanham, MD: Rowman & Littlefield.

Kapstein, E. (1989) 'Resolving the regulator's dilemma: international coordination of banking regulations', *International Organization*, 43, 2: 323–47.

—— (1992) 'Between power and purpose: central bankers and the politics of international regulation', *International Organization*, 46, 1: 265–87.

Kassim, H., Peters, G., and Wright, V. (eds) (2000) *The National Co-ordination of EU Policy: The European Level*, Oxford: Oxford University Press.

Katz, R. S., and Wessels, B. (1999) *The European Parliament, the National Parliaments, and European Integration*, Oxford: Oxford University Press.

King, M. (2007) *Turmoil in Financial Markets: What Can Central Bankers Do?*, paper submitted to the Treasury Committee by the governor of the Bank of England.

Kjaer, A.-M. (2004) *Governance*, Cambridge: Polity.

Knill, C. (2001) 'Private governance across multiple arenas: European interest associations as interface actors', *Journal of European Public Policy*, 8, 2: 227–46.

Knill, C., and Lehmkuhl, D. (1999) 'How Europe matters: different mechanisms of Europeanization', *European Integration Online Papers*, 3, 7; http://eiop.or.at/eiop/texte/1999-007a.htm.

—— (2002) 'Private actors and the state: internationalization and changing patterns of governance', *Governance*, 15, 1: 41–63.

Kohler-Koch, B. (1999) 'The evolution and transformation of European governance', in B. Kohler-Koch and R. Eising (eds), *The Transformation of Governance in the European Union*, London: Routledge, pp. 14–35.

—— (ed.) (2003) *Linking EU and National Governance*, Oxford: Oxford University Press.

Kohler-Koch, B., and Rittberger, B. (2006) 'The "Governance Turn" in EU Studies', *Journal of Common Market Studies*, annual review, 44: 27–49.

Kynaston, D. (2001) *The City of London: A Club No More, 1945–2000*, Vol. 4, London: Chatto & Windus.

Laffan, B. (1997) 'From policy entrepreneur to policy manager: the challenge facing the European Commission', *Journal of European Public Policy*, 4, 3: 422–38.

Lannoo, K. (2005) 'The transformation of financial regulation and supervision in the EU', in D. Masciandaro (ed.), *Handbook of Central Banking and Financial Authorities in Europe*, Cheltenham: Edward Elgar, pp. 485–513.

Lastra, R. (2003) *The Governance Structure for Financial Regulation and Supervision in Europe*, LSE Financial Markets Group, Special Paper 149.

Lewis, J. (2002) 'National interests: Coreper', J. Peterson and M. Shackleton (eds), *The Institutions of the European Union*, Oxford: Oxford University Press.

—— (2005) 'The Janus face of Brussels: socialization and everyday decision-making in the European Union', *International Organization*, 59: 937–71.

London Economics (2005) *Securities Trading, Clearing, Central Counterparties and Settlement in EU 25 – An Overview of Current Arrangements: Report*, London: 30 May.

London Stock Exchange (2004) *Response to the Communication on Clearing and Settlement in the European Union*, London: 30 July.

London Stock Exchange, PR Newswire, Investor Relations Society, Association of British Insurers, Confederation of British Industry, Waymaker, Quoted Companies Alliance, National Association of Pension Funds, Association of Private Client Investment Managers and Stockbrokers, London Investment Banking Association, Institute of Chartered Secretaries and Administrators and British Bankers' Association (2003) *News Dissemination and the EU Transparency Directive*, June.

Lütz, S. (1998) 'The revival of the nation state? Stock exchange regulation in an era of globalised financial markets', *Journal of European Public Policy*, 5, 1: 153–68.

—— (2004) 'Convergence within national diversity: the regulatory state in finance', *Journal of Public Policy*, 24, 2: 169–97.

Macartney, H. (forthcoming) 'Variegated neo-liberalism: transnationally oriented fractions of capital in EU financial market integration', *Review of International Studies*, pp. at proof stage.

Macartney, H., and Moran, M. (2008) 'Banking and financial market regulation and supervision', in K. Dyson (ed.), *The Euro at Ten*, Oxford: Oxford University Press, pp. 325–40.

McCreevy, C. (2006) *Clearing and Settlement: The Way Forward*, speech delivered to the Economic and Monetary Affairs Committee of the European Parliament, Brussels, 11 July.

McNamara, K. (1998) *The Currency of Ideas: Monetary Politics in the European Union*, Ithaca, NY: Cornell University Press.

Maes, I. (2007) *Half a Century of European Financial Integration*, Brussels: Mercato-fonds.

Majone, G. (1996) *Regulating Europe*, London: Routledge.

Marcussen, M. (2000) *Ideas and Elites*, Aalborg: Aalborg University Press.

Masciandaro, D. (ed.) (2005) *Handbook of Central Banking and Financial Authorities in Europe: New Architectures in the Supervision of Financial Markets*, Cheltenham: Edward Elgar.

Masciandaro, D., and Quintyn, M. (eds) (2007) *Designing Financial Supervision Institutions*, Cheltenham: Edward Elgar.

Maurer, A., and Wessels, W. (eds) (2001) *National Parliaments on their Ways to Europe: Losers or Latecomers?*, Baden-Baden: Nomos.

Mayes, D., Halme., L., and Liuksila, A. (2001) *Improving Banking Supervision*, Basingstoke: Palgrave Macmillan.

Moloney, N. (2002) *EC Securities Regulation*, Oxford: Oxford University Press.

—— (2006) 'Effective policy design for the retail investment services market: challenges and choices post FSAP', in G. Ferrarini and E. Wymeersch (eds), *Investor Protection in Europe*, Oxford: Oxford University Press, pp. 379–442.

Moran, M. (1991) *The Politics of the Financial Services Revolution: The USA, UK and Japan*, Basingstoke: Macmillan.

—— (1994) 'The state and the financial services revolution: a comparative analysis', *West European Politics*, 17, 3: 158–77.

—— (2000) 'From command state to regulatory state', *Public Policy and Administration*, 15, 4: 1–13.

—— (2002) 'Understanding the regulatory state', *British Journal of Political Science*, 32: 391–413.

Moran, M., and Macartney, H. (2009) 'Central banking and financial supervision: internationalization, Europeanization and power', in K. Dyson and M. Marcussen (eds), *The Changing Power and Politics of European Central Banking: Living with the Euro*, Oxford: Oxford Uhniversity Press.

Moravcsik, A. (1993) 'Preferences and power in the European Community: a liberal intergovernmental approach', *Journal of Common Market Studies*, 31, 4: 473–524.

—— (1998) *The Choice For Europe*, London: University College London Press.

Moravcsik, A., and Nicolaides, K. (1999) 'Explaining the Treaty of Amsterdam: interests, influence, institutions', *Journal of Common Market Studies*, 37, 1: 59–85.

Mügge, D. (2006) 'Reordering the marketplace: competition politics in European finance', *Journal of Common Market Studies*, 44, 5: 991–1022.

National Bank of Belgium (2006), *Target 2 – Securities: Initial Assumptions and Questions: Report of the National Bank of Belgium on the Outcome of the Meeting with the Belgian Market*, 11 September.

Norman, P. (2007) *Plumbers and Visionaries*, Chichester: John Wiley.

Nouy, D. (2007) *Presentation before the Economic and Monetary Affairs Committee of the European Parliament*, 2 October.

Nugent, N. (2001) *The European Commission*, Basingstoke: Palgrave Macmillan.

Oatley, T., and Nabors, R. (1998) 'Redistributive cooperation: market failures, wealth transfer and the Basle Accord, *International Organization*, 52, 1: 35–54.

O'Brennan, J., and Raunio, T. (eds) (2007) *National Parliaments within the Enlarged European Union: From 'Victims' of Integration to Competitive Actors?*, London: Routledge.

Olson, M. (1971) *The Logic of Collective Action: Public Goods and the Theory of Groups*, London: Harvard University Press.

Oosterloo, S., and de Haan, J. (2004) 'Central banks and financial stability: a survey', *Journal of Financial Stability*, 1, 1: 257–73.

Padoa-Schioppa, T. (1999a) 'EMU and banking supervision', *International Finance 2*, 2: 295–308.

—— (1999b) 'Payments and the Eurosystem', *Speech to SIBOS*, 13 September.

—— (2002) *Parliamentary Hearing of the Committee on Economic and Monetary Affairs of the European Parliament*, 10 July.

—— (2003) 'Central banks and financial stability: exploring a land in between', in European Central Bank, *The Transformation of the European Financial System*, Frankfurt: ECB.

—— (2004a) *The Euro and its Central Bank*, London: MIT Press.

—— (2004b) *Regulating Finance: Balancing Freedom and Risk*, Oxford: Oxford University Press.

—— (2007) Letter to the ECOFIN Council, 26 November.

Pagoulatos, G. (1999) 'European banking: five modes of governance', *West European Politics*, 22, 1: 68–94.

—— (2003) 'Financial interventionism and liberalisation in Southern Europe: state, bankers and the politics of disinflation', *Journal of Public Policy*, 23, 2: 171–99.

Parsons, C. (2000) 'Domestic interests, ideas and integration: lessons from the French case', *Journal of Common Market Studies*, 38, 1: 45–70.

—— (2002) 'Showing ideas as causes: the origins of the European Union', *International Organization*, 56, 1: 47–84.

Pauly, L. W. (2008) 'Financial crisis management in Europe and beyond', *Contributions to Political Economy*, 27, 1: 73–89.

—— (2009) 'The old and the new politics of international financial stability', *Journal of Common Market Studies*, 47, 5: 955–75.

Peters, B. G. (2004) *The Politics of Bureaucracy*, London: Routledge.

Peters, B. G., and Pierre, J. (1998) 'Governance without government? Rethinking public administration', *Journal of Public Administration Research and Theory*, 8, 2: 223–43.

Peterson, J. (1995) 'Decision-making in the EU: towards a framework for analysis', *Journal of European Public Policy*, 2, 1: 69–93.

Pierre, J., and Peters, B. G. (2000) *Governance, Politics and the State*, London: Macmillan.

Pollack, M. (2001) 'International relations theory and European integration', *Journal of Common Market Studies*, 39, 2: 221–44.

—— (2003) 'Control mechanism or deliberative democracy? Two images of comitology', *Comparative Political Studies*, 36, 1–2: 125–55.

Porter, T. (2003) 'Technical collaboration and political conflict in the emerging regime for international financial regulation', *Review of International Political Economy*, 10, 3: 520–51.

—— (2005) *Globalization and Finance*, Cambridge: Polity.

Posner, E. (2005) 'Sources of institutional change: the supranational origins of Europe's new stock markets', *World Politics*, 58: 1–40.

—— (2007) 'Financial transformation in the European Union', in S. Meunier and K. McNamara (eds), *Making History: European Integration and Institutional Change at Fifty*, Oxford: Oxford University Press.

—— (2009a) *The Origins of Europe's New Stock Markets*, Cambridge, MA: Harvard University Press.

—— (2009b) 'Making rules for global finance: transatlantic regulatory cooperation at the turn of the millennium', *International Organization*, 63, 4: 665–99.

PricewaterhouseCoopers (2004) *Study on the Financial and Macroeconomic Consequences of the Draft Proposed New Capital Requirements for Banks and Investment Firms in the EU*, final report, 8 April.

Prodi, R. (2002) *Implementation of Financial Services Legislation in the Context of the Lamfalussy Report*, intervention by President Romano Prodi to the European Parliament's plenary session, Strasbourg, 5 February.

Quaglia, L. (2007) 'The politics of financial service regulation and supervision reform in the European Union', *European Journal of Political Research*, 46, 2: 269–90.

—— (2008a) *Central Banking Governance in the European Union: A Comparative Analysis*, London: Routledge.

—— (2008b) 'Setting the pace? Private financial interests and European financial market integration', *British Journal of Politics and International Relations*, 10, 1: 46–64.

—— (2008c) 'Committee governance in the financial sector in the European Union', *Journal of European Integration*, 30, 3: 565–80.

—— (2008d) 'Explaining the reform of banking supervision in Europe: an integrative approach', *Governance*, 21, 3: 439–63.

—— (2009a) 'Political science and the Cinderellas of Economic and Monetary Union: payments services and clearing and settlement of securities', *Journal of European Public Policy*, 16, 4: 623–39.

—— (2009b) 'The "British plan" as a pace-setter: the Europeanisation of banking rescue plans in the EU?', *Journal of Common Market Studies*, 47, 4 [special issue].

—— (2009c) *The Politics of Regulating Credit Rating Agencies in the European Union*, Working paper of the Centre for Global Political Economy at the University of Sussex, no. 5, June.

—— (2009d) 'The politics of insurance regulation and supervision reform in the European Union', *Comparative European Politics*, pp. at proof stage.

Quaglia, L., De Francesco, F., and Radaelli, C. (2008) 'Committee governance and socialisation in the EU: the state of the art', *Journal of European Public Policy*, 15, 1: 1–12.

Quaglia, L., Eastwood, R., and Holmes, P. (2009) 'The financial turmoil and EU policy cooperation: the dog that did not bark?', *Journal of Common Market Studies Annual Review*, 47, 1: 1–25.

Radaelli, C. (1999) 'Harmful tax competition in the EU: policy narratives and advocacy coalitions', *Journal of Common Market Studies*, 37, 4: 661–82.

Reid, M. (1988) *All-Change in the City: The Revolution in Britain's Financial Sector*, Basingstoke: Macmillan.

Rhodes, R. (1996) 'The new governance: governing without government', *Political Studies*, 44, 4: 652–67.

—— (1997) *Understanding Governance: Policy Networks, Governance, Reflexivity and Accountability*, Buckingham: Sage.

Sabatier, P. A. (1998) 'The advocacy coalition framework: revisions and relevance for Europe', *Journal of European Public Policy*, 5, 1: 98–130.

Sandholtz, W., and Stone Sweet, A. (1998) *European Integration and Supranational Governance*, Oxford: Oxford University Press.

Scharpf, F. (1997) 'Introduction: the problem-solving capacity of multi-level governance', *Journal of European Public Policy*, 4, 4: 520–38.

—— (1999) *Governing in Europe: Effective and Democratic?*, Oxford: Oxford University Press.

Scheller, H. (2004) *The European Central Bank*, Frankfurt: ECB.

Scully, R. (2005) *Becoming Europeans? Attitudes, Behaviour, and Socialization in the European Parliament*, Oxford: Oxford University Press.

Simmons, B. (2001) 'The international politics of harmonization: the case of capital market regulation', *International Organization*, 55: 589–620.

Singer, D. A. (2004) 'Capital rules: the domestic politics of international regulatory harmonization', *International Organization*, 58: 531–65.

Smith, J. (1999) *Europe's Elected Parliament*, Sheffield: Sheffield Academic Press.

Speyer, B. (2006) 'Governing global financial markets – Basel I and II: the role of non-state actors', in G. Folke Schuppert (ed.), *Global Governance and the Role of Non-State Actors*, Baden-Baden: Nomos, pp. 101–16.

Story, J., and Walter, I. (1997) *Political Economy of Financial Integration in Europe: The Battle of the System*, Manchester: Manchester University Press.

Summit of European G8 Members (2008) *Statement*, Paris, 4 October.

Thatcher, M., and Stone Sweet, A. (2002) 'Theory and practice of delegation to non-majoritarian institutions', *West European Politics*, 25, 1: 1–22.

Tietmeyer, H. (1999) *International Cooperation and Coordination in the Area of Financial Market Supervision and Surveillance*, Basel, 11 February.

Toniolo, G. (2005) *Central Bank Cooperation at the Bank for International Settlements, 1930–1973*, Cambridge: Cambridge University Press.

Treasury Committee, House of Commons (2006) *European Financial Services Regulation*, London: Stationery Office.

—— (2008a) *The Run on the Rock*, Fifth Report of Session 2007–8, London: Stationery Office.

—— (2008b) *Financial Stability and Transparency*, London: Stationery Office.

Treasury Committee, House of Commons Treib, O., Bähr, H., and Falkner, G. (2007) 'Modes of governance: towards a conceptual clarification', *Journal of European Public Policy*, 14, 1: 1–20.

Trondal, J., and Veggeland, F. (2003) 'Access, voice and loyalty: the representation of domestic civil servants in EU committees', *Journal of European Public Policy*, 10, 1: 59–77.

Tsebelis, G. (1990) *Nested Games: Rational Choice in Comparative Politics*, Berkeley: University of California Press.

Underhill, G. (1991) 'Markets beyond politics? The state and the internationalisation of financial markets', *European Journal of Political Research*, 19: 197–225.

—— (1995) 'Keeping governments out of politics: transnational securities markets, regulatory cooperation and political legitimacy', *Review of International Studies*, 21, 3: 251–78.

—— (1997) 'The making of the European financial area: global market integration and the EU single market for financial service', in G. Underhill (ed.), *The New World Order in International Finance*, London: Macmillan.

Underhill, G., and Zhang, X. (2008) 'Setting the rules: private power, political underpinnings, and legitimacy in global monetary and financial governance', *International Affairs*, 84, 3: 535–54.

van Kersbergen, K., and van Waarden, F. (2004) '"Governance" as a bridge between disciplines: cross-disciplinary inspiration regarding shifts in governance and problems of governability, accountability and legitimacy', *European Journal of Political Research*, 43: 143–71.

Verdun, A. (1999) 'The role of the Delors Committee in the creation of EMU: an epistemic community?', *Journal of European Public Policy*, 6, 2: 308–28.

—— (2000) 'Governing by committee: the case of the monetary committee', in T. Christiansen and E. Kirchner (eds), *Committee Governance in the European Union*, Manchester: Manchester University Press, pp. 132–45.

Vogel, S. (1996) *Freer Markets, More Rules: Regulatory Reform in Advanced Industrial Countries*, Ithaca, NY: Cornell University Press.

Wallace, H. (1999) 'Piecing the integration jigsaw together', *Journal of European Public Policy*, 6, 1: 155–60.

Wallace, H., and Young, A. (eds) (1997) *Participation and Policy Making in the European Union*, Oxford: Oxford University Press.

Wallace, W. (1983) 'Less than a federation, more than a regime: the Community as a political system', in H. Wallace, W. Wallace and C. Webb (eds), *Policy-Making in the European Community*, New York: John Wiley, pp. 403–36.

Westlake, M., and Galloway, D. (2004) *The Council of the European Union*, London: John Harper.

Westrup, J. (2005) 'Ireland', in D. Masciandaro (ed.), *Handbook of Central Banking and Financial Authorities in Europe: New Architectures in the Supervision of Financial Markets*, Cheltenham: Edward Elgar, pp. 355–72.

——(2007) 'The politics of financial regulatory reforms in Britain and Germany', *West European Politics*, 30, 5: 1096–119.

Wincott, D. (1995) 'Institutional interaction and European integration: towards an everyday critique of liberal intergovernmentalism', *Journal of Common Market Studies*, 33, 4: 597–609.

Wood, D. (2005) *Governing Global Banking*, Aldershot: Ashgate.

Woods, N. (1995) 'Economic ideas and international relations: beyond the rational neglect', *International Studies Quarterly*, 39, 2: 161–80.

Wymeersch, E. (2006) 'Securities clearing and settlements: regulatory developments in Europe', in G. Ferrarini and E. Wymeersch (eds), *Investor Protection in Europe*, Oxford: Oxford University Press, pp. 465–83.

Yee, A. (1996) 'The causal effects of ideas on policies', *International Organization*, 50, 1: 69–108.

Zentraler Kredit Ausschuss (2003) *Stellungnahme des Zentralen Kreditausschusses zum Konsultationspapier des Baseler Ausschusses zur Euregelung der angemessenen Eigenkapitalausstattung von Kreditinstituten vom 29. April 2003 (Basel II)*, Berlin, 17 July.

Zysman, J. (1983) *Governments, Markets, and Growth: Financial Systems and the Politics of Industrial Change*, Ithaca, NY: Cornell University Press.

Index